The Agendas of Tibetan Refugees

STUDIES IN FORCED MIGRATION
General Editor: Dawn Chatty

Volume 1
A Tamil Asylum Diaspora: Sri Lankan Migration, Settlement and Politics in Switzerland
Christopher McDowell

Volume 2
Understanding Impoverishment: The Consequences of Development-induced Displacement
Edited by Christopher McDowell

Volume 3
Losing Place: Refugee Populations and Rural Transformations in East Africa
Johnathan B. Bascom

Volume 4
The End of the Refugee Cycle? Refugee Repatriation and Reconstruction
Edited by Richard Black and Khalid Koser

Volume 5
Engendering Forced Migration: Theory and Practice
Edited by Doreen Indra

Volume 6
Refugee Policy in Sudan, 1967–1984
Ahmed Karadawi

Volume 7
Psychosocial Wellness of Refugees: Issues in Qualitative and Quantitative Research
Edited by Frederick L. Ahearn, Jr.

Volume 8
Fear in Bongoland: Burundi Refugees in Urban Tanzania
Marc Sommers

Volume 9
Whatever Happened to Asylum in Britain? A Tale of Two Walls
Louise Pirouet

Volume 10
Conservation and Mobile Indigenous Peoples: Displacement, Forced Settlement and Sustainable Development
Edited by Dawn Chatty and Marcus Colchester

Volume 11
Tibetans in Nepal: The Dynamics of International Assistance among a Community in Exile
Ann Frechette

Volume 12
Crossing the Aegean: An Appraisal of the 1923 Compulsory Population Exchange between Greece and Turkey
Edited by Renée Hirschon

Volume 13
Refugees and the Transformation of Societies: Agency, Policies, Ethics and Politics
Edited by Philomena Essed, Georg Frerks and Joke Schrijvers

Volume 14
Children and Youth on the Front Line: Ethnography, Armed Conflict and Displacement
Edited by Jo Boyden and Joanna de Berry

Volume 15
Religion and Nation: Iranian Local and Transnational Networks in Britain
Kathryn Spellman

Volume 16
Children of Palestine: Experiencing Forced Migration in the Middle East
Edited by Dawn Chatty and Gillian Lewando Hundt

Volume 17
Rights in Exile: Janus-faced Humanitarianism
Guglielmo Verdirame and Barbara Harrell-Bond

Volume 18
Development-induced Displacement: Problems, Policies and People
Edited by Chris de Wet

Volume 19
Transnational Nomads: How Somalis Cope with Refugee Life in the Dadaab Camps of Kenya
Cindy Horst

Volume 20
New Regionalism and Asylum Seekers: Challenges Ahead
Edited by Susan Kneebone and Felicity Rawlings-Sanaei

Volume 21
(Re)constructing Armenia in Lebanon and Syria: Ethno-Cultural Diversity and the State in the Aftermath of a Refugee Crisis
Nicola Migliorino

Volume 22
'Brothers' or Others? Propriety and Gender for Muslim Arab Sudanese in Egypt
Anita Fábos

Volume 23
Iron in the Soul: Displacement, Livelihood and Health in Cyprus
Peter Loizos

Volume 24
Not Born a Refugee Woman: Contesting Identities, Rethinking Practices
Edited by Maroussia Hajdukowski-Ahmed, Nazilla Khanlou and Helene Moussa

Volume 25
Years of Conflict: Adolescence, Political Violence and Displacement
Edited by Jason Hart

Volume 26
Remaking Home: Reconstructing Life, Place and Identity in Rome and Amsterdam
Maja Korac

Volume 27
Materialising Exile: Material Culture and Embodied Experience among Karenni Refugees in Thailand
Sandra H. Dudley

Volume 28
The Early Morning Phone Call: Somali Refugees' Remittances
Anna Lindley

Volume 29
Deterritorialised Youth: Sahrawi and Afghan Refugees at the Margins of the Middle East
Edited by Dawn Chatty

Volume 30
Politics of Innocence: Hutu Identity, Conflict and Camp Life
Simon Turner

Volume 31
Zimbabwe's New Diaspora: Displacement and the Cultural Politics of Survival
Edited by JoAnn McGregor and Ranka Primorac

Volume 32
The Migration-Displacement Nexus: Patterns, Processes and Policies
Edited by Khalid Koser and Susan Martin

Volume 33
The Agendas of Tibetan Refugees: Survival Strategies of a Government-in-Exile in a World of Transnational Organizations
Thomas Kauffmann

The Agendas of
Tibetan Refugees

SURVIVAL STRATEGIES OF A GOVERNMENT-IN-EXILE IN A
WORLD OF TRANSNATIONAL ORGANIZATIONS

By
Thomas Kauffmann

berghahn
NEW YORK · OXFORD
www.berghahnbooks.com

First published in 2015 by
Berghahn Books
www.berghahnbooks.com

Library of Congress Cataloging-in-Publication Data
Kauffmann, Thomas, 1975-
 The agendas of Tibetan refugees: survival strategies of a government-in-
exile in a world of transnational organizations / by Thomas Kauffmann.
 pages cm. --   (Studies in forced migration; volume 33)
 Includes bibliographical references and index.
 ISBN 978-1-78238-282-9 (hardback: alk. paper) --
ISBN 978-1-78238-283-6 (ebook)
 1. Tibetans--Government policy--Western countries. 2. Refugees--
Government policy--Western countries. 3. Tibetans--Western countries--
Politics and government. 4. Governments in exile. 5. Tibet Autonomous
Region (China)--Politics and government--1951- I. Title.
 DS786.K3253 2015
 325'.21089954101821 dc23
                                                        2015003138

British Library Cataloguing in Publication Data
A catalogue record for this book is available
from the British Library

Printed on acid-free paper

ISBN 978-1-78238-282-9 (hardback)
EISBN 978-1-78238-283-6 (ebook)

Contents

Foreword   vii

Acknowledgements   x

Introduction   1

1. Rehabilitation and Development in Exile   13

2. The Central Tibetan Administration   35

3. The Political Agenda   60

4. The Religious Agenda   84

5. Reception of the Tibetan Agendas in the West: Constitution of
   the Global Tibet Movement   111

6. A New Model of Partnership and its Adaptability   131

7. Challenges to the Model   152

Conclusion   181

Bibliography   189

Index   203

Figures follow p. 110

Foreword

After the Palestinians, the Tibetans in exile constitute the oldest internationally-recognized refugee community in the world. The majority of them live in India, which, ever since Jawaharlal Nehru's invitation to the fugitive Dalai Lama to settle in his country in 1959, has been as generous and accepting a host nation as one could ever hope to find. The bulk of the funding for the exile community, however, comes from international – mainly Western – donor organizations. The question that Thomas Kauffmann sets out to answer in this book is straightforward enough: 'How, after more than fifty years of exile, are the Tibetan refugees still able to attract such substantial assistance..., unlike other populations of refugees who are largely or totally forgotten?' Two obvious answers come to mind. First, because the Tibetan refugees are poor and needy. Perhaps so; but it has often been observed – in India, but more so in Nepal – that Tibetan refugee camps are islands of relative prosperity in seas of far greater indigence. So if it is not because of their property, is it because they are refugees? Between 1990 and 1996 the government of Bhutan, a Himalayan country with a population of under a million, embarked on a policy of ethnic cleansing that resulted in the exodus of over 100,000 citizens, a figure larger than the number of Tibetans who fled the Chinese communists in 1959. The expulsion resulted in the highest per-capita refugee crisis precipitated by a nation state that has ever been recorded. But the world knows little about the crisis, and cares less. If the Tibetan refugees have been the recipients of international aid for so long, then, it is clearly neither because they are poor, nor because they are refugees.

If the answer is not to be found in the obvious places, perhaps it has something to do with Western perceptions of Tibetans. Several authors have charted the history of Western attitudes to Tibetans, from the earliest accounts of the Jesuit missionaries, through the era of the so-called 'colonial encounter' with the British, and down to the present day. Up to the end of the nineteenth century the attitude was broadly consistent, insofar as it was sympathetic towards ordinary Tibetans and utterly contemptuous of their religion and their clerical institutions. The latest phase, as we know, has been marked by unqualified adulation. For all its positive qualities, this development is not without its critics, who argue that the spiritual infallibility attributed to religious figures is all well and good, but that it oversteps the mark, trespassing on domains beyond faith while claiming critical immunity of grounds of cultural exclusiveness. To challenge historical scenarios founded on apocryphal 'treasure texts', or on the spiritual authority of the writer, is likely to be regarded less as good critical practice than as sacrilege. The *omertá* surrounding scholarly insufficiency, say the critics, carries a certain danger: that it contributes to the exclusion of Tibet from the free market of intellectual exchange.

The image of Tibet has been the subject of an interesting debate in recent years. The argument on one side has it that Tibetans are helplessly trapped in a gilded Never Never Land that has been generated by the spiritual hunger of the West; the opposing view holds that, far from being the victims of the process, the Tibetans have themselves engineered this image to their advantage. A more refined perspective suggests that it is not a matter of manipulation on the part of one side or the other, but the result of a particular relational dynamic, a dynamic that has its origins in the 'patron-priest' (*chöyön*) model that effectively provided the template for Tibet's international relations since the thirteenth century.

It is this model that Thomas Kauffmann – rightly in my opinion – sees as providing the charter for the relationship between the Tibetan refugees and their Western patrons. 'Tibetans', of course, do not constitute a homogenous entity, but in the present context the term is synecdochic for the Central Tibetan Administration (the 'Tibetan Government-in-Exile'), which provides the point of contact and the public face of the Tibetan refugee community and articulates its relationship with Western donors.

Having identified the general model for the relationship, what is the motive for the Western agencies' perpetuation of their support? The mechanism, Thomas Kauffmann suggests – and this is the central insight of the work – is a phenomenon that he describes as 'spiritualization'. What exactly the author means by this, and the compelling evidence he presents to support his argument, are best left to him to explain, but it is worth mentioning that the general concept receives unexpected support from an early critic of Tibetan Buddhism, Jean-Jacques Rousseau. In *The Social Contract*, Rousseau condemned what he called 'the religion of the lamas', on the grounds that (like Roman Catholicism and Japanese religion) it fused institutional religion with individual faith. But Rousseau understood the social potential of religious belief, and advocated cultivating it in the interest of political conformity and service to the state. Religious belief, he suspected, was the most effective method of stultifying the critical faculties of the general populace and ensuring that they did not question too rigorously the rational basis for their actions. Once a particular form of conformity was translated from a social desideratum into a religious dogma, no amount of rational argument to the contrary could ever shake it.

The conclusions drawn by Thomas Kauffmann are not based on armchair theorizing but extensive fieldwork, not confined to Tibetan refugee camps but embracing the Tibet Autonomous Region and, most crucially, the offices of several international donor agencies. The enduring support of Western (and now, increasingly, Asian) welfare organizations for Tibetan refugees has been a matter of bewilderment for many. This careful study by someone who has not only studied Tibetan language and civilization, but who has long professional experience in the world of NGOs, offers an intelligent, sympathetic and persuasive answer to the question.

Charles Ramble
Directeur d'études – Sciences historiques et philologiques
Ecole Pratique des Hautes Etudes – Paris, France

Acknowledgements

A book is never written alone, especially an anthropological one. It is a collective work, the fruit of innumerable experiences and meetings. Such a project is shaped by what people really want to give to you and share with you, and by what they are ready to invest in it. I was especially lucky during the construction of this book to be surrounded by very generous people, including my family, friends and supervisors, as well as my Tibetan friends and informants. I cannot name here all the many people who provided me with insights, ideas and support for this work, but they will recognize themselves and they know well my gratitude.

I would particularly like to thank the woman who became my wife in the course of this project, Laurence. None of the work would have been possible without her and her constant support – so I would like to dedicate this book to her and to our son Matthieu.

'The excellence of a gift lies in its appropriateness rather than in its value.'
– Charles Dudley Warner, 1873

Introduction

Among the populations of refugees in the world, the Tibetans have a special place. Crossing the Himalaya at the end the 1950s to escape the Chinese invasion of their country, the Tibetans, led by their charismatic leader the Dalai Lama, still see their story spread and listened to, after more than fifty years. The Tibetan refugees are nowadays known, in the West and elsewhere, as a population trying to regain their freedom by peaceful means, following their religion, Buddhism, and their leader, the Dalai Lama.

In 1998, I came to Dharamsala (Himachal Pradesh, India), capital of the Tibetan 'government-in-exile', and home of the Dalai Lama and some ten thousand of his fellow refugees, while conducting research for my master's degree in anthropology. I arrived replete with fantasies and dreams about Tibetan culture and religion, which had been instilled by readings on Tibet and the manner in which this country reached me through the media and on the cultural and artistic stage of France. Yet my first contacts with Tibetans, lay and clerical, showed me that they were not 'magicians and mystics' (David-Néel 1971), but rather people confronting difficult times, trying to keep their culture alive while surviving in a foreign land.

Looking at the community, the Tibetans seemed to have met both these challenges successfully, an impression reinforced during my frequent travels there and to other Tibetan refugee communities in India and Nepal. I also observed real economic development within the refugee community. The Tibetan-owned shops, farms and construction sites, often from positions of economic strength, employed Indian labourers, even in remote settlements like Tezu in the far north-east of India. This economic development is in many settlements in striking contrast with that of the local population. Observing this phenomenon, I have through the years wondered why the poverty narrative is still so prevalent among the refugees.

I have been impressed by the increasing numbers of Western individuals and organizations that are assisting[1] the Tibetans through welfare, development and political activism. Dharamsala became an international hub for all well-wishers of the Tibetan cause. Thanks to several years of experience in non-governmental organizations (NGOs), I became aware of the questions raised by foreign assistance, prevalent in every Tibetan settlement, and of the sharp contrast between the level of assistance to Tibetans and that to other populations, even those living adjacent to the Tibetan settlements. Thus I decided to write this book – based on my doctoral research – on the interplay between Tibetan refugees and their Western benefactors.[2] The main question that I want to answer is this: How, after more than fifty years of exile, are the Tibetan refugees still able to attract such substantial assistance from Western governments, NGOs, other organizations and individuals, unlike other populations of refugees who are largely or totally forgotten?

This issue has been addressed by a number of authors, all of whom, however, adopt the point of view of Western individuals or organizations in their relations to the Tibetan refugees. From these works, one has the impression that the Tibetans are, if not totally powerless, then shaped by the foreign aid they receive. Moreover, in the larger anthropological critique of the development framework, the relationship between a population and their developers is almost always described from the latter's point of view in terms of power, influence and transformations. Here, I attempt to give the Tibetans a voice, and to study their own role in their successful attraction of Western support, by examining their discourses and actions towards their patrons and the ways in which they negotiate and mediate their position in such a relationship.

While discussing with Tibetans their success in attracting foreign – and especially Western – assistance, I was struck by the homogeneity of their answers. For them, this success is due not to chance or foreign charity, but to the charisma of their leader, the Dalai Lama, to their religion, from which the entire world has something to learn, to the justness of their cause, and to their own honest and hard-working community. These are the characteristics that, for Tibetans, explain their popularity among Western individuals and organizations. I was, at first, surprised by the absence of foreign influences in these explanations – the Tibetans give all the credit to themselves. I discovered, through my research, that the refugees have indeed managed to perpetuate the attraction of foreign resources thanks both to the establishment of a strong leadership – the Central Tibetan Administration (CTA), known informally as the Tibetan 'government-in-exile', – and to the preservation in exile of a traditional mode of governance that joins politics with religion (a union referred to as *chos srid zung 'brel*).[3] Furthermore, the ongoing Western support is guaranteed by the existence of a strong movement of Western supporters – a movement that, as I will show, arose from an intense interest in the political and religious agendas launched by the Tibetan refugees themselves. However, I will argue that, contrary to what my informants claim, this success cannot be understood without further contextualization.

This context includes, first, favourable conditions surrounding the installation of the Tibetans in exile; second, a long-standing Western fascination with everything Tibetan; and, third, a Western search for a new paradigm of the development relationship. The Tibetan leadership, their agendas, and the reception of these agendas in the West, constitute the main focus of this book.

Contextualization

It is important at this stage to clarify my understanding of certain general terms that have been used so far. Other concepts and expressions will be explained as they appear in the subsequent chapters.

Tibet

Delimiting Tibet is a contentious matter, as the Central Tibetan Administration and the Chinese authorities make very different claims as to its political and historical boundaries (see Powers 2004). Historically, during the time of the first kings, from the early seventh to the ninth centuries, the ethnic Tibetan populations were united under the Yarlung Dynasty. These populations were located in central Tibet: the regions of Ü (*dbus*), whose capital is Lhasa (*lha sa*), and Tsang (*gtsang*), which constitute the core of the Chinese Tibet Autonomous Region (TAR) created in 1965. Tibetan populations also existed to the north and east, in regions called Amdo (*a mdo*) and Kham (*khams*) by the Tibetans, which the Chinese have now integrated into the provinces of Qinghai, Sichuan, Gansu and Yunnan. Finally, the Tibetan Empire also controlled ethnic Tibetan populations to the north-west and west of central Tibet in what is now the Uighur Autonomous Region of Xinjiang, as well as in parts of present-day India, such as Ladakh, Sikkim, Northern Uttar Pradesh and Arunachal Pradesh, and also parts of northern Nepal and Bhutan. This period represented the peak of Tibetan power, when the empire's territory was as large as Western Europe.[4] The Tibetans even briefly captured Ch'ang-an (today's Xian), the then Chinese capital (Snellgrove and Richardson [1968] 2003: 31). After the assassination of King Langdarma (*glang dar ma*) in 842, the empire collapsed, and the central power in Lhasa never regained such a vast territory (ibid.), even during the reign of the fifth Dalai Lama (1617–1682) and his reunification of the country.

Different authors make a distinction between 'political' Tibet (central Tibet, where power was located in Lhasa) and 'ethnic' or 'ethnographic' Tibet, a much larger entity where 'Tibetan civilization' (Stein [1962] 1972) once flourished. Actually, different Tibetologists remark that if the Tibetans refer to *bod* (the Tibetan word for 'Tibet') for central Tibet and its inhabitants, they refer to *nang pa* ('those from inside') for the followers of *chos* (meaning Dharma and, consequently, religion, as elaborated below), which is the main marker of their collective identification and, hence, applies to an area much larger than central Tibet (Kolas 1996: 52ff.).

Today, 'political' Tibet is more or less coextensive with the Tibet Autonomous Region (TAR). However, the Tibetan leadership in exile claims the three main provinces (*chol kha gsum*) of Tibet: Ü-Tsang, Kham and Amdo, which are much larger than the TAR. In this book, I shall use the name Tibet in both its political and ethnographic senses, and will specify the intended meaning as required.

Tibetan Refugees

As stated in the 1951 United Nations Convention Relating to the Status of Refugees, a refugee is a:

> [p]erson who is outside his or her country of nationality or habitual residence; has a well-founded fear of persecution because of his or her race, religion, nationality, membership of a particular social group or political opinion; and is unable or unwilling to avail himself or herself of the protection of that country, or to return there, for fear of persecution. (United Nations High Commissioner for Refugees 2008: 6)

Today, 16 million refugees exist throughout the world (not counting the so-called 'internally displaced persons'). The largest of these communities is the Palestinians (around 4.6 million), followed by refugees from Syria and Afghanistan (around 2 million each), Iraq (around 2 million), Sudan (around 700,000), Somalia (around 460,000), Congo (around 400,000), Burundi (also around 400,000) and Vietnam (around 370,000) (ibid.). The Tibetan refugees in the world numbered 127,935 in 2009, according to the second official survey (Planning Commission 2010). Yet because of various complicating factors, such as continued migration from Tibet to Nepal and India, it remains very difficult to estimate their total numbers. An official from the CTA gave me a figure of 150,000 as the government's estimate of the number of exiles,[5] which would make the Tibetans between the tenth and fifteenth largest refugee community in the world.

About 147 states have signed the 1951 UN Convention or its 1967 Protocol, but India has not. As a consequence, Tibetans who escaped their country and settled in India are not protected by the UN Convention. Nonetheless, from the very beginning the Indian government has recognized these Tibetans as refugees.[6] As such, they have the right to stay in India and can work, even though considered foreigners. It must be noted – and this will become clear in the following chapters – that India granted unique relief and rights to the Tibetans. The Tibetans who arrived between 1959 and 1979, and their children born in India since then, can obtain a Residential Certificate (RC), the Indian legal recognition of their status, which has to be endorsed every six or twelve months (depending on the settlement's location) by the Foreign Registration Office (FRO), as in the case of every other foreign resident in India. This RC entitles them to receive an Identity Certificate (IC), which permits them to travel abroad. Refugees who arrived after 1979 are in limbo; they are allowed to stay in India but are not entitled to any Indian official documents.

On the Tibetan side, the CTA provides a 'green book' (named after its colour, see Chapter 2), which acts as an identity card. Under the Tibetan Charter of 1991, every Tibetan should possess such an identity card, but for obvious political reasons Tibetans living in Tibet cannot obtain one. This document is valid only within the sphere of influence of the CTA, and entitles holders to claim such services as schooling and welfare from the Tibetan administration. As further described in Chapter 2, the CTA recognizes Tibet as the three provinces of Ü-Tsang, Kham and Amdo, and hence Tibetans and Tibetan refugees from these three regions, or those who have at least one parent from anywhere in 'ethnographic' Tibet, can claim such a Tibetan identity card.

My research concentrates on the Tibetan refugee community in India, the largest in the world (accounting for around 70 per cent of the 150,000 Tibetan refugees). Occasional comparisons are, however, drawn with other countries such as Nepal, where the CTA is well represented but where the socio-economic conditions of the Tibetan community are quite different. As always in such a project, the scope of the work is constrained by that fact that not all aspects of the central question can be dealt with exhaustively. I therefore limit myself to examining Western assistance to Tibetan refugees, in full awareness that they are also helped by traditionally Buddhist countries like Taiwan, Japan and Thailand, and, importantly, by their main host country, India.[7]

Tibetan Religion

My understanding of Tibetan 'religion' corresponds to what the Tibetans call *chos*, the Tibetan word for the Sanskrit word *dharma*: the teaching of the Buddha. According to the 1998 survey on Tibetans in exile, 99 per cent of the refugees living in India and Nepal are Buddhists, calling themselves *nang pa*, literally 'insiders' (Planning Council 2000: 201). They belong to one of the four prominent sects (or schools) of *Vajrayana* (the Adamantine Vehicle, also called *Tantrayana* or Tantric Vehicle), the latest of the three main phases of Buddhism. The schools in question are Nyingma (*rnying ma*), Kagyu (*bka' rgyud*), Sakya (*sa skya*) and Gelug (*dge lugs*). Buddhism came to Tibet in two phases: the Early Diffusion, which extended from the seventh to the ninth centuries, and the Late Diffusion, which began in the late tenth century.

Besides *chos*, the Tibetans in exile officially recognize a 'fifth school': this is Bon (*bon*) – not Buddhism but a religion certainly influenced by it. Bon is known to Tibetan historians as the indigenous religion of Tibet. The mutual influences between Buddhism and Bon in Tibet are recognized, and the actual practice of Bon resembles Buddhism.[8] As a Gelug master wrote in the eighteenth century: 'Bon is so mingled with Buddhism and Buddhism with Bon that my analytic eye fails to see the difference between them' (Karmay 1998: 533).

In exile in 1977, Bon was, for the first time in Tibet's history, recognized by the official Tibetan leadership as a Tibetan religious tradition, when it was politically represented at the Tibetan Assembly alongside the four main schools of Buddhism. In exile, Bon followers represent less than 1 per cent of the refugee community, and most of them are concentrated in Dolanji (Himachal Pradesh, India), but their official visibility has become much greater thanks to their new seat in the Assembly.

At present, for reasons described below, the Tibetan leadership has adopted a broad definition of 'religion'. This is consistent with the position expressed by the Dalai Lama in his first autobiography: 'Roughly speaking, any noble activities of mind, body and speech are Dharma, or religion' (Dalai Lama [1962] 1997: 204).

The West

The use of the term 'West' as a totalizing concept does not mean that it describes a single, homogeneous reality. However, my use of the term follows that of the population I study: the Tibetans refer to 'Westerners' as *dbyin ji* (pronounced 'yinji'), a term that means 'Englishman' but also, by extension, any (white) foreigner coming from Europe or the New World.

The Tibetan refugees have the opportunity to meet different *dbyin ji* in India and Nepal: tourists and travellers, Dharma and New Age followers, sympathizers with the Tibetan cause, researchers, and others. The Tibetans hold certain preconceptions about the *dbyin ji* they meet. I am one of these *dbyin ji*, and I was often surprised to hear of the expectations that the Tibetans had of me, as much as they must have been to learn of my expectations of them as Tibetans. By and large, the Tibetans call anyone of Caucasian type *dbyin ji*. People of other ethnic backgrounds are more commonly referred by their colour. Finally, my understanding of assistance as 'Western' is those organizations and individuals from Western Europe, South Africa, North, Central and South America, Australia and New Zealand.

Methodology

The research undertaken for this book has been in the form of fieldwork, involving 'participant observation'. I understand fieldwork as a qualitative method involving the immersion of the researcher within the studied population, as well as the holistic study of this population's behaviour and customs. The understanding of the latter, however, arises from a wide range of contacts, interviews, surveys, participation in the community's life, and other observations. As a result, such a method enables the researcher to acquire an inductive form of knowledge.

Since 1998, I have conducted three principal rounds of fieldwork in India, the longest of these being for doctoral research, when I spent one year (2006) in different settlements. My different stays in Tibetan settlements since 1998 amount to a total of two and a half years. I chose to conduct my main fieldwork in three places, selected for their representativeness of the Tibetan community in India. I spent the longest period in Dharamsala, capital of the Tibetan diaspora and the transnational location where Western individuals and organizations meet the refugees. I spent a shorter period in Tezu (Arunachal Pradesh), a remote settlement difficult of access, because I wanted to see how the Tibetan Agency (i.e. the CTA) and Western organizations worked there. I also spent time in Bylakuppe (Karnataka), the largest and oldest Tibetan settlement, and, moreover, the one most fully documented since the earliest time of exile, and whose subsequent evolution I wished to understand.

In Dharamsala, through contacts and interviews, I gained a thorough overview of the organization and management of the CTA. I conducted research in every department of the administration, with a special emphasis on the Planning Commission. The people interviewed in this commission were willing to assist me, and provided as much information as I needed – information all the more significant because foreign researchers do not apparently approach the commission as frequently as they do other departments. I also spent much time in the Library of Tibetan Works and Archives, reading different reports and literature from or about the CTA – documentation that is unavailable in European libraries. Thanks to an accreditation letter issued by the CTA, I could interview officials who were not normally willing to answer questions (such as those in the Department of Finance). Armed with this letter, and with personal contacts, I organized my journey to the settlement in Tezu (Arunachal Pradesh), which, for political and geographical reasons, is very difficult to visit. My interviews there gave me insights into the power and authority of the CTA over the remotest Tibetan settlement, as well as on the impact of foreign assistance in a place where no Westerners (tourists or development professionals) had stayed for at least the previous seven years. My stay in Bylakuppe was also fruitful, for the same reasons, and I was able to observe relations between the largest Tibetan settlement outside Tibet and both the CTA and Western organizations. I also spent time in the Tibetan area of Darjeeling, as well as in all the settlements of Arunachal Pradesh, including Shimla. In 2007, I spent three months with two organizations based in Europe and worked with Tibetans, inside and outside Tibet, as I wanted to understand how they negotiated with the Tibetan administration. My internships in both organizations gave me insights concerning their work, their internal management, their engagement with the CTA and Tibetans, and the individuals working there as well as members and donors. Finally, I spent three months in Tibet itself, mostly in Lhasa, the capital, since I wanted to understand the contacts between Western organizations and Tibetans in a different setting. This rich experience allowed me to better situate relations between Tibetans living inside and outside Tibet, between Western organizations working inside and outside Tibet, and between Tibetans living in Tibet and the Western organizations in a wider context. In Tibet, I was able to interview many informants working in Western organizations. All were anxious that I should preserve their anonymity. Some even postponed our meetings continuously because they did not want to meet me, but wished to avoid refusing an appointment directly. The level of paranoia I discovered in Lhasa seemed to be an excuse for the organization not to communicate; but it is true that in the People's Republic of China (PRC) the work of these bodies is never guaranteed, and their presence is contingent on their absolute neutrality on the Tibet issue.

To respect my informants in Tibet, I decided to preserve strict anonymity of individuals and organizations throughout the book, with some exceptions where I received formal authorization. I have thus changed the names of my informants, and have avoided, to the best of my ability, giving information that could lead to their identification. However, none of the characters or situations in this book is fictitious; all are represented as I genuinely saw, understood and lived with them.

This book is built upon more than 150 structured or semi-structured interviews that I conducted, the numerous notes I took from my observations and from secondary sources. The interviews were mostly conducted in English, because I was more at ease with this than with the Tibetan language, although a translator helped me on a few occasions. Conducting the interviews in English was not a problem because most of the people I interviewed spoke it well. During my fieldwork, I collected a variety of important materials: reports from the CTA, from Tibetan and Western organizations, and from meetings of these different groups; various internal documents on these organizations; and various materials published by the organizations themselves, such as flyers and booklets. These documents represent an important way to understand how these organizations are established and managed, and how they communicate and disseminate their work. I will use some of these extensively because they underpin my arguments. I refer to the relevant internet addresses whenever these are available, in order to allow the reader easy access to them and to further reading.

Finally, I would like to finish this section on methodology by raising a point that is rarely mentioned in research on Tibet and Tibetans: the position of the researcher. It should be remembered – especially in the domain studied here, where passion, emotion and politics rule – that ethnographies are shaped by the ethnographer himself.[9] Thus, allow me a few words about myself. I indeed conducted this research following my own opinions, which could be defined, in the words of my own informants, as a 'middle-way approach'. This means that I am not a Buddhist, but neither am I against Buddhism; I feel close to the Tibetans, but am not against the Chinese; I place myself between theoretical perspectives on NGOs and their day-to-day practices. As a result, my research was built not on any conscious preconceived agenda, but by following a middle path in trying to understand and shed light on difficult questions. This was even more important given the fact that, in different presentations of my work, I encountered often very emotional, if not extreme, reactions from people who thought that I was showing the Tibetans as maliciously controlling their donors, or on the contrary, as being 'too clever'. I think instead that, like many refugees in the world, the Tibetan refugees developed certain successful survival strategies.

Chapter Outlines

Every chapter in this book is a brick in the structure of explaining the Tibetan refugees' success in the West.

Chapter 1 presents the historical context of the settlement and rehabilitation of Tibetans in India. It details the key historical, political and socio-economic events that allow for an understanding of the argumentation developed in the following chapters. Moreover, this diachronic study gives insights into how the CTA could and did emerge as a developmental agency, thanks to the help of the host and Western countries. This chapter proceeds through the distinct historical phases that the Tibetans themselves recognize, giving an original and updated context for the Tibetan refugees. It is built out of my fieldwork as well as original secondary sources from, for example, NGO archives, as well as published and unpublished materials.

Chapter 2 studies the Tibetan administration, the CTA – its history, its organization, and the principal discourses that provide it with legitimacy and power within the Tibetan community. As Chapter 1 shows, the collective memory of shared sufferings was important in the creation of a diaspora. Chapter 2 describes how the CTA continues to use this memory, and other symbols and institutions, to create the sense of belonging to a diaspora with nationalist objectives. This chapter describes also how the Tibetan administration negotiated its position as a local partner for the organizations that work with Tibetans. These organizations are then described together with the type of resources that they bring. Finally, the chapter addresses the concept of *chos srid zung 'brel* (religion and politics joined), and how this has led to the construction of two interconnected agendas. This chapter shows that the Tibetan leadership has been absolutely instrumental in the Tibetan refugees' success – a point neglected by the existing literature.

Chapters 3 and 4 study, respectively, the political and the religious agendas that the CTA has developed in order to maintain its presence on the international stage and perpetuate foreign support for the refugees. In Chapter 3, the political agenda is described in terms of the deployment and display by the Tibetan administration of the main concepts, ideas and values expected of the local partner by the Western organizations in the development relationship. Chapter 4 focuses on the religious agenda – that is, how the Tibetans came to launch what I call a religious strategy. They have managed indeed to present themselves as invaluable in their relationship with their Western patrons: by reorganizing their religion in exile; by presenting their Western patrons as being in need of this religion; and by operating what I call a 'spiritualization' of the received support. These two chapters show that the Tibetans have not only a political and religious power able to represent them, but one that has launched proactive agendas to keep the Tibet cause alive and to perpetuate the attraction of Western resources. In so doing, the Tibetan refugees have accommodated their patrons' expectations, as described in the literature on development and on Tibetans, and have also created their own model, their own specificities in the relationship with their patrons.

Chapter 5 describes the reception in the West of these two agendas, and how a transnational community, which I call 'the Global Tibet Movement', was created around the Tibet cause. It shows the prevailing stereotypes of Tibet and Tibetans in the West, ones that validate the reception of the Tibetan agendas. This chapter, through a discursive analysis, shows how the Global Tibet Movement is the platform for the Tibetan agendas in the West, in terms not only of assistance but also of discourse and action.

Chapter 6 analyses the developmental relationship between the Tibetans and their Western supporters. It shows how a kind of model relationship could arise from the different elements described in the previous chapters. The model proposed by the Tibetans initiated what I call the 're-enchantment' of the development relationship, which is described in this chapter. I propose here a new way of understanding relations between the Tibetans and their patrons, and study the adaptability of such a model.

The last chapter, Chapter 7, describes the challenges induced by the relationship on the Tibetan refugee community. It analyses the latest developments in the community from the perspective of Western patronage.

Notes

1. I use the terms 'assistance', 'support' and 'aid' interchangeably to refer to the allocation of political, material or symbolic resources (see Chapter 1) from donor countries, organizations or individuals.
2. Similarly, I use the terms 'benefactors', 'patrons' and 'donors' interchangeably to refer to the individuals or organizations that provide assistance to Tibetans (see Chapter 2).
3. As a rule, I will give the Wylie transliteration (written in italics) of every Tibetan term I use. However, having transliterated it, I will usually go on to use its common form, where such exists: for example, *mchod yon* will always be written as such, but *khams* will be presented as Kham. As for Sanskrit terms, I will write these in italics without diacritics and follow the same principles as for the rendering of Tibetan terms.
4. See, amongst others, Stein ([1962] 1972: Chapter 1), Snellgrove and Richardson ([1968] 2003: Chapter 1) and Goldstein (1994: 76ff.).
5. The 2008 edition of *World Refugee Survey* counts 110,000 Tibetan refugees in India (U.S. Committee for Refugees and Immigrants 2008: 31) and 20,500 in Nepal (ibid.: 24).
6. The only community apart from Sri Lankan Tamils to have this recognition in India.
7. Although Western assistance to Tibetans has been addressed by a number of works, non-Western support, especially Indian, which has been crucial to the Tibetans' successful rehabilitation and development, tends to be overlooked in literature on Tibetan refugees. Studies of this non-Western assistance to Tibetans are needed, not least because Asian assistance, both inside and outside Tibet, is increasing.
8. For further reading on Bon, see, amongst others, Skorupski (1981), Kvaerne (1990), Kvaerne and Thargyal (1993), Kumar (1997), Karmay (1998), and Karmay and Watt (2007).
9. A recent development in ethnography has reshaped and reconfigured some classical dichotomies used in the field, such as local/global, inside/outside, tradition/modernity, 'us'/'them', and so on. This deconstruction has been brought about by a self-reflexive rethinking on the part of ethnography itself, initiated by a variety of post-modern, post-structuralist and post-colonial thinkers such as Clifford (Clifford, Marcus et al. 1986; Clifford 1983, 1988, 1997), Jameson (1991), Pratt (1992), Gupta and Ferguson (1992, 1997), Bhabha (1994), Marcus (1995) and Appadurai (1990, 1996), to name but a few.

1

Rehabilitation and Development in Exile

Arrival in Exile

In 1911, the Chinese Revolution and the collapse of the Qing dynasty marked the beginning of de facto independence for Tibet. A convention in Shimla (India) in 1914 between Chinese, British and Tibetan representatives attempted to settle the boundaries of Tibet. The British admitted Chinese 'suzerainty'[1] over Tibet, but the treaty was never signed by China. The First World War and the 'warlord era' in China kept Tibet safe from colonial intentions for some years. The thirteenth Dalai Lama was thus able to rule his country until his death in 1933. During his reign, he introduced some practical reforms, developed the army and affirmed Tibet's independence.

After the thirteenth Dalai Lama's death, Reting Rinpoche (*rwa sgreng rin po che*) was appointed regent and headed the Kashag (*bka' shag*, the Tibetan Cabinet) for seven years. His main task was to find the reincarnation of the Dalai Lama. The quest was arduous and marked by political pressures. Only in 1940 was the new Dalai Lama formally proclaimed. Born in July 1935 in a small village in Amdo, the boy who would be renamed Tenzin Gyatso (*bstan 'dzin rgya mtsho*) was brought to Lhasa, where he began his monastic education. In 1941, Reting was accused of being too close to China and deposed. After the Second World War, the fragile independence of Tibet, in any case not recognized by any country or international organization, collapsed. In 1947, the British left India, and in October 1949 the People's Republic of China (PRC) was proclaimed. One of the first declarations by Mao Zedong addressed the 'Peaceful Liberation' of Tibet. However, in 1950 the Chinese People's Liberation Army (PLA) attacked the town of Chamdo (*chab mdo*, Eastern Tibet) and advanced towards Lhasa. The Tibetan army, outnumbered and outmatched, was eventually crushed easily by the PLA.

The Dalai Lama, enthroned hurriedly in 1950 at the age of fifteen, sent messages to Western countries seeking support, but without success. The Dalai Lama recalls:

> The British government expressed their deepest sympathy for the people of Tibet, and regretted that owing to Tibet's geographical position, since India had been granted independence, they could not offer help. The government of the United States also replied in the same sense and declined to receive our delegation. (Dalai Lama [1962] 1997: 60)

The Dalai Lama, shortly after his enthronement, fled to Yatung (*gro mo*) on the Indian border to escape from the advancing Chinese troops. He had been well advised to send part of his personal fortune to a secure location. Hence, he was followed in Yatung by more than a thousand animals laden with gold, silver and centuries-old coins, a procession that continued on to Sikkim. The treasure was hidden in the Sikkimese king's stables until 1960, when it was sent to Calcutta by trucks to be converted into currency. This amount, almost US$1 million at that time, constituted the Dalai Lama's Charitable Trust and contributed to the financing of the rehabilitation of Tibetan refugees (Avedon 1994: 91). As early as 1950, the Tibetan leaders appealed to the United Nations (UN) against China, but only El Salvador brought the question to the UN, and no further action was taken because too few countries were interested in raising the issue (Holborn 1975: 717). Interestingly, a U.S. representative explained that, as a Roman Catholic country, El Salvador was following the personal inclination of Pope Pius XII, and the Vatican's official will, to bring Tibet's fate to the international stage (Knaus 1999: 74).

In 1951, with no alternative in the face of the inexorable advance of the PLA, a Tibetan delegation was sent to Beijing by the Dalai Lama to negotiate with the Chinese authorities. Instead of negotiations, however, the Tibetan emissaries found that the Chinese, in a position of strength, were dictating to them. With forged seals – as they were not entitled by the Dalai Lama to sign any treaty – the Tibetans signed the so-called 'Seventeen Point Agreement'. This agreement, rejected later by the Dalai Lama as his first significant political act in exile, stated that Tibet was an inalienable part of the 'big family of the motherland' (China), but that the status and prerogatives of the Dalai Lama and the Panchen Lama should be respected (Goldstein 1989: 737ff.). The years of de facto independence were over.

During the same period, the United States was at war with the communist regime of North Korea. Tibet thus acquired a new strategic importance, and the U.S. government decided to support Tibetan resistance to the Chinese invaders. This support, both overt and covert, was economic and military. An unofficial statement by the United States proposed help that would 'facilitate Tibetan wool marketing in the United States, conduct marketing surveys for other Tibetan products, buy up unspecified "strategic Tibetan products which otherwise might go to China", offer Tibet economic aid, ... offer military assistance to the extent permitted by Indian law' (Knaus 1999: 81). Later, the United States also secretly proposed to the Dalai Lama, still in Yatung, that he should organize his escape to India, Ceylon or another 'friendly place' until he could go back to his country as 'head of an autonomous and non-Communist country' (ibid.: 102). This proposal used the term 'autonomous' because the United States still recognized the Chinese Nationalists' claims to Tibet. But the Dalai Lama had already taken his decision to return to Lhasa and to temporize with the Chinese. In 1954, the Tibetan leader went to Beijing to meet Mao Zedong, who appointed him Vice-Chairman of the First National People's Congress of China. After one year in China, and before returning to Lhasa, the Dalai Lama had his last meeting with the Chinese leader, who told him: 'Religion is poison. It has two great defects: it undermines the race, and secondly it retards the progress of the country' (Dalai Lama [1962] 1997: 88).

In India, a form of political resistance was being simultaneously organized by Tibetans. Gyalo Thondup, the Dalai Lama's brother, installed in Darjeeling (West Bengal), expanded diplomatic contacts with Western chancelleries, and especially that of the United States, in order to gain support. Knaus recounts how Gyalo Thondup, together with other Tibetans, created in 1954 what can be seen as the first relief organization for Tibetans, in Kalimpong. The 'Tibetan Welfare Association' had as its principal goal the sending of relief and support to the victims of a flood that had affected Gyantse, the fourth largest Tibetan city. The association was financed initially by the Indian government, and then by the sale of Indian whisky and tea to the Chinese troops in Tibet (Knaus 1999: 123–24). Later on, this association continued its activities by sending pamphlets and information to Tibet about the situation and the Chinese occupation. This continued until 1959, when it was dismantled.

In 1956, Gyalo Thondup went to the U.S. embassy in Calcutta and asked for military help. He got it, beginning one of the most secretive operations of the Cold War. The aim of the United States was not so much to liberate Tibet from its occupiers as 'to impede and harass the Chinese Communists' (Knaus 1999: 139), and they organized airdrops of arms and ammunitions between 1958 and 1961. They also trained Khampa fighters in a top-secret camp built in Colorado, and planned to parachute leaders of the guerrilla force into Tibet. After 1959, the guerrillas were relocated to Mustang until 1974, when the resistance was disbanded under tragic circumstances.[2] The resistance, christened the 'Volunteer Freedom Fighters for Religious and Political Resistance',[3] enjoyed significant successes, but covert U.S. support was never enough to threaten the Chinese presence in Tibet. Moreover, the U.S. support was more anti-communist opportunism than genuine support for an independent Tibet; and in 1972, when Richard Nixon went to Beijing to meet Mao Zedong and Zhou Enlai to formalize the rapprochement of the two countries, all support for the Tibetan resistance ceased.

In Tibet, from 1950 onwards, Tibetan discontent against Chinese rule gained momentum. This passive resistance culminated in the Lhasa uprising of 10 March 1959. The uprising, which was severely crushed, led to the flight of the Dalai Lama to India. This day is now remembered, commemorated and celebrated in Tibetan settlements as 'Uprising Day', and is an important marker of the Tibetan nationalism built in exile. The Dalai Lama himself recounts his memory of the flight into exile in *My Land and My People* (Dalai Lama [1962] 1997): how he was in disguise when leaving his palace, how he and one hundred of his ministers and household members crossed the Lhasa River, and how they travelled on foot and by horse to reach India. They crossed the Indian border on 30 March 1959, after reinstating the Tibetan Government in a ceremony in Lhuntse Dzong, close to the Indian border. Thousands of Tibetans, hearing that their leader had escaped, decided to follow him.

On the Indian side, on 4 April 1959, the Indian Prime Minister, Jawaharlal Nehru, stated at a press conference in New Delhi that, 'India's policy was governed by three factors: the preservation of the security and integrity of India; India's desire to maintain friendly relations with the People's Republic of China; and India's deep sympathy for the people of Tibet' (Holborn 1975: 719). At that time, the Tibetan refugees and the Indian government still believed that the problem with China would be quickly solved and that the former would soon be able to return to their country.

In the following months, thousands of Tibetans continued to flee their country. In 1964, an estimated 40,000 lived in India, 11,000 in Nepal, 6,700 in Sikkim and 3,000 in Bhutan (Holborn 1975: 720, 723, 746). These Tibetans represent the first wave of refugees and as such the core of the actual refugee community in exile. No more important wave of refugees would be seen again before the end of the 1980s, because of the tight control of the Chinese authorities during the Cultural Revolution and the closed nature of the country. The limited opening of the Tibet Autonomous Region (TAR) at the end of the 1980s, and the repression of demonstrations from 1987 onwards, would lead more Tibetans to make their way into exile. Since then, refugees have continued to arrive every year, at various rates depending on the political situation in the TAR; but an average of 2,000 to 2,500 refugees crossed the border yearly before 2008.

Memories of these early escapes remain vivid and emotional among the Tibetans who arrived in India, Nepal or Bhutan at that time. Palden Tashi,[4] a young monk in 1959, told me how he escaped on 18 March, leading the sixteenth Karmapa Lama's horse, and how they reached Bhutan after several weeks of exhausting and dangerous travel. At that time Bhutan, not recognized by the UN as an independent state, was under the control of Indian police and, as such, safe for many Tibetan refugees. After two months in Bhutan, they left for Sikkim, where they settled permanently in Rumtek. Nowadays, Palden Tashi is not a monk anymore, but an official for the Tibetan government; he lives in Dharamsala, where he settled with his family. He told me his personal story from more than forty years ago, as vividly and clearly as though it had happened the previous day. Like Palden Tashi, all the Tibetans who fled in 1959 or in the 1960s can still vividly remember their 'way to freedom', and these memories constitute the first seminal element in the establishment of a new Tibetan community in exile, a narrative that would subsequently become a myth of creation of a new Tibetan society for the younger generations born in exile. This narrative is constantly revived by new refugees who continue to arrive every year and who have to follow the same way – a long escape route of around three weeks on foot across the Himalayas, made mostly during winter because the frontiers are less controlled in this season. This escape marks them forever, and their experiences are added to similar ones of their fellows and melded into the collective memory.

The Rehabilitation Phase

Early Centralization: The Central Relief Committee for Tibetans

In its response to the mass influx of Tibetan refugees, in April 1959 the Indian government immediately created two transit camps, one in Missamari (in present-day Assam) and the other in Buxa (in West Bengal). Problems of acclimatization quickly became obvious: the climate in India was difficult to endure for the Tibetans, who were used to the dry, cold air of high altitudes; Tibetans could not speak Indian languages, nor locals the Tibetan language; and the refugees who managed to bring some belongings were forced to sell them and quickly ran out of resources. Epidemics unknown in Tibet began to develop, claiming a large number of victims in the camps.[5] Moreover, the refugees continued to pour into the camps, which rapidly became overcrowded. The refugees nevertheless endured these conditions in the hope and belief that they were only temporary, and that they would soon be able to return to their country.

The Indian government placed responsibility for the refugees not with the Home Ministry but with the Ministry of External Affairs, whose head was Prime Minister Nehru (Dawa Norbu 2001: 9). It did so for three main reasons. First, India's leaders wanted to isolate the Tibetan issue in order to avoid problems with China. Second, the government did not want to give the impression to existing refugees, like the Bengalis, that the Tibetan refugees were receiving better treatment. Third, Nehru wished to be personally in charge of the refugee issue to counter those opponents who reproached him for his policies towards China and considered the situation in Tibet to be a consequence of his policy failure. As a result, Nehru placed the Tibetan refugees high on his agenda, in a gesture that Dawa Norbu calls 'humanitarian work as political compensation' (ibid.).

To avoid problems with China and with other refugees in India, the Indian government at first wanted to avoid the creation of large refugee centres. The result was that, until the settlements were eventually created, many Tibetans had to survive on their own, scattered around the northern areas of the country. They lived by begging, or on the food distributed by relief or missionary organizations, or by working as road builders. Woodcock, founder of Canada's Tibetan Refugee Aid Society (TRAS), wrote in a 1962 report:

> In Kalimpong, 3,390 refugees queued up on the day [I] visited the town, for a distribution of powdered milk – the only food available – by a Christian organization. In Darjeeling the Dalai Lama's representative in charge of relief said that 1,200 destitute people came regularly for the twice-weekly distribution of powdered milk and a little rice. (Woodcock 1970: 415)

Many refugees were nevertheless working on road construction sites in the Himalayan regions of north India and making a living, but this work was more than exhausting, and many died as a direct consequence. In 1969, there were still sixteen thousand Tibetan road workers waiting to be rehabilitated in one of the existing settlements (Office of His Holiness the Dalai Lama 1969: 3).

In April 1959, the Indian government launched the Central Relief Committee for Tibetans (CRCT), which would channel and control the aid of various international organizations to the two camps. This international assistance was organized and made available from the early days of the Tibetan exile. Travis Fletcher, field director of the American Emergency Committee for Tibetan Refugees (AECTR), founded in 1959 by Lowell Thomas,[6] wrote:

> The speed and efficiency with which help was made available to the Tibetans in those early days of the programme amazed most sceptics ... As the Dalai Lama crossed the border into India, I despatched a cable to Mr Thomas, asking him to appeal to the American people for medicines, cash and supplies. The speed with which Mr Thomas and his [c]ommittee met this crisis was amazing. Within two days a contribution of 5,000 dollars was cabled to the Acharya Kripalani[7] [chairman of the CRCT] and his [c]ommittee, followed within two weeks by another contribution of 10,000 dollars. Forty-eight hours after my cable was sent, a Pan Am Cargo plane landed at the airport in New Delhi with approximately four thousands pounds [worth] of antibiotics and other valuable drugs. (Central Relief Committee for Tibetans 1961: 24)

The American organization CARE, founded in 1945, provided 95 per cent of the food rations in Missamari during eight months of operation. The AECTR provided medical supplies and money. American Christian organizations, such as the Church World Service (CWS), the National Christian Council, the United States Catholic Conference, the Church's Auxiliary for Social Action, the Lutheran World Federation (LWF), the Catholic Relief Services (CRS) and the Young Men's Christian Association (YMCA), also helped with refugee aid through the CRCT (Central Relief Committee for Tibetans 1960: 17). Quickly, other organizations, such as the Swiss Red Cross and the International Red Cross, the Tibet Society of Great Britain, Oxfam, the Norwegian Refugee Council, the United Nations High Commissioner for Refugees (UNHCR), the TRAS, and many more (see Information Office of His Holiness the Dalai Lama 1981: 72), joined the international movement to assist the Tibetan refugees.

Centralization through the CRCT facilitated the relief of the refugees in the camps of Missamari and Buxa. As Travis Fletcher wrote in 1961:

> [T]his programme was a new experience to me, and no doubt to representatives of other voluntary agencies, in that we were working through a Central Relief Committee, and not independently. At first there was some doubt in my mind as to whether this could be done effectively. It did not take long, however, to realise that *working through a central coordinating agency made up of prominent and devoted Indian people*[8] *would result in better coordination, which is so desirable but rarely accomplished in any relief programme* ...
>
> By working through the Central Relief Committee, confusion and duplication were avoided. The voluntary agencies did not find themselves, as is frequently the case, contributing the same items to the refugees while other items were in short supply. (Central Relief Committee for Tibetans 1961: 24, emphasis added)

This centralization and long-term planning, which would later be continued through the Central Tibetan Relief Committee (CTRC)[9] and the Central Tibetan Administration (CTA), are a main factor behind the constitution of the latter as a developmental agency. They are indeed instrumental in the explanation of a successful or unsuccessful relief programme. Castles, describing migratory movements in Asia, identifies lack of long-term planning as a common trend (Castles and Miller 1998: 175). Such a lack is absolutely not the case with Tibetans. When centralization and long-term planning are missing, a lot of effort and funds can be lost, as seen in programmes linked to the 2004 tsunami in Asia and the 2010 earthquake in Haiti.[10]

The Resettlement Programme

Politically, the Indian government tried at the outset not to harm its relations with China. It therefore refrained from seeking international help for the refugees, and kept control of the relief coming from foreign countries. But after its humiliating defeat and the demonstration of Chinese power in the border war of 1962,[11] India changed its policy towards the Tibetan refugees. As an example, India came to support the UN resolutions on Tibetans. In 1965, the Indian delegate to the UN made this address:

> Although the relationship between Tibet and India ... has flourished all through the ages ... we have always taken care not to make that relationship a political problem ... we have exercised the greatest caution, for we believe that what should concern all of us is the much larger human problem, namely, *the plight of these good and innocent people who are being victimized merely because they are different, ethnically and culturally from the Chinese.* (Office of His Holiness the Dalai Lama 1969: 301, emphasis added)

Furthermore, militarily, India understood that it needed a special force capable of defending its borders in remote Himalayan regions, where it had been weakened by the Chinese invasion and the blatant incapacity of its own army to prevent it. The Indian army accepted the principle of a Tibetan force in its own ranks, called officially the 'Special Frontier Force' (SFF) and known by the Tibetans as 'HQ 22' (after the identification number of their squadron). Envisaged at the beginning to include six thousand soldiers, the force today is double that size, with two companies of women (Knaus 1999: 272).[12] 'The Indians now had their own special units of Green Berets (they wore red), and they were Tibetans' (ibid.: 273). But, like the United States, which actually had a different agenda from the liberation of Tibet, the Indians saw the SFF more as a force to defend its borders than, as the Tibetan fighters saw it at the beginning, as one to fight for Tibet. Nowadays, the SFF, which distinguished itself in 1971 during the fight for the independence of Bangladesh and more recently during the 1999 war with Pakistan in Kargil (Jammu-and-Kashmir), is integrated into the Indian army as an elite company, and many Tibetan refugees get their resources from it.

Thus, from 1962 onwards, the Indian Government sought permanent solutions to settle the Tibetans in an environment where they could re-establish their culture, and accepted the principle of the creation of large settlements that could also provide employment for the refugees, many of whom continued to work on the gruelling and deadly road construction crews in the Himalayas. Nehru asked the Indian states to provide land for the new refugees, as many as fifteen hundred of whom were arriving each week during these years (Holborn 1975: 718). Several states answered positively, giving (mostly poor-value) land to install the settlements. This permanent solution sought by the Government of India gave the Tibetans the opportunities to transform their community from homeless exiles to refugees who could thus re-create their cultural, social and political environment. The transit camps were transformed into settlements, which rapidly took the shape of villages, far from the common plight of other refugee populations in Asia (for example, the Bhutanese refugees in Nepal),[13] and far from the UNHCR refugee camps of tents, which strew poor countries. The fact that India accepted the principle of niches of preserved Tibetan culture on its territory, and participated materially and financially in their implementation, is central to understanding the successful rehabilitation of the Tibetans.

The first agricultural settlements were built at the beginning of the 1960s on the plains of South India: one in Bylakuppe (State of Mysore, now Karnataka), created in 1961, one in Mainpat (Madhya Pradesh), created in 1962, one in Mundgod (Mysore), created in 1963, and one in Chandragiri (Orissa), created in 1963. The climatic conditions caused suffering for the refugees, and many of them died. Furthermore, few exiles knew about agriculture, and even Tibetan farmers did not at first know how to handle these low-altitude lands and crops. The Tibetans themselves executed all the work of land clearing; they had to cut trees, remove the trunks and roots, and dig the soil. Many died in the course of this effort, either killed by the work itself, disease or by wild animals living on these lands (Avedon 1994: 88ff.). In 1961, two other settlements were created in the North-East Frontier Agency (later the State of Arunachal Pradesh): one in Changlang[14] and one in Tezu. These were both in 'protected areas', close to the Chinese border. According to Holborn, '[t]his fact has had a marked effect on the amount of assistance forthcoming from private agencies, as well as on the establishment of government services' (Holborn 1975: 722).

The first two workshops for the production and selling of carpets were created, for Tibetans who were not farmers, in Darjeeling (West Bengal) and in Dalhousie (Himachal Pradesh) near Dharamsala, at the end of 1959 (Subba 1990). The Tibetan carpets, a traditional Tibetan craft, were to become world famous, and would eventually support and even create fortunes for refugees in Nepal. Other employment opportunities were proposed in different settlements by the Tibetan Industrial Rehabilitation Society (TIRS), established in 1965. These projects included, amongst others, woollen mills, tea estates, Tibetan crafts, and handicraft centres. The TIRS provided care and education for the people involved in these projects, funded by foreign organizations.

In April 1960, the Dalai Lama settled permanently in MacLeod Ganj, a locality on the heights of Dharamsala,[15] Himachal Pradesh (Dalai Lama [1962] 1997). He installed and organized the Central Tibetan Administration (CTA) there. India refused to recognize it, but, as the host country, nonetheless gave relative independence to the Dalai Lama, allowing the

Tibetan administration to manage and administer all the refugee settlements. These settlements, as well as the different organs of the CTA, are registered legally in India as charities (under the Societies Registration Act XII of 1860). Most of these organs are also registered under the Foreign Contribution Act, which allows them to receive foreign funds.

Given the reality that the period of exile might last longer than expected and that the difficulties in the Tibetan settlements needed attention, the Indian government decided to give greater responsibility and power of decision-making to the international agencies working through the CRCT. In 1964, the CRCT presented a Master Plan for the rehabilitation of the Tibetan refugees in India. This plan was supported by all the donor agencies working with the CRCT, as they had some part in its design: they were able to draw up individual projects and submit them for inclusion (Holborn 1975: 725). This Master Plan marked the transition from an emergency relief situation to the rehabilitation of the Tibetan refugees.

It is important to note, nevertheless, that the idyllic picture painted by Fletcher in 1961 and quoted earlier was not shared by all organizations. A report written the same year by a representative of the Swiss governmental organization Schweitzer Auslandhilfe in Nepal reassesses the reasons for the exile:

> It is difficult to understand why Tibetans have fled; only the big landlords and lamas have been in danger. Indeed, the farmers and labourers have today under Chinese occupation a better living than before under the Dalai Lama. This explains the high percentage of monks who are predominantly charlatans amongst the refugees. (Forbes 1989: 26)

Moreover, the danger of the donors forgetting the Tibetan plight already existed after the emergency of the first years. The director of CARE India wrote in 1961:

> Another problem: like all disasters, *like all refugees, the Tibetans in time begin to lose their novelty and dramatic appeal.* In the United States, it may be possible to sustain interest and sympathy with pictures, and by continuing to tell the remarkable story of the Tibetan refugees. *Public response – through CARE and other agencies – to the distress of the Tibetan refugees has been one of the most generous on record,* including aid to the Hungarians. (Central Relief Committee for Tibetans 1961: 30, emphasis added)

To avoid this danger, and to perpetuate the success of the refugees by attracting more help and by avoiding negative statements such as the Swiss remark, the different organizations decided, in 1963, to work under the coordination of the International Council of Voluntary Agencies (ICVA), which was to bring its own expertise to bear on the settlement issue of Tibetan refugees. In April of the same year, ICVA presented its findings at a seminar held in Geneva, where forty NGOs were present, as well as representatives of the UNHCR, the government of India, and the Dalai Lama. The principal conclusions were that the international agencies should assist the Indian government (through the CRCT Master Plan) in the creation of further settlements to absorb fifteen thousand more Tibetans (Holborn 1975: 726).

In 1964, the UNHCR's director of operations for India and Nepal reported the success and effectiveness of these different bodies in coordinating assistance to Tibetans, and accounted for the following improvement of the situation:

> Nearly one year ago I visited India and so, on this occasion, was able to compare the situation of the Tibetan refugees and the progress made in the last year. *At the outset, I would like to state that the progress achieved since I last visited India must give great satisfaction to the Government of India, H.H. the Dalai Lama, the Central Relief Committee and all the voluntary agencies giving assistance to the refugees.* Not only is there a marked improvement in the physical condition of the refugees, but *the whole structure of the Central Relief Committee has developed in such a way as to ensure a steady improvement of the situation of the refugees.* The emergence of a Master Plan Sub-Committee should lead to a comprehensive plan for the solution of the problem. (UN General Assembly 1964: 1, emphasis added)

A Collective Memory and the Rise of a 'Diaspora'

The rehabilitation phase is known in the collective memory of the Tibetan refugees as a time of terrible circumstances and hardship, followed by a fantastic recovery that makes them proud of their achievements. Indeed, a succession of difficulties created a sense of belonging to the same community. These hardships were, first, the escape into exile, then the road construction sites, and, finally, the building of the settlements that prompted more casualties. As one of my informants put it:

> I was born in India [in 1977] when my parents were already financially more at ease. It is hard for me to imagine the hardship they had to endure when they arrived in India in 1962, from Tibet. They left behind them all their belongings, having heard that His Holiness [the Dalai Lama] was in India and arrived first in Nepal. Then they tried to reach Dharamsala to be close to His Holiness but did not find any work there. They were sent to Manali [Himachal Pradesh] to work on the road construction sites. There they lived in tents in a climate close to the Tibetan, with really little to eat. It was terrible and my father speaks very little about this period. After some years they managed to buy some clothes with the little money they could save and they installed a small stall in a street in Manali. Now [1999], they have a proper shop in a concrete building and can make a living out of it. I had the opportunity to go to school and to improve a lot the life and education level of my family ... We, Tibetans, are now

very successful, having started from nothing. This is just amazing. (Personal Communication #A 1999)

Many refugees were similarly engaged on road construction sites in Himachal Pradesh, in the regions of Shimla, Chamba, and the Kulu and Kangra valleys (Office of His Holiness the Dalai Lama 1969: 129). According to one relief organization, there were over twenty-one thousand refugees in 1967 who were working on road construction and as contract labourers – which is a significant proportion of the estimated total of sixty-seven thousand refugees in India at this time (The Tibet Society 1967: 39). This collective memory of the hardships at the beginning is carefully maintained by official institutions, like schools. A Tibetan Children's Village (TCV) school history book for grade VIII recounts the following, next to pictures of the early time in exile:

> Many people today know the stories of their parents' and grandparents' hazardous and challenging life at work on roads …

> Children, women and men were all working side by side in unusual groups: former nuns, farmers, monks, officials, all thrown together. They had to endure a full day's hard physical toil under a mighty sun, followed by nights crammed into tiny tents. Fresh from the highland plateaux, they entered a new world of rain and jungle for which their thick chuba and high boots were unfit, dramatising their entry into a life for which they have had almost no preparation.

> After the first of the refugees were sent to the mountains of northern India to do the road work, refugees were sent off in crowded trucks to various other locations. Many people today know the stories of their parents' and grandparents' work on these roads. (TCV 2000: 5–6)

These hardships nevertheless led to practical results: most of the Indian roads in the Himalayan region of Himachal Pradesh were built by Tibetan refugees. The Tibetans are proud of this result, and as such do not consider themselves just passive beneficiaries of Indian assistance, but rather the deserving earners thereof.[16] Many of my older informants recollected their days in these road construction camps with sadness, but were also proud to tell me that the roads that I was using when visiting other settlements in Himachal Pradesh were built by them.

The same self-awareness of their merit is grounded in the fact that the refugees built their settlements themselves (preparing the lands and building the houses). These settlements, a melting pot of refugees from different socio-economic as well as geographical origins, acted as the 'technology of power' (Foucault and Gordon 1980) to propagate the new exile identity, forged in the experience of the same hardships and diffused throughout the settlements. The history book gives this description of the building of the settlements:

In all the settlements, when the refugees would arrive, temporary huts served as shelter until permanent houses were completed. In most instances the refugees were paid minimum wages to drill wells, clear forests and prepare the land for agriculture ...

The first Tibetan settlement, called Lugsung Samdupling Tibetan Settlement, was started on 16 December 1960 on the outskirts of Mysore in dense forest at Bylakuppe. The site was gradually cleared and made fit for cultivation through the painstaking work of the first Tibetan settlers. The new land consisted of undeveloped jungle. Apart from the intense heat, wild animals posed great danger to human lives. The trees and undergrowth were backbreaking and exhausting to remove. Many died, but the remaining Tibetan settlers kept working and made the best of the wretched conditions ... Today, it is one of the largest Tibetan settlements in India. It is fully self-sufficient and has a number of schools and monasteries including Sera Monastery, which had been one of the three largest in Tibet. (TCV 2000: 6)

The history of these different apocalyptic traumas – carefully kept alive in the collective memory for the younger generations – is dramatically different from the present situation, making it even more powerful, and strengthening the feeling amongst refugees that they not only miraculously survived but have flourished thanks to their own merit and hard work (a feeling that I will analyse later and call the 'self-sufficiency narrative'). This shared history of the Tibetan refugees, shattering the socio-political and economic organization of Tibetan society, created a new society of refugees, freed from their early differences and equal in their plight. This new society, crystallized around this vivid collective memory, which takes on the characteristics of a myth of creation, recognizes one man as its saviour: the Dalai Lama. The Dalai Lama is the central figure of this new community of refugees. He is not only the ultimate temporal and spiritual leader but the source, the genesis of the community. Everything started from him[17] and the refugees to whom I talked about the hardships of the beginning all related their strength and hope for a better future to the privilege of being with their god-leader. In practice, before the Dalai Lama introduced elections and democracy in his community, the government and its offices were labelled as belonging to the Dalai Lama: for example, the ministries were called 'offices of His Holiness the Dalai Lama', and the settlement officers were 'representatives of His Holiness the Dalai Lama' (See Office of His Holiness the Dalai Lama 1969).

As Malkki observes, every refugee population tends to create a common history, a sort of collective capital of archetypes, whence it can draw its narrative for the present and the future (Malkki 1995). The Tibetans did this, and the new community, formed in exile around a shared apocalyptic history and one charismatic leader, can now be defined as a diaspora, as it has all the characteristics of such a society. Safran lists six defining characteristics:

[The concept of diaspora can] be applied to expatriate minority communities whose members share several of the following characteristics: 1) they, or their ancestors, have been dispersed from a specific original 'centre' to two or more 'peripheral', or foreign, regions; 2) they retain a collective memory, vision, or myth about their original homeland – its physical location, history and achievements; 3) they believe that they are not – and perhaps cannot be – fully accepted by their host society and therefore feel partly alienated and insulated from it; 4) they regard their ancestral homeland as their true, ideal home and as the place to which they or their descendants would (or should) eventually return – when conditions are appropriate; 5) they believe that they should, collectively, be committed to the maintenance or restoration of their original homeland and to its safety and prosperity; and 6) they continue to relate, personally or vicariously, to that homeland in one way or another, and their ethnocommunal consciousness and solidarity are importantly defined by the existence of such a relationship. (Safran 1991: 83)

Indeed, following his definition point by point, one can see that the Tibetan refugee community forms a diaspora.[18] However, I would add to Safran's second point that the Tibetan refugees retain a collective memory not only of their homeland but also of their arrival in exile, as seen earlier. And to complete Safran's definition, the Tibetans do not want to be integrated into their hosts' culture or even society, as a self-chosen policy of keeping their own culture as authentic as possible for their return. Finally, the conceptualization of the notion of diaspora[19] is holistic and implies the deployment of a strong leadership for the community. This is also the case for the Tibetan refugees.

The End of the 1960s, and the 1970s

The refugees' situation improved rapidly after the terrible circumstances attending the beginning of exile. At the end of the 1960s, many settlements, like Bylakuppe, were self-sufficient in the sense that their inhabitants were no longer dependent on external resources for their daily survival (Conway 1975: 79ff.; Goldstein 1975a, 1975b).

By the end of the 1970s, the refugees had been able to create in exile not only viable settlements, but Tibetan environments. Some later works even spoke of a 'renaissance of the Tibetan civilization' (Fürer-Haimendorf 1990). They did so by re-establishing religious institutions, developing the teaching of the Tibetan language, culture and history, and increasing socio-economic conditions that could perpetuate their survival in exile and safeguard their identity. These achievements were made possible by the help of the Indian government, and the continuous help of international organizations. These years mark the establishment in exile of the socio-political conditions that would lead to the consolidation of the Tibetan refugees' system as an administration with a government, as well as an aid agency for the refugees.

During the same period, the thirty-five settlements that can be found today in India were all built: sixteen are based on agriculture, fourteen on agro-industrial activities, and five on the production and selling of handicrafts (mostly carpets). If the scattered concentrations of Tibetans in India – who are not living in settlements but whose communities are organized in like manner (with a welfare officer as leader) – are added to the settlements, the number of Tibetan colonies in India under the jurisdiction of the CTA increases to fifty-six: forty are located in the north (Himachal Pradesh and Ladakh); seven in the north-east (Sikkim and east of Bhutan); two in Delhi; two in the centre; and five in the south (Planning Council 2000: 71ff. See Figure 1 for a map of the settlements in India, Nepal and Bhutan).

The end of the 1970s marks the end of what the Tibetans call the 'rehabilitation phase' and the beginning of the 'development phase', as told to me by an official from the CTA. At this time, many organizations made the assessment that their help was no longer needed and terminated it, which is the case with most of the Christian organizations cited previously. Some made this evaluation much earlier, in the 1960s, and of all the organizations working with the Tibetans in 1960, only a few have remained until today. These organizations were replaced by new ones, many created exclusively to help Tibetans, sustaining a process that created a real transnational community centred on the refugees.

The Development Phase

Stabilization in Exile

At the end of the 1970s, the Tibetan leadership assessed that the exile could last for much longer than the twenty years that had already elapsed, and that the Tibetan community should now be developed in exile in order for it to flourish and be strong enough to attain its main goals: saving its culture and regaining a free country.

'The development stage [after 1980] is marked by "stabilization" of Tibetans in India where they themselves are now being asked to take the responsibility of development projects and activities' (Office of Planning Commission 2004: 19). This 'stabilization' and awareness of the situation, along with the recent material development, pushed the Tibetan leadership to plan for the future in exile. In doing so, the Tibetan community broadened its activity from preoccupation with the concerns of refugees alone to become a community in development. The CTA accordingly asked a U.S. expert on development, Richard Weingarten, to compile a report on the needs of the community in terms of planning and structural management (as further described and analysed in Chapter 2), which led to the first 'Integrated Development Plan' (Planning Council 1992).

At the same time, in 1979 and 1980, three fact-finding missions of emissaries from Dharamsala visited Lhasa and Tibet, and came back to report the overwhelming and jubilant reception they had received as the Dalai Lama's representatives. The Chinese authorities had not expected such reactions from the Tibetans; they thought that these emissaries would be ignored and that Chinese power was now really accepted in Tibet. They had to cancel a fourth mission in order not to lose face (Avedon 1994: 323ff.). These missions came back with a message from Deng Xiaoping, then general secretary of the Chinese Communist Party, noting that, except for independence, everything could be discussed on the Tibetan issue. The Dalai Lama, acknowledging this fact, abandoned the Tibetan claims to independence in 1987.

In parallel, the attributes of a democratic state were developed further by the CTA, including the adoption of a Charter in 1991, the increase of direct suffrage for elections, and the installation and improvement of a 'welfare state'. This period marks the deployment of the Tibetan administration as an important Agency, which developed political as well as religious agendas. As soon as the Tibetan refugees were self-sufficient, they developed the will to show the world what they could have achieved socially and economically without the presence of the Chinese.[20] Being successful in exile, the refugees wanted to make void China's claim of Tibetan backwardness and show the world what they were capable of.

With a strong legitimacy of leadership, because the Dalai Lama had re-created in exile the same temporal and spiritual system of power as had existed in Tibet, and because of the support and recognition of his authority shown by the Tibetans inside Tibet during the fact-finding missions, the Tibetan refugees could claim that their success was their own and that they would have reached it in Tibet without Chinese power. This continuity with the past is indeed what appeals to Western organizations working with Tibetans, represented by what Tibetans call the *chos srid zung 'brel* or 'politics and religion in one'. Stabilization in exile was contingent on the strengthening and perpetuation of the community's resources for its survival. The launch of an 'international campaign' by the Dalai Lama, as well as different events in Tibet and in the West in the 1980s and 1990s, guaranteed the continuation of Western support.

The International Campaign

In 1972, the U.S. reconciliation with the Chinese regime marked a shift in the strategic and political importance of Tibetans for the United States, who no longer needed the Tibetans as a lever in anti-communist strategy, and so its direct support to the Tibetans ended. The Tibetan leadership became aware of the danger of this new situation. The challenge was to find a way of compensating for the U.S. government's drastically reduced support. The target was the U.S. population itself, as well as U.S. non-governmental organizations (NGOs). From October 1987, the date of the Dalai Lama's second public press conference since 1959 (Dalai Lama 1995: 17), the Tibetan leader began to address and convey a political message to the West, because so far he had only been engaging with international leaders as a religious leader.[21] He also redirected the contents of his message from

> the arena of geopolitical national interests to the sphere of core U.S. values – to the U.S. ideological commitment to freedom and human rights. The goal was to create a momentum that would lead the United States to support Tibet because it was the just and right thing for freedom-loving Americans to do. (Goldstein 1997: 76)

Clifford Bob, in 'Merchants of Morality', describes how a leader of a local cause can be transformed into an 'international icon' on the 'global morality market' (Bob 2002: 45), a process that can be translated to the Tibetan leader:

> What transforms insurgent leaders into international icons? Eloquence, energy, courage, and single-mindedness can undeniably create a charismatic mystique. But transnational charisma also hinges on a host of pedestrian factors that are nonetheless unusual among oppressed groups. *Fluency in a key foreign language, especially English; an understanding of Western protest traditions; familiarity with the international political vogue; and expertise in media and NGO relations – all these factors are essential to giving leaders the chance to display their more ineffable qualities.* (ibid.: 42, emphasis added)

In the middle of the 1980s, in order to strengthen this goal, an 'international campaign' was launched with the help of Western supporters and donors; in 1988, the International Campaign for Tibet (ICT) was created. Chaired by U.S. actor Richard Gere, it is now one of the most important Tibet support groups in the world in terms of activities of awareness, advocacy and development. Even if the organization claims that it is independent from the CTA, it is often considered as one of its extensions, or at least as its closest ally, and Lodi Gyari, the executive chair of its board, is also 'Special Envoy to the Dalai Lama for North America'. Moreover, according to McLagan, the ICT is partly financed by the CTA, which transfers funds via Switzerland (McLagan 1996: 327). Similarly a 'Year of Tibet' (10 March 1991 to 10 March 1992) was launched in the United States, consisting of religious and cultural performances, a giant Kalachakra initiation by the Dalai Lama in New York in October 1991, and other events aimed at raising popular awareness of the situation in Tibet (ibid.: 370ff.).

The International Campaign for Tibet involved these organizations, as well as the CTA, in being more visible on the international stage and in the media through different activist actions. Different events in the 1980s and 1990s gave this international campaign an important springboard, and the Tibetan refugee cause was publicized more than ever. From this time onwards, Tibetan support groups mushroomed throughout the world, keeping alive in the West the 'Tibet cause' and the refugees' plight. This movement took the shape of a transnational community, which I shall call 'the Global Tibet Movement'.

Decisive Events in the 1980s and 1990s

The Dalai Lama presented a 'Five-Point Peace Plan' before the U.S. Congress in September 1987. This peace plan was the Dalai Lama's first step towards abandonment of the independence claim in favour of the autonomy demand. It had serious political consequences. The Dalai Lama formally presented this autonomy demand one year later, in June 1988, in front of the European Parliament in Strasbourg. He said:

> The whole of Tibet, known as Cholka-Sum (U-Tsang, Kham and Amdo), should become a self-governing democratic political entity founded on law by agreement of the people for the common good and the protection of themselves and their environment, in association with the People's Republic of China. The government of the People's Republic of China could remain responsible for Tibet's foreign policy. (Dalai Lama 1995: 38)

The Chinese government, in its effort to open the country to the international community, opened Tibet for foreign tourists at the beginning of the 1980s. Western tourists began to flow in freely for the first time in Tibet's history. They could see the situation in the country and be aware of the Tibetans' claims. The Dalai Lama's reception by Congress in 1987 was regarded inside Tibet (as well as in exile) as a great opportunity to make official such claims, and to win the political support of the United States. In Lhasa, a group of Tibetan monks began to shout anti-Chinese and pro-independence slogans to show their support for the Dalai Lama. This triggered a series of riots in Tibet, which were repressed severely by the police (whose ranks included many Tibetans). These tensions lasted until at least 1989, and the Chinese government quickly closed Tibet's borders and imposed martial law. But this came too late, as many Westerners had witnessed the riots and documented them. Some were even in the middle of the demonstrations, and could later recount what they had seen. Amongst them were Robbie Barnett, who created the Tibet Information Network, and John Ackerly, now a board member of the ICT. Later in 1989, the Chinese student demonstrations and their violent suppression in Tiananmen Square, shown on television throughout the world, strengthened the feeling in the West, whether true or not, that a very violent kind of repression was happening in Tibet.

In 1989, the Dalai Lama received the Nobel Peace Prize for his non-violent struggle for freedom, implying Western recognition thereof. This kind of support was not, however, translated into political action, as no country has to date dared to challenge directly the Chinese authorities on the political issues of Tibet. Later, in the middle of the 1990s, two Hollywood films relaunched and strengthened the world's awareness and support for the Tibetans. Both *Seven Years in Tibet* (directed by Jean-Jacques Annaud) and *Kundun* (directed by Martin Scorcese) present the vision of a lost paradise, invaded and raped by evil Chinese forces. These successful films galvanized support for the Tibetan cause.

All these events created large movements of support in the West, and in the decade between 1985 and 1995, Tibetan support groups and NGOs helping Tibetans grew quickly. ICT membership, for example, went from five thousand in 1995 to eighty thousand in 2000 (Pike 2001: 30), and is at more than one hundred thousand today (http://savetibet.de/ict/). As will be described in Chapter 5, these groups decided to join together in an international network, the International Tibet Support Network (ITSN), which counts more members than there are Tibetans living in exile.

In 1991, the Dalai Lama declared in front of the Tibetan Parliament: 'In the 1960s, many non-Tibetans, who were genuinely concerned with our cause, suggested to me that the cause of Tibet was a dead one and that there was no hope for us. Now, thirty years later, we see the resuscitation of Tibet's cause' (Dalai Lama 1995: 132). The Tibetan cause was not only resuscitated, it took on such importance that the exiled community embarked on a new period, which I call the 'globalization phase'. During this last phase, beginning in the 1990s, the Tibetan refugees were confronted by outside influences, inside changes and material successes, and they began to encounter different challenges, which I will study in the last chapter of this book.

Notes

1. A vague term with regard to international laws, but used on purpose (see Goldstein 1989).
2. On this subject, read Knaus (1999) for the best documentation of these events; also Jamyang Norbu (1994) for the account of an ex-fighter, and McGranahan (2005) and Dunham (2005) who also study the Tibetan resistance and its end. Works on these events are scarce.
3. This unified the different resistance movements including the largest, created in Kham (*khams*) and called Chushi Gangdrug (*chu bzhi sgang drug*, 'four rivers and six ranges', a sobriquet of Kham) (Knaus 1999: 144ff.). Note also the reference to both religion and politics in the name of the unified movement.

4. In order to respect the anonymity of some of the people I interviewed, their names have been changed.

5. For a description of the hard conditions in these transit camps, see the account by the famous Tibetologist Hugh Richardson of his visit to Missamari in 1960 (Richardson [1962] 1984: 234ff.); see also Avedon (1994: 76ff.).

6. The AECTR ceased its operation suddenly in 1968, without having seen its developmental projects through to their end (Office of His Holiness the Dalai Lama 1969: 21). The AECTR staff declared that their organization was conceived with a view to providing relief in an emergency situation (archive material #84 2008) – but this did not explain why they left their projects unfinished.

7. Acharya Kripalani (1888–1982) is an important figure in Indian contemporary history. He led the Congress Party at the time of Indian partition. His role as chairman of the CRCT helps to explain the success of such an organization. His wife, Sucheta, became the first woman to lead an Indian state, Uttar Pradesh. She is recognized by the Tibetans as a 'friend' and is described as having been very active with regard to assistance for the Tibetan refugees (Information Office of His Holiness the Dalai Lama 1981: 109).

8. Travis Fletcher notices also that because the majority of CRCT members were also members of the Indian Parliament, many administrative obstacles in the delivery of aid to Tibetans were quickly relieved; this also explains the success of the emergency programme (ibid.).

9. The CTRC is the Tibetan legatee and successor of the CRCT. Although very close in their names and missions they should not be confounded.

10. See evaluations of the humanitarian answers to these crises at http://www.alnap. org/resource/3530 and http://www.alnap.org/current/Haitilearningportal. The website addresses given in the book change frequently. They were last checked in June 2015.

11. See an exhaustive description of this war in Knaus (1999: 260ff.).

12. This figure is very high: if 12,000 Tibetans are engaged on the SFF, they represent more than 12 per cent of the roughly 94,000 Tibetans who were surveyed in India in 2009 (Planning Commission 2010). Interestingly, however, this figure is not noted in any official Tibetan document, and the two demographic surveys conducted since 1998 make no mention at all of this military commitment. One of my informants, a former SFF soldier, gave me the same figure of enrolment, but at the time I thought he was exaggerating. An official website of the Indian army announces 10,000 men (not only Tibetans) in the SFF (http://www.bharat-rakshak.com/ARMY/units/87-SFF.html) but given the secret or sensitive nature of their operations the reality could be different from the communication.

13. There are about 110,000 refugees from Bhutan, with Nepalese origin (or BONO, 'Bhutanese of Nepalese Ethnic Origin'), living in camps under UNHCR management in South Nepal (Subedi 2001: 77). They left Bhutan in the beginning of 1990s after the Bhutanese king, worried about their growing number, edicted a law to fix the Bhutanese identity. These refugees are quite forgotten on the international stage, especially as Bhutan is seen in the West as an ideal monarchy, living in peace and developing trendy concepts such as the 'Gross National Happiness'. See more on these refugees' issue in Hutt (1996), Lay Lee (1998), Subedi (2001) and Kharat (2001).

14. Later shifted to Miao (Arunachal Pradesh) in 1976.
15. See Anand (2002) for the choice of the name 'Dharamsala' instead of the more accurate 'MacLeod Ganj'. The appellation 'Dharamsala' tends to be preferred by Tibetans, Indians and Westerners when talking about the Tibetan government and the Dalai Lama's residence.
16. Similarly, as will be seen in the ensuing chapters, some Tibetan refugees feel as deserving earners of assistance from other countries' organizations and individuals.
17. Actually, the Tibetan cosmogony reports that the Tibetan race descends from the union of a deity, Avalokiteshvara, with a local goddess, and the Dalai Lama is recognized by the Tibetans as the reincarnation of Avalokiteshvara.
18. The term 'diaspora' has been applied to Tibetan refugees for some years now. It was first used in the works of Nowak (1983), Fürer-Haimendorf (1990), Klieger (1991) and Barnett and Akiner (1994). It was further developed and conceptualized in two books edited the same year by Korom (1997a, 1997b): *Constructing Tibetan Culture* and *Tibetan Culture in the Diaspora* (proceedings of the panel on refugees at the Seventh Seminar of the International Association of Tibetan Studies). Anand (2003) presents a comprehensive study of the Tibetan community as a diaspora.
19. There has been a proliferation of studies on diaspora as a concept, and also as a concrete fact. Diaspora theories are linked with purity, hybridization, deterritorialization, cosmopolitanism and transnationalism. Vertovec gives three different meanings to diaspora: '"diaspora" *as social form*, "diaspora" *as type of consciousness*, and "diaspora" *as mode of cultural product*' (Vertovec 1997: 277, original emphasis). Cohen provides a typology of diasporas 'based on their most important characteristics, naming classical, victim, labor, imperial, trade and cultural diasporas' (in Anand 2003: 218). One can also refer to Hall (1990), Tölölyan (1996) and Clifford's chapter 'Diasporas' in *Routes* (Clifford 1997).
20. See the article of Dawa Norbu (1999) where he discusses the compatibility of Buddhism, and especially Tibetan Buddhism, with democracy. The author wants to show in this article that the Tibetans could have reached democracy by themselves without any external influences.
21. Magnusson describes the Dalai Lama's international travels since 1959, which he calls 'promotional world tours':

> After his 1959 exile to India it was not until 1967 that he could travel further abroad. The first countries he visited were Japan and Thailand. On most of these early tours he met mainly with people interested in Tibetan Buddhism and with Tibet supporters. There was no official meeting with governments and he avoided bringing up political matters. In 1973 the Dalai Lama visited the Pope in Rome and went on to Switzerland and the Netherlands. He continued to Iceland and Norway, went through Sweden and Denmark, and to the UK. In 1974 and 1978 he went briefly abroad but it was not until the extensive 1979 tour covering Mongolia, Switzerland, Greece and the USA that he accessed non-religious forums. In 1980 he once again visited the Pope on his way to Canada. In 1981 he led the

first so-called Kalachakra initiation in Tibetan Buddhism outside Tibet and India. In 1982 he visited South East Asia, Australia, Mongolia, the Soviet Union and Europe. In the years that followed his touring intensified and a more systematic interaction with actors in world politics developed. An indicator of his global prominence was when he was awarded the Nobel Peace Prize in 1989. (Magnusson 2002: 205, emphasis added)

2

The Central Tibetan Administration

The Rise of a Local Partner

Transition from Rehabilitation to Development Phase

In 1975, the vice-chairman of the Tibetan Refugees Aid Society (Conway 1975), based in Canada, wrote that the end of the rehabilitation phase led to three possible approaches to future developments by organizations working with Tibetans. First, some groups believed that the refugees' problems were over: the Tibetans were self-supporting and could survive on their own. According to Conway, the United Nations High Commissioner for Refugees (UNHCR) at the time concluded that the 'Tibetan programme' must be phased out, and that member governments were insisting that resources should be transferred to other needs.

A second approach, given that the settlements were self-supporting, felt that any further assistance would run the danger of elevating the refugees to a more developed stage than their local hosts, which would create tensions. 'In the case of more universal aid agencies, therefore, it is argued that once a level of subsistence equal to that of the local community is attained, resources can be given elsewhere. In the case of agencies solely concerned with the Tibetans, these should now close their books and dissolve their organizations' (ibid.: 82).

A third group of agencies argued that the refugees were now integrated into an 'underdeveloped' country and, as such, should have access to the same developmental projects as their hosts. 'Th[is] will, it is hoped, provide greater opportunities for economic and social growth, and preferably be of a kind to benefit not just individual Tibetan communities but also their neighbours and hosts as well' (ibid.). It is this third approach that has prevailed, and various organizations have continued to help the Tibetan refugees to this day.

Conway remarks that this third approach required a change in the mode of fundraising by the foreign agencies. Rather than the small amounts donated by different organizations, there would need to be substantial and guaranteed investment. Such investment could only be provided through cooperation between these organizations and governmental institutions. Conway notes that an initial experiment in Canada was carried out with the government's Canadian International Development Agency (CIDA). This agency helped the non-governmental organizations to enter into the modernist theory of development: '[these NGOs were] encouraged – even prodded – into thinking in developmental terms, rather than in terms of charitable "do-goodism"' (ibid.: 84). Thanks to CIDA's support, the Tibetan Refugee Aid Society could continue to work much more effectively with its beneficiaries.

Moreover, the Central Tibetan Administration (CTA) organized itself as such an institution, entitled to receive foreign assistance by virtue of the fact that it was considered as a local partner by foreign organizations. This new model still allowed the Tibetan refugees to be helped by foreign donors, and to make a smooth transition between successful rehabilitation and economic and material development.

Constitution as a Local Partner

Korff and Schrader (2004: 12ff.) propose a history of development by decades since the 1950s. They show that the development world was reorganized in the middle of the 1970s to make it more professional, with structured procedures for the attribution, realization, monitoring and evaluation of projects. At the same time, non-governmental organizations began to work with governmental funds, which meant more control and monitoring thereof, and the entire sector was revolutionized (Korten 1990). This process is still ongoing. Moreover, since the end of the 1990s, the emphasis in development has been placed on the defence of the environment, 'sustainable development', as well as the local people. Whenever the latter mismanage their environment or put it in danger, they have to be reformed.[1] Development is no longer merely social, political and economic, but also environmental. 'Sustainability proved quite successful as an instrument of "de-politicising" development by naturalising it' (ibid.: 14). New concepts were recently injected into development, such as 'mainstreaming' and 'up-scaling'. The population in development now has to be 'empowered', and 'capacities' have to be 'built', leading the same authors to note that these populations are still considered powerless (ibid.: 15).

An American expert in finance and development, Richard Weingarten, co-founder of the Tibet Fund in the United States in 1981, understood that Tibetans in exile had to recast their financial and material necessities within these new developmental requirements if they wanted to continue to attract international assistance.[2] In the mid-1980s, Mr Weingarten talked with the Dalai Lama about economic development and the future of the refugees. The Dalai Lama worried that the educated younger generation, who were finding jobs only outside the settlements, might lose their culture. Following that discussion, the American expert agreed to evaluate how the Tibetans should manage their settlements for the future, and to look at economic development and culture preservation. Weingarten spent nine months in twenty-five settlements, and presented to the Dalai Lama, in September 1987, a 200-page unpublished report called the 'Tibetan Economic Development Project Report' (Weingarten 1987).

This report gave a planned framework to the Tibetan community, which had to deal, from this time onwards, with two strains: the arrival of new refugees from Tibet, who created a demographic challenge in the community; and the rise of an educated youth with no employment prospects inside the community.[3] The report's main objective was to address these two challenges both by giving proposals for transforming the community and creating employment opportunities inside the community, and by securing international assistance through the adoption of modern economic management methods. These objectives are summarized thus in the report:

> While planning is primarily done for the purpose of problem solving and increasing the livelihood of obtaining desired results, it is also a fundamental constituent of successful fundraising in the economic development arena. This arena is relatively new for the community, and must be entered with understanding. Funding here is not based on an easily perceived and imminent human need, but rather on the soundness of an economic concept, its financial feasibility, the manner and professionalism with which it is presented, the establishment of criteria for evaluating its success or failure, and cultivated personal relationships with funding agency staff. The audience for proposals in this area is generally quantitative by nature and might be a bank, a bi- or multilateral agency, or an international charitable organization specializing in economic development. (Weingarten 1987: 19)

The report's main suggestions were for the Central Tibetan Administration to create: (a) a 'Planning Council', an office in charge of the economic planning of the entire community; (b) employment opportunities by developing vocational training, expanding the carpet business and the handicraft centres, creating processing plants for agricultural products like maize and dairy products, and launching small-scale industries like a sweater manufacturing plant; and (c) a revolving loan fund to act like a 'central bank'. Similar proposals were made for each settlement, given their local specificities.

Mr Weingarten told me that the first reaction of the Tibetan officials was one of doubt because they did not see the usefulness of developing the economy in exile, given that their objective was to go back to Tibet. In answer to such hesitation, the expert answered that, whatever the future of Tibet, the leadership and the community needed to develop modern methods of economic management. The Dalai Lama adopted this point; he understood the importance of having an economically integrated approach, and, as Mr Weingarten told me, 'it may have influenced the Dalai Lama's view that going back to Tibet and focusing on the social issues rather than on the political issues was quickly a successful strategy and a political compromise'. Indeed, in June 1988 the Dalai Lama formally ceased his call for the independence of Tibet; and the report, showing the importance of economic and social issues, was perhaps connected with this decision.

The first suggestion adopted by the CTA was the creation in 1988 of the 'Planning Council' (PC, renamed lately as the 'Planning Commission'). This council published a 'CTA Projects Needs Support Directory' (Planning Council 1990), which prefigured what would later be called the 'Integrated Development Plan' (IDP).[4] In 1994, the Social and Resource Development Fund (SARD) was created under the Department of Finance of the CTA. This new office manages the financial aspects of the projects and works closely with the PC. The SARD was registered in 1997 under India's Societies Registration Act 1860. As such, it can raise, manage and receive foreign funds and act as an intermediary between donor agencies and the different CTA departments managing the projects. Subsequently, the CTA set up the first revolving loan fund – the first time the Tibetans had borrowed money. They borrowed US$1 million, and then had to learn how to manage the interest rates and increase the value of their loan, as well as justifying and documenting it. A Tibetan, Ngodup Dorjee, had been trained specially at a German university in how to manage such funds. The budget set for this fund, now called the 'Corpus Fund', for 2008 was 140 million Indian rupees (approximately US$3 million). The main income of the fund came from donations and fundraising events (Office of Planning Commission and SARD 2005: 29).

Thanks to these new organs, the Tibetans in exile could secure and continue to receive foreign resources. Today, the CTA supervises through these offices almost every project developed by foreign donor agencies, and it evaluates many of these projects, working therefore quite independently. The fact that the CTA centralizes and coordinates all projects for the refugees creates ideal conditions for the attraction of foreign assistance. Practically, it works like a local partner or an independent NGO, having its own offices for fundraising, management and evaluation of the projects. The CTA is, as such, entitled by the international organizations working with the Tibetans to receive funds and manage projects, yet with the added and important advantages of indigenous knowledge and expertise. In the professionalized world of development, it is indeed very important for Western organizations to guarantee the efficiency and transparency of their projects as well as the involvement of their beneficiaries.[5] The Tibetans managed indeed to place themselves in such a position.

These international organizations, working with the CTA, recognize the Tibetan administration as the legitimate leadership of the Tibetans. Even though the CTA is not recognized politically by any country, different intergovernmental organizations treat it as a partner; for example, the UNHCR finances the reception office of new refugees in Kathmandu, but the office is managed by the CTA. The administrative costs of the CTA, which are about 20 per cent of the total budget (Office of Planning Commission and SARD 2005: 28), are financed entirely by the Tibetans themselves through voluntary taxes, donations of the Dalai Lama, and income generated by the Corpus Fund. Hence, no organizations finance the CTA directly, the totality of the international funds channelled through the CTA can be allocated solely to projects, and this Tibetan aid agency is thus a perfect partner with no administrative costs. In their communication, these international organizations can thus announce that all their funds go directly to the only beneficiaries. This is a very strong argument in development.

Richard Weingarten's expertise led to the emancipation of the refugees concerning the management of their own development, unlike during the 'rehabilitation phase' (see previous chapter), when they were totally dependent on the foreign development organizations' decisions. Thus, with centralized institutions that could organize both individual and institutional assistance, the CTA assured its transition from the rehabilitation phase to the development phase, and prevented the Tibetan refugees' plight from being forgotten.

This success of the CTA as a local partner for foreign organizations is rooted in the centralization, from the outset, of assistance to the Tibetan refugees. The Central Relief Committee for Tibetans (CRCT, see Chapter 1) was created in 1959 and controlled by the Indian government. Its Tibetan legatee, the Central Tibetan Relief Committee (CTRC), was set up by the Dalai Lama in 1981 to 'look after the welfare and socio-economic development of the Tibetan refugees living in settlements and other scattered communities in India, Nepal and Bhutan' (Central Tibetan Relief Committee 2003: 8). Finally, the centralization and management of the projects were made possible by the PC and SARD under the coordination and leadership of the CTA.

Thanks to these conditions, the CTA today successfully attracts funds for the different projects planned and identified by itself. It can then implement and conduct these projects through redistribution to different ministries and other independent bodies. These projects are finally evaluated and audited by the Tibetan administration. In the management of the entire cycle of development projects,[6] the CTA has become more than a simple local partner for other organizations, and is a developmental agency with its own budget. To become such an agency, the Tibetan administration has had to learn the language of the development world.

A Learned Language

As seen in the reports on different projects produced from the end of the 1970s onwards, the Tibetan leaders quickly met the conditions for receiving and managing foreign assistance: they knew how to write applications for projects and their reports and were successful in the fulfilment of their objectives. One example is the financing by the NGO Oxfam of a dispensary in the settlement of Chaundragiri in Orissa, India. In 1978, the settlement's leader applied for subsidies for the dispensary (Nyima 1978). The application states:

> This being a remote area, lack of proper medical care and facilities is a big problem here and normally the death rate use to be higher than birth rate. Hence, we are trying to have a dispensary within our colony to minimise the problem, but success of it will largely depend on the aid we could receive for maintenance of establishment cost and medical facilities from ou[t]side aiding agencies …

> In spite of various other shortcomings and lack of sufficient fund, the construction work of dispensary building with three rooms has already reached at completion state with available fund and if we could get more fund for medicines, establishment cost and construction of few bedrooms, staff quarter, and a diseal [*sic*] ambulance van, the benefit from services of such a dispensary in these areas to the people will be immense and need not be over emphasised. From this year a medical team from Christian hospital, Berhampur, use to visit once a month to check up the health conditions of people here and use to supply information and medicines of which benefit is immense. Therefore if we have a reasonably equipped dispensary here, the benefit will be immense. (ibid.: 2–4)

The arguments presented here are elaborated in form and content, the incomes and outcomes of the project are clear, and, as a result, Oxfam accepted the application (under reference ORS-38) and financed the dispensary from 1978 until the end of 1982. Since that date, the Tibetans have financed it themselves (Lata Manjari Parhi 1983: 2). Every year, the Tibetans sent in a report on the evolution of the project, with data about the different diseases and the number of patients treated at the dispensary (Nyima 1980, 1982). In 1981, a reporter for Oxfam wrote: 'I was very impressed to see how beautifully they have made use of [the] Oxfam grant. I feel that from the agricultural profit, they will be able to support [the] dispensary completely from next year' (Battacharya 1981: 2).

More recently, an application presented by the Federation of Tibetan Co-operatives in India Ltd (FTCI) presented a 'business plan' to raise funds for the acquisition of two hotels and the business unit of the handicraft centres sold by the CTA.[7] This plan is well structured, with lots of figures, indicators, charts and calculations of business indexes, such as the 'Net Present Value', as seen in its table of contents:

Executive Summary; Background and Objectives; Organizational Structure; Project Description; Budget; Federation Summary; Project Description; Need Assessment; Goal; Objectives; Activity and Timeline; Output; Outcome; Monitoring, Evaluation and Audit; Budget Estimation; Sustainability; Important Assumptions; Net Present Value (NPV); Annexure. (Federation of Tibetan Co-operative in India Ltd 2006)

Besides the language habitus learned by the Tibetans, they appropriated and built different tools to professionalize their management of the projects they implemented or monitored. Different guidelines, procedures and manuals were thus adopted.[8]

More will be said in the next chapter on the issue of language and concepts used by the Tibetans to paste their needs into the general framework of actual development. In this section, we have seen how foreign experts helped the Tibetans to acquire and appropriate for themselves the technical knowledge and tools needed by the modern development world. In addition, we learned how the CTA could become such an indispensable partner for international organizations willing to work with Tibetans.

The Central Tibetan Administration's International Partners

Nature of the International Organizations

The CTA is financed by three main sources of income: first, the refugee community, through donations of the Dalai Lama and a voluntary tax, which finances the expenses of the administration; second, the Indian government, which finances, among other things, a share of the education system; and third, international organizations, which finance more than 80 per cent of the CTA's total budget and therefore deserve further description.

The international organizations and individuals assisting Tibetans can be categorized into five groups:

(1) Intergovernmental and Governmental Organizations
   These organizations work with the refugees through different projects. The CTA receives their resources directly, through the fundraising activities of the SARD, or indirectly, through an intermediate organization. For example, the Canadian International Development Agency (CIDA) financed the Tibetan Refugee Aid Society for its projects in India and Nepal, and in Tibet.
      These organizations do not officially recognize the CTA as a government, and so they only finance overtly what they consider to be politically neutral projects. The UNHCR thus collaborates with the

CTA in its Kathmandu office – the Tibetan Refugees' Welfare Office (a reception centre for all new refugees arriving from Tibet via Nepal) – which is managed by the CTA and whose director is also the Dalai Lama's representative in Nepal. This office is the UNHCR's 'implement partner'. Likewise, the European Commission is developing agricultural projects in Tibetan settlements in southern India.

Some politicized agencies also finance the refugees, such as the U.S. organization National Endowment for Democracy (NED), funded by the U.S. government 'to strengthen democratic institutions around the world through non-governmental efforts' (http://www.ned.org/about). Knaus (1999: 310ff.) claims that, even though the CIA stopped its direct support of Tibetan guerrillas in the early 1970s, the agency has since continued to finance the CTA covertly. I am unable to confirm such a claim, but the fact that different agencies linked to the U.S. government, like the NED, are working with the refugees indicates the continuation of such links.

(2) Non-governmental Organizations (NGOs)

The term NGO is a general one, but I understand it to mean organizations that manage developmental projects with the Tibetans and do not engage in political activism (these are listed in the next category). Some of these organizations work with Tibetans and other populations, while some were created solely to assist the Tibetans. Most NGOs present during the rehabilitation phase no longer work with Tibetan refugees (although some have stayed, like the Norwegian Church Aid and Catholic Relief Services). Other NGOs are more willing to work in Tibet itself now, like the Swiss Red Cross and Save the Children. The NGOs working with Tibetans only are well represented in exile, but most of these do not have a local office, and work through the CTA. Examples are the Tibet Foundation and the French organization Solhimal.

The CTA coordinates their activities through its PC and SARD offices, and organized a joint conference for the first time in 2005 under the title First Donors Conference (Office of Planning Commission and SARD 2005). This conference had weak participation: only 30 organizations attended, out of the 140 invited. Many participants cancelled their visit because of relief operations following the Indian Ocean tsunami of December 2004.

(3) 'Friends of Tibet' or 'Tibet Support Group' (TSG) Organizations

These are political activist organizations for the 'Tibet cause'. Most of them have regrouped under the International Tibet Network (ITN, formerly known as International Tibet Support Network). In 2012, this network included some two hundred organizations from over fifty countries, and claims to have more than a hundred thousand members[9] (i.e. as many people as there are Tibetan refugees living in India and Nepal). These TSGs represent an important turning point in the history of development for Tibetans, and have multiplied greatly since the end of the 1980s. 'Although many of the TSGs are a hybrid of campaigning and relief work, around 150 [of the organizations which are members of the ITN] are solely "political" campaigning organizations, i.e., their work is dedicated to bringing about a change in the political status of Tibet' (Reynolds 2003: 448).

These organizations create and manage development projects, together with activist projects such as demonstrations, petitions and targeted actions. They are the most active – and certainly the most influential – group among the five categories, in the creation and perpetuation, in the West, of the discourse on Tibet. Many of these organizations have, however, a short life span; they are often founded by enthusiastic amateurs (who perhaps return from a visit to some Tibetan settlements in South Asia, or who hear about the 'Tibetan cause' and want to do something for it), who sometimes fail to grasp the requirements for a successful organization and its sustainability.

The TSGs coordinate their actions through the ITN and develop joint projects; many are very structured and have held an international meeting every four years or less since 1990. The first conference was organized in Dharamsala by the CTA in accordance with the International Campaign for Tibet (ICT) described previously. This networking is in striking contrast with the lack of information sharing and cooperation between the various NGOs working with the Tibetans (apart from the recent initiatives to regroup them for a conference).

(4) The 'Dharma Followers'

These are people who call themselves Buddhist and are important patrons of the religious institutions both in exile and in Tibet. Given that the traditional economic system of support to the clergy collapsed when it arrived in exile, new ways of subsistence had to be found. A Western interest in Buddhism, and especially Tibetan Buddhism, provided a good opportunity to find new sponsors. Many monks and respected religious masters have built 'Dharma Centres' (religious centres where Buddhism is taught) and other religious institutions in Western countries (as well as in China, Taiwan[10] and Japan), thus creating new sources of income for their institutions in exile.[11] What Miller (1993: 224) characterizes as a 'Dharma Industry' will be developed further in Chapter 5.

Different NGOs or TSGs reproach members of this group for only funding and helping religious institutions. They are thus criticized for lack of involvement in the lay community and in politics. However, I have observed that this is a generalization and that many Dharma followers are also involved in other activities to assist Tibetans. They indeed support sponsorship programmes as well as other development projects. They actually share with the other groups an interest in the Tibetan people and culture, even if their main interest is the religion and its institutions. Accordingly, donors who would not characterize themselves as Buddhists can support religious institutions. Hence, the different groups are permeable and often interconnected.

(5) Voluntary Supporters

The fifth category is composed of people who regularly volunteer in the Tibetan settlements or give financial support, without being formally part of a structured NGO or TSG. They may organize language courses or take part in the various volunteer organizations to be found in the settlements (see, for example, http://www.lhasocialwork.org/volunteer. html).[12] They are an important group, and it is no exaggeration to say that in every Tibetan restaurant or coffee shop in tourist settlements like Dharamsala, one can encounter Westerners teaching Tibetans on a variety of subjects, but principally the English language. This group also creates vocations and motivations for these individuals to create or work for a settled organization.

Assistance Provided by the International Organizations

Roemer (2008) remarks that that the Tibetan government-in-exile is backed up by an international community, which is the ideal case theorized by Shain. Indeed, the five groups described above provide three kinds of assistance (following Frechette 2002: 7ff.).

(1) Human resources: skills development, teaching and training in languages, communication, and more. This category consists of different projects that 'build capacities' through the training and education of Tibetan official and administrative staff, but also of the population, through vocational and technical training. Examples of such projects are the Fulbright Scholarship for CTA staff: each year, opportunities to study in the United States are offered to Tibetan administrative staff. Some projects enhance and develop the communication and organization of the CTA, the Weingarten report being an example (Weingarten 1987). Volunteering initiatives are mushrooming in the Tibetan settlements, where foreigners teach English or other foreign languages, computer skills, and other subjects. Further projects aim to improve the production by and employment for, the refugees; for

example, an Italian NGO, COSPE, developed a pilot project in twelve settlements in India to launch organic agriculture, and an Israeli NGO is training several dozen Tibetan farmers each year at *kibbutzim* in Israel to teach them modern agriculture methods.

(2) Material resources, of two types:
  (a) The 'welfare state', described below and organized by the CTA and other Tibetan institutions. This assistance is successful; the director of a Western NGO told me that the Tibetans were receiving more proposals for sponsorship than were needed. It is provided mostly by TSG organizations, and has succeeded thanks to the human values that the sponsorship implies, and also because it is easy to implement and develop: the only task for a Western organization is to enter into relations with a Tibetan institution, which will then manage everything. Another wing of the 'welfare state' comprises the infrastructural projects, like construction or renovation of public buildings (schools, hospitals, nursing homes), which are financed by numerous organizations.
  (b) Cultural assistance to monasteries and other religious institutions, and to cultural institutions (including, in exile, the Tibetan Institute of Performing Arts, and the 'Norbulingka', a craft arts conservatoire, established by a Western anthropologist). Help to religious institutions is provided mostly by Dharma followers, and help to the cultural institutions comes from a variety of organizations.

(3) Symbolic resources: personal recommendations, marketing assistance and public statements of support. This is mainly a political form of help provided by the TSGs, such as campaigns for 'Free Tibet', or for respect for human rights in Tibet. These resources also help the Tibetans to realize their agendas (studied in the following chapters) on the international stage, as the TSGs communicate and work in harmony with the CTA.

The total budget managed by the Tibetan administration – the administration costs and development project funds for the community – has grown quickly since the launch of the international campaign. Richard Weingarten told me that, at the time of the report (1987), the annual budget for the entire community was about US$100,000, and is now around US$18 million (of which US$3 million represents the sole administration costs).[13] On the one hand, this explosive growth has increased the dependency of the CTA on foreign (mostly Western) donors, whose assistance now represents, according to the Planning Commission, around 80 per cent of the Tibetan refugees' total budget (personal communication). On the other hand, the success of the Tibetans in the West gives them the power to choose their partners: the PC has had to refuse projects through lack of human resources to manage them (ibid.). We see that the welfare state provided by the CTA is perpetuated thanks to foreign assistance, yet the Tibetan administration spends a considerable part of its functioning budget (about half according to the Planning Council 1994: 10) to run its representative offices – which are rather like political, economic and socio-cultural embassies – in the West, South Africa and Japan.

The Rise of a Leadership

Contextualization

Goldstein has traced the evolution of the Tibetan political system in various works.[14] The regime was already beginning to be centralized in the thirteenth century, but it is only under the reigns of the Dalai Lamas, starting in the seventeenth century, that a 'state type of political structure', with a bureaucracy, emerged (Goldstein 1968: 144). From then on, the territory under the power of the central government based in Lhasa (*bod gzhung*) began to be divided into districts (*dzong*). These districts were organized around 'aristocratic and religious feudal-type estates with attached serfs' (ibid.: 18). Such estates were able to run their internal affairs relatively independently of the central government, but would refer to the latter when more important decisions were at stake. They also had to pay taxes to the central government, represented by appointed district commissioners (*dzong pon*). The system was a 'delicate balance between centralized and decentralized (feudal-like) political authority' (Goldstein 1971a: 171). The central government maintained a monopoly over the army, means of transportation and communication, money and coinage, and a 'court-of-last-appeals' for justice, all of which gave it an 'overall superordinate position' (ibid.: 176). The Dalai Lama, or the regent, was the head of the government. Under him sat a Council of Ministers, or Kashag (*bka 'shag*), composed traditionally of three lay officials and one monk (Goldstein 1968: 161). The council had important powers and was the 'administrative centre of the Tibetan government' (ibid.: 173). It did not, however, influence religious matters, which were dealt with by the Ecclesiastical Office composed of monks. Other offices existed, such as a Foreign Affairs Office, a Judicial Office and an Agricultural Office.

Apart from these political bodies, there were different assemblies, of which the most important was the General Assembly (*tshogs 'du rgyas 'dzoms*), gathered by the council with the ruler's authorization, with a consultative role for major decisions (ibid.: 188). These assemblies 'represented primarily the two great political groupings: the monks of Sendregasum [the three main Gelug monasteries] and the bureaucratic officials' (ibid.). The thirteenth Dalai Lama created the position of 'Chief Minister' (*srid blon*), who acted as a prime minister during the ruler's exile in Mongolia in 1904 (ibid.: 183). The title would die with the thirteenth Dalai Lama, and only reappear when the current Dalai Lama recreated it in exile.

When fleeing the Chinese authorities in March 1959, the Dalai Lama did not know from the outset that he would become a refugee in India. He first tried to flee the tense situation in Lhasa and thought that he could stay for some time near the border, as he had done at Yatung eight years previously. When the Chinese authorities heard that the Dalai Lama was missing, they dissolved the Tibetan government. A few days later, the Dalai Lama re-established it as the 'temporary government of Tibet', in Lhuntse Dzong (*lhun rtse rdzong*), after having performed different religious and secular rituals (Dalai Lama [1962] 1997: 173). After only a few days in Lhuntse Dzong, however, the situation became dangerous, as the Chinese army was approaching, so the Dalai Lama and his entourage understood that they had no choice but to escape to India. Shortly after his arrival in Tezpur (in present-day Assam, India), on 18 April 1959, the Dalai Lama gave a press conference where he declared that he was rejecting the '17-Point Agreement' and would not be bound by it any longer (ibid.: 182). Two days later, he left for Mussoorie, where he stayed for one year with his government,[15] before settling for good in Dharamsala. On 24 April 1959, the Dalai Lama met, for the first time since his arrival, the Indian prime minister, Jawaharlal Nehru. He recounted: 'I mentioned casually to Pandit Nehru ... that we had established a temporary government in southern Tibet. He became slightly agitated. "We are not going to recognize your government", he said immediately' (Avedon 1994: 70).

This temporary government, created hastily in southern Tibet, would eventually become the Central Tibetan Administration (CTA), known also as the 'Tibetan Government-in-Exile' (TGIE), which has never been recognized by any country. Nevertheless, India gave latitude to this government installed on its soil (TCV 2000: 60), a condition that permitted the CTA's success.

Then, on 20 June 1959, the Dalai Lama declared at a press conference: 'Where I am, accompanied by my government, the Tibetan people recognize us as the government of Tibet' (Avedon 1994: 72). This statement is still true after fifty years: the TGIE is recognized by the Tibetan refugees as the only Tibetan government, just as it is by many Tibetans inside Tibet, who call it the *bod gzhung* – literally, the 'government of Tibet'. The composition of this government is the same as its predecessor in Tibet: the Kashag is made up of seven ministers, heading seven departments (Home, Education, Religion and Culture, Finance, Security, Health, and Information and International Relations). Before 2001, the Dalai Lama had directly headed the Kashag, but in that year, for the first time, Samdhong Rinpoche, a member of the clergy, was directly elected as prime minister by the population. Finally, in 2011, a new prime minister, Lobsang Sangay, was nominated as 'Tibetan Political Leader' (Sikyong or *srid-skyong*), thus marking the complete political retreat of the Dalai Lama. Besides the Kashag and the ministries, the TGIE counts forty-four members elected by the population and these represent the different regions and religious schools of Tibet. These universal elections, created in exile by the Dalai Lama, and the abandonment of a set ratio between clergy and lay people within the political administration, marked a dramatic shift from the previous situation. In addition, the election of women has been a profound change.

Thus the CTA now enjoys undeniable legitimacy in the eyes of Tibetans, thanks in large part to the recognition of the Dalai Lama as the ultimate temporal and spiritual leader, but also to the major role played by the Dalai Lama in reorganizing a Tibetan political system in exile. That reorganization was effected through the re-establishment in exile of an administration and all the symbols of a nation, as well as the creation of a welfare state with the help of foreign aid. All of these factors have led to a new form of political apparatus in exile.

An Imagined Community

The official programme of the CTA is expressed as follows:

> Right from its inception, the CTA has set itself the twin task of rehabilitating Tibetan refugees and restoring freedom and happiness in Tibet. The rehabilitation agenda includes three important programmes: (a) promoting education among the exile population; (b) building a firm culture of democracy; and (c) paving the way for self-reliance so that the Tibetan people are able to survive with self-esteem and confidence that flows from not having to depend on external assistance. (Dorjee Thinley 2005: 62)

Beside these programmes, the Tibetan leadership understood the importance of unifying the refugee community through a common cultural and ethnic self-definition, thus improving the group's solidarity, in order to fulfil its two tasks described in the above quotation. This process took two forms: first, the creation of a form of nationalism; and second, the construction of shared history and traditions.

The Tibetan leadership developed in exile the symbols of a Tibetan nationalism, its main organ being the government itself. An official flag was adopted, based on a drawing made by the thirteenth Dalai Lama.[16] Likewise, a national anthem and a national emblem were adopted, following exactly what Hobsbawm and Ranger describe as elements constitutive of a nation, which 'in themselves ... reflect the entire background, thought and culture of a nation' (Hobsbawm and Ranger 1992: 11). The national plight is commemorated yearly on 10 March, the anniversary of the Lhasa uprising in 1959, and the Tibetans consider this celebration as their national day. Different authors have remarked that these forms of nationalism were created in exile as a result of the Chinese occupation and the arrival in exile.[17] They all note the importance of Tibetan Buddhism as the main marker of Tibetan national identity.[18] Dreyfus, in his article 'Tibetan Religious Nationalism' (Dreyfus 2002: 37ff.), argues that the Tibetan religion is the native element constituting the nationalism created in exile. For him, Tibetan nationalism is not a secular and exogenous phenomenon, imported from the West through the process of modernization, as analysed by Gellner (1983), nor an artificial creation through 'inventions of tradition' (Hobsbawm and Ranger 1992), nor an 'imagined community' (Anderson 1991). Dreyfus (2002: 37) argues further that these visions of nationalism are 'also often combined with a critique of Orientalism, which views non-Western nationalism as an introjection of Orientalist visions'. He proceeds to show that nationalism can be religious and indigenous, as in the Tibetan context: 'The use by many Tibetans of religious motives to define themselves as a nation shows the degree to which the analysis of non-Western nationalisms as internationalisations of Western orientalist discourse misses the mark' (ibid.: 49).

As we will see later in this chapter, Dreyfus is correct when he associates religion and nationalism on the Tibetan political stage, since these two concepts are intrinsically joined (through the *chos srid zung 'brel* concept of politics and religion joined together, studied below). The national symbols and rituals, described earlier, further incorporate religious elements. However, mundane elements of history and tradition were also deployed by the Tibetan community to create a sense of nation and unified community, as described by Hobsbawm and Ranger (1992) and Anderson (1991).

Authors working on forced migration recognize a 'myth of home', alongside a 'myth of returning home',[19] whereby communities idealize their lost homeland. The creation of this idealized homeland implies the polishing of disintegrative elements of the past. These elements from Tibet included differences of religious sects, differences of dialects, and the significant distances of geographically isolated Tibetan groups from each other. As will be evidenced in the following chapters, these differences were erased in exile. The 'myth of home' plays an integrative role and gives the refugees a strong identity. The Tibetan 'imagined community' (Anderson 1991), or the 'imagined return community' as Stepputat (1994) would put it, is more unified in exile than it ever was before.

Different facts explain such a new communal identity in exile. First, as seen in Chapter 1, the collective traumas have coalesced into a shared history, creating a sense of belonging to the same community, to a diaspora. Second, the settlements, which regrouped, for the first time in Tibetan history, people from various geographical and socio-economic backgrounds, have operated like a mould for a new unified community. Malkki (1995: 498ff.) sees the refugee settlements as a 'device of power' for their administrators: in the Tibetan context, they are instrumental in the creation of a new community. And third, new conceptions about Tibet or the reading of its history arose among the exiled community.

Among refugees, Tibet is presented as though it were a paradise before the Chinese occupation, and the Chinese forces are portrayed as truly evil, the organizers of genocide against Tibetans. I have constantly heard such assumptions from the Tibetan refugees with whom I have talked. An example is the view expressed by Tempa Tsering, secretary of the CTA's Department of Information and International Relations:

> The Tibetan tragedy has all [the] elements [of apartheid in South Africa or ethnic cleansing in Balkans], including the elements from the horrors of the Jewish holocaust. How is it that we Tibetans have suffered so much and yet are unable to articulate our suffering in inspired term? Here are some new words which might set you thinking. *The first one is culturecide. The next is Tibetocide. The third and last is deshangrilised.*[20] (Department of Information and International Relations and Friedrich-Neumann Stiftung 1996: 66, emphasis added)

During my interviews with refugees from different settlements in India and Nepal, I was struck by the cohesion they displayed, which contrasted with what I had heard in Tibet. Hence questions about their social, religious and geographical origins seemed irrelevant to many of these informants, who answered that 'we are all Tibetans, fighting for our rights under the leadership of His Holiness [the Dalai Lama]'. This cohesion and sense of community is carried forward by the education system, which teaches a unique Tibetan language, the Lhasa dialect (*lha sa skad*), and a unique form of history and even religion (see Nowak 1978b on this issue). Moreover, facts that could cast any doubt on this unity and shared representation are ignored in the official Tibetan history as elaborated in exile. One such fact is the Tibetan armed resistance to the Chinese occupation, which was conducted mostly by Khampas, and was not non-violent. The truthful narration of this historical episode would go against both the presented unity of the Tibetans and their supposed non-violent nature. McGranahan calls such selection 'historical arrest', which keeps some historical facts – like armed resistance to the Chinese invasion – as Foucauldian 'subjugated knowledge' (McGranahan 2005: 570ff.). Jamyang Norbu, a Tibetan intellectual and former guerrilla, elaborates further on the same issue:

> There has ... been a singular lack of enquiry into the resistance movement on the part of the exile Tibetan government. This government has always had an uneasy relationship with the resistance. The wide extent and popularity of the resistance highlighted the failure of the government's policy of cooperation with the Chinese occupation forces. (Jamyang Norbu 1994: 186)

History is not the only unified and 'smoothed' domain of Tibetan society. Religion itself was also affected (see Chapter 4), as was Tibetan identity and political presentation (see Chapter 3).[21]

The government of Tibet, reinstalled in exile by the Dalai Lama, has gained strong legitimacy thanks to its continuity with the past and also its deployment of a nationalism based on different elements and carried out in the community through the establishment of an education system (see Chapter 3). This new Tibetan community, created in exile, gave its leadership to the CTA as its sole representative. The CTA could further enhance its own legitimacy and power thanks to its constitution as a state-like apparatus, which was even able to develop a welfare state for its 'citizens'.

The Welfare State

The CTA, which Tibetans inside and outside Tibet call *bod gzhung*, the 'government of Tibet', acts like a real government, with different ministries, a head of state (until recently the Dalai Lama) and an administration. This government is not recognized by any other country, even if, as will be seen in the following sections, international governments and organizations (including those of India and Nepal) work with it.[22] In addition to the Tibetan state symbols, the CTA edits official documents for its nationals, that is, Tibetan refugees. Since 1972, the Tibetan refugees have been invited to contribute to the income of their government. A 'voluntary tax' (*dpya khral*, or Chatrel in the anglicized version) is collected by the Tibetan administration from every refugee. It is voluntary because the CTA has no legal right or means to levy a tax; however, the refugees have to pay it in order to have access to the various services provided by the CTA. This tax, proportionate to the person's income, is now a duty for each Tibetan refugee according to Article 3(4) of the Charter. Moreover, the tax represents an overt link between the Tibetan refugees and their government, as stated officially: 'The existence of Chatrel symbolizes the Tibetan people's recognition of CTA as their legitimate representative. Chatrel payment exhibits Tibetan people's support for CTA's financial needs until Tibet regains freedom' (http://tibet.net/support-tibet/pay-green-book/). Payment of this tax is recorded in an individual document, the 'Green Book' (*rgya che mang dngul*),[23] which is in effect a 'passport' for the refugees to both prove their identity and claim their rights from the Tibetan administration. I recall a meeting in my house between a Tibetan recently arrived from Amdo and a Tibetan refugee born in South India. They could not converse in Tibetan because they spoke different dialects, so they switched to English, to their profound distress. The refugee told me that he became aware for the first time that people could be Tibetan 'without speaking *lha sa skad* [the language of Lhasa spoken in exile] and owning a Green Book'.

Moreover, thanks to steady improvements in the material conditions of the settlements and the unbroken support from foreign organizations and donors, the CTA has, over the years, been able to develop what can be seen as a 'welfare state'. The welfare of the refugees is actually written into the Charter under Article 16 (Social Welfare) as a duty of the CTA: 'The Tibetan Administration-in-Exile shall endeavour to secure appropriate means of providing sources of livelihood, happiness and mental and physical well-being for the Tibetan people' (http://www.tibetjustice.org/materials/tibet/tibet6.3.html). In effect, the CTA controls such resources as housing, access to schooling and scholarship opportunities, healthcare benefits, pensions, direct aid to the desperately poor, and employment in the administration and different affiliated institutions that it manages in the settlements. The Tibetan administration is able to manage such a welfare state thanks to the help of international organizations and a well-organized scheme of assessment of the different needs of the Tibetan population and good management of the projects devised to answer these needs. This welfare state is implemented in the settlements through the 'Tibetan Settlement Offices' (formerly known as 'Tibetan Welfare Office') operating under the Home Ministry, which are responsible for taking care of the different social, health and economic problems the settlers might have.

In 1990, the CTA published a list of needs for the Tibetan community under the title *CTA Project Needs Support Directory* (Planning Council 1990), which led to the publication in 1992 of the extremely successful first 'Integrated Development Plan' (IDP) (Planning Council 1992). This IDP, drawn up with the advice of Mr Weingarten, was followed by three others, which have been published periodically up to the present day. In the different IDPs, necessary projects are listed for each department, and sub-listed for each settlement, and their financing has to be guaranteed by foreign support.[24] The needs are evaluated by the 'settlement officers' or 'welfare officers', most of them sent by the CTA into the different Tibetan communities, who report back to Dharamsala. The listed projects include the rehabilitation of unsettled Tibetans in new settlements (ibid.: 12); the financing of 'irrigation, handicraft centres, tractors, sanitation, electricity, … aged/infirm relief' in Tezu (Arunachal Pradesh) (ibid.: 15); the development of 'income-generating schemes for second generation Tibetans [*sid*]' (ibid.); and the financing of 'upgrading and expansion of Paonta Sahib [Himachal Pradesh] school' (ibid.: 22).

The latest (fourth) integrated development plan, from 2009 to 2013, has continued the list of practical projects needed for the Tibetan community. The four development plans give the impression of a strong follow-up to all projects, and also the perpetuation of the welfare state. The fourth plan focuses on different objectives, listed by categories such as the 'middle-way approach policy'; 'strengthening religious culture programme';[25] 'promotion of organic agriculture system'; 'Tibetan cooperatives support programme'; 'implementation of Basic Education Policy'; 'Tibetan public health programme'; 'youth empowerment programme'; 'strengthening Tibetan democracy programme' (Planning Commission 2009: 4). As seen before, the CTA acts as an intermediary between the Tibetans and the foreign organizations: the administration redistributes the funds received. The organizations can choose which project they want to develop, but the genesis of the projects, their implementation, management and final evaluation, are left to the CTA.

In parallel, the CTA has developed a broad scheme of sponsorship in order to sustain individuals with special needs (students, elderly, destitute, sick or physically challenged people). The scheme is also extended to monks and nuns who have no other means of support. The needs directory of 1990 lists different sponsorship programmes, such as 'Adopt-A-Granny (or Granddad)', where the sponsors have to pay a certain amount every month to sustain the cost of living of the sponsored person (Planning Council 1990: 17).[26]

The different departments of Education, of Religion and Culture, and of Home, are responsible for the management of these sponsorships.[27] As for the development projects, individual needs are assessed in the settlements by the relevant staff of the CTA. Again, the administration is at the core of this relationship between donors and refugees, and this increases its power and authority. By providing such a welfare state at every settlement, including remote Tezu, the CTA can maintain strong authority over the refugees, yet without having a coercive state apparatus like an army, a police force, courts and prisons. De Voe recounts how the administration is using access to the welfare state as a means of power:

> As Tibetan government offices concerned with education and welfare came to have more pull with aid agencies, some Khampa and Amdowa groups [in Nepal] not in good standing with the Tibetan Government began to feel slighted in settlement funding ... Loyalty to the Government became, essentially, an unwritten criteria for an aid recommendation: if the Tibetan middle level did not approve of a project and issue the aid request, aid agencies would not accept it. (De Voe 1983: 10)

Klieger remarks also that the Tibetan 'welfare state within a state [i.e. India]' (Klieger 1991: 102), 'although still dependent on distant patronage, is in a socio-economic position of being able to circumvent immediate host dependency and subsequently certain forces of primary assimilation' (Klieger 1991: 21).

The Tibetan Way to Govern: The *chos srid zung 'brel*

In Western societies, an understanding of the term 'political' generally highlights those elements that are secular in nature, in opposition to the term 'religious'. In short, the dualism lies between the sacred and the profane. Broadly speaking, Western societies understand 'political' power to be that which rules in secular matters, and religious power as being devoted to sacred matters (I return to the Western dichotomy of sacred and profane in Chapter 4). From this perspective, an analysis of societies where this distinction is remote, or even absent, is sometimes difficult for a Western mind. In Tibet, this lack of distinction is precisely the case, and the two forms of power,[28] political and religious, have traditionally been combined, yet at the same time kept distinct, in what Ruegg calls a 'diarchy':

> It is what we indicate by the Tibetan naming of *lugs* [*zung*] 'combined order' and *lugs* [*gnyis*] 'double order' or *tshul* [*gnyis*] 'double rule' ... in other words, the coordination (literally 'sizygy') of the order of Dharma or of the Priesthood and of the order of Regnum/Imperium (*chos srid zung 'brel*). (Ruegg 1995: 18)[29]

The same author remarks that, in the Tibetan context, the union (Gk: '*suzugia*') of the two forms of power – which are therefore no longer opposed – is known as *chos* [Dharma, religion] *srid* [temporal, worldliness] *zung 'brel* [joined]; this replaces the opposition of 'sacred' and 'profane', 'dear to the historians of religion' (ibid.: 25). Hence, Tibet's traditional political system integrated these two forms of power, whereby both had their own sphere of influence but also interacted intimately, such as in the bureaucracy where lay official positions were doubled by monk officials.

Ruegg describes the relation between the two forms of power, and notices that they can be either distributed between two associated persons, such as the king (*rgyal po*) and the religious hierarchy (*bla mchod* or *mchod gnas*), who will develop a patron–priest relationship (*mchod yon*); or, alternatively, exercised by the same person, who will be a 'monk-king' or, in other words, a 'hierocrat' (ibid.), as exemplified by the figure of the Dalai Lama.

The Fourteenth Dalai Lama as Embodiment of the chos srid zung 'brel

The fifth Dalai Lama was recognized as a manifestation of Avalokiteshvara, a divine emanation, but also as the reincarnation of King Songtsen Gampo (*Srong btsan sgam po*), the first religious king (*chos rgyal*) (Ishihama 2003). The Dalai Lamas, since the fifth, representing the 'Hierocrat' or 'Bodhisattva-King',[30] have thus historically embodied the diarchic model of *chos srid zung 'brel*.[31]

Once the fourteenth Dalai Lama arrived in exile, he soon became the hope of the refugees who followed him. They looked to him to find a solution not only for regaining the freedom of their country, but also for their daily survival in exile and the safeguarding of their culture and religion. Enjoying considerable indulgence (Dawa Norbu 2001: 9) from Nehru, the Indian prime minister, the Dalai Lama was able to suggest the creation in India of infrastructure sufficient to guarantee the survival and rehabilitation of the Tibetan refugees and the perpetuation of their culture (as seen in Chapter 1). His legitimacy was thus not only guaranteed inside the Tibetan communities in exile, and amongst the Tibetans living in Tibet for whom he symbolized freedom, but also within the Indian government and its agencies, which considered him the natural Tibetan ruler. Soon, the Dalai Lama also began to be considered as the only legitimate Tibetan ruler by the Western media and even the Western political world.

With the growing popularity in the West of Tibetan Buddhism (described in the following chapters), the Dalai Lama came to be regarded more and more like a religious leader, and he is nowadays presented quasi-unanimously by Western organizations and media as the temporal and spiritual leader of the Tibetans.[32] This double function is not without its problems: the *chos srid zung 'brel* and the particular status of the Dalai Lama are often disjoined in international discussions on Tibet. Indeed, because not one country recognizes the Tibetan government-in-exile, the Dalai Lama has always been received by Western politicians and officials as a religious leader, an international and personal advocate of non-violence and a winner of the Nobel Peace Prize. Even though the Dalai Lama is formally recognized by the U.S. Congress as the 'spiritual and temporal leader of the Tibetan people',[33] he remains a charismatic leader, and not the historical chief of a government-in-exile. This mode of reception is debated and discussed in the West. Activists' organizations (see Chapter 5) push their governments to address the political side of the Tibet issue with the Dalai Lama, while governments themselves try not to enter into political matters that might irritate Chinese authorities and jeopardise commercial exchanges with China. Such a dilemma sometimes leads to novel compromises. During a visit to France in August 2008, the Dalai Lama was received not by the French president, but by his wife, giving thus a formal but unofficial touch to the Tibetan leader's visit. On the other hand, the Chinese government regards the Dalai Lama as a political dissident and does not even take his religious function into consideration. As such, the Dalai Lama is labelled by the Chinese as a 'splittist', and every government or official who receives him is seen as interfering in China's internal affairs.

The dilemma in which the Dalai Lama was trapped – until recently – by his double function of political and religious leadership sums up the entire situation of the Tibetan refugees and the Tibet issue. The Dalai Lama is well aware of this dilemma, and Knaus (1999: 213) recalls that, at first, the Tibetan leader 'refused to be received anywhere except as a chief of state'. It was only with the launch of the International Campaign for Tibet at the end of the 1980s (see Chapter 1) that the Dalai Lama accepted to be received as the spiritual leader of his people. Nonetheless, he always tries to stress to his hosts the political situation of his country and people; he constantly articulates and joins his two forms of power, as expressed in 1991 at the Oxford Union:

> The question of the Tibetan national struggle is not just a mere political one. I believe it is a more spiritual involvement. I myself feel that, as a Buddhist monk, if the Tibetan national struggle was just purely political, then I must consider whether my involvement is appropriate or not. But since this national struggle is for more than political freedom, and is also for spiritual freedom, which is not only of benefit to Tibetans alone, but also to larger communities, as a simple Buddhist monk involved in that kind of national struggle, I consider it as spiritual work and as part of my own spiritual practice. (Dalai Lama 1995: 161, grammar respected)

In this statement, the Tibetan leader is not referring to his embodiment of the *chos srid zung 'brel*, but instead presents his task as that falling to a Buddhist monk. His presentation as a simple monk was indeed repeated in all his speeches to Western audiences after the launch of the international campaign, and is often linked to his declaration that, if Tibet were free, he would return to the life of a simple monk (Dalai Lama 1995: 169). In his memoirs, however, written much earlier in 1962, the Dalai Lama wrote about his dual form of leadership at the time of popular unrest in Tibet in the 1950s:

> My dual position as Dalai Lama, by which Tibet had been happily ruled for centuries, was becoming almost insupportable. In both my capacities as religious and secular leader, I felt bound to oppose any violence by the people. I knew the Chinese were trying to undermine my political authority ... Yet even if people lost faith in me as their secular leader, they must not lose faith in me as religious leader, which was much more important. *I could delegate or abdicate my secular leadership, but the Dalai Lama could never abdicate as religious leader, nor would I ever dream of doing so.*
>
> Thus I began to think it might be in the best interests of Tibet if I withdrew from all political activities, in order to keep my religious authority intact. Yet while I was in Tibet, I could not escape from politics. To withdraw, I would have to leave the country. (Dalai Lama [1962] 1997: 108, emphasis added)

This text, written more than fifty years ago, is still relevant to the actual situation of the Dalai Lama. Recently, however, in a historic move, the Dalai Lama declared in March 2011 that he would resign from all political responsibilities. He put this into practice in the following weeks, and at present the Tibetan leader no longer heads the political body of his community. In spite of such a decision, the Dalai Lama is still considered by friends and enemies alike as both the temporal and spiritual leader of Tibet.

The Central Tibetan Administration Agendas According to the chos srid zung 'brel

The CTA, with strong legitimacy constructed in exile for both the refugees and the international community, has been able to negotiate a new international profile for the Tibetans, based on the narrative of successful Western concepts, such as democratization, liberal humanism, environmentalism, and human rights, but above all, on profound spirituality. This idealistic presentation of themselves has guaranteed an ongoing international awareness of their cause, as well as their own survival in exile through the consequent attraction of assistance. It is not by chance that the CTA turned its political focus towards the West; indeed, there was a definite strategy to seek support from these countries, as summarized by Barnett: 'The Tibetan exiles … turned for support to former colonizers rather than to the formerly colonized, and chose public relations rather than political alliance as its form of politics' (Barnett 2001: 279).

Tibetan politics, however, is more than just 'public relations'. I have identified two main agendas that the Tibetans are using for such representation: political and religious. These two agendas, which constitute the core description and analysis of chapters 3 and 4 respectively, are, according to the diarchic concept of the *chos srid zung 'brel*, interconnected. It will become clear that politics and religion are inter-instrumentalized by the Tibetans. Indeed, the political agenda is the way in which the Tibetans present the management of their governance, which they often justify with religious arguments; just as the religious agenda is the way in which the Tibetans present their religion in order to obtain what would be seen in the West as political goals. These two agendas do not represent opposing secular and religious spheres, but rather the joining of these spheres, according to the concept of *chos srid zung 'brel*. The power of this mode of governance and its attraction for Western supporters help to explain the unique success of the Tibetan refugees on the international stage.

Notes

1. Like the Tibetan nomads in the grasslands, who are accused by the Chinese government of destroying their environment (see, for example, Fischer 2005).
2. The information given here on Mr Weingarten's work was gathered thanks to several conversations with him in 2008 and the reading of his unpublished report, which he was kind enough to send me.
3. These two challenges will be further described and discussed in the following chapters.
4. The first one, for the years 1992–1997, was published by the Planning Council in 1992 with the help of an NGO, the Vikasoko Development Exchange. This NGO employed Vijay Mahajan, currently a leading figure in micro-credit in India, and Thomas Fisher, a graduate from the University of Oxford who lived for three years in Dharamsala, to continue Weingarten's work of expertise and guidance (personal communication).
5. See the OECD 'Paris Declaration' and 'Accra Agenda for Action' which, in 2005, put the emphasis on these criteria (http://www.oecd.org/dac/effectiveness/parisdeclarationandaccraagendaforaction.htm).
6. See https://ec.europa.eu/europeaid/sites/devco/files/methodology-aid-delivery-methods-project-cycle-management-200403_en_2.pdf
7. In 2001, the former prime minister, Samdhong Rinpoche, decided to sell all the private businesses owned by the CTA, as he considered that it was unethical for his government to be involved in business (personal communication). They then sold the hotels that they owned as well as the export unit of the handicraft centres, which had been built and acquired partly with funds from international organizations. In the business plan presented by the FTCI, the raised funds needed are presented as follows: 'The overall costs of the above three business units are estimated at Rs. 57,156,000/- (approx $1.33 million). So towards this end, we plan to raise … 50 per cent in the form of soft loan (Debt financing) and the remaining 50 per cent is to seek from foreign donor as grant. Hence the amount requested for the soft loan is Rs. 28,578,000/- and we prefer if it is offered interest free' (Federation of Tibetan Co-operative in India Ltd 2006: 2).
8. See for example the audit manual of the CTA: http://tibet.net/wp-content/uploads/2012/02/Audit-Manual.pdf
9. See www.tibetnetwork.org
10. Individual assistance from Taiwanese Buddhists became very important recently.
11. See Chapter 4, as well as Ström (1994, 1995 and 2001) and Frechette (2002), for the most important works on the reinstallation of the religion in exile.
12. See Chapter 5 for a further discussion on these individual initiatives.
13. It is difficult to find accurate figures of the CTA's budget. According to the Charter, the budget should be published every year but I have never found such a document either in Tibetan or in English (some members of the CTA staff even denied the existence of such a document). However, through different discussions on the subject and different documents, such as the last Integrated Development Plan (Planning Commission 2009: 56, which budgets all projects

for the period 2009–2013 to US$13 million – without administrative running costs), it is possible to confirm this estimation.

14. See his works from 1968, 1971a, 1971b and 1973.
15. Composed of around seventy members (Avedon 1994: 67).
16. See, respectively, http://tibet.net/about-tibet/the-tibetan-national-flag/; and http://tibet.net/about-tibet/tibetan-national-anthem/
17. See, amongst others, Nowak (1978a: 214ff.; 1983), Klieger (1991: 144ff.), and Dreyfus (2002).
18. See the works quoted in the previous note, and also Moran (2004: 192), who describes religion as the Tibetan national identity.
19. See, for example, Al-Rasheed (1994) and Zetter (1999), as well as Chapter 5, for further discussion of this point.
20. Grammar respected: from 'Shangri-la': a Western myth on Tibet as a lost paradise (see Chapter 5).
21. A parallel can be made, in another context, with what Anderson (1991: 163) says about the nation-building of 'recently decolonised states', which involves 'both a genuine, popular nationalist enthusiasm, and a systematic, even Machiavellian, instilling of nationalist ideology through the mass media, the educational system, [and] administrative regulations'.
22. The Tibetan Administration shares some similarities with what Wolch (1989: 201) calls a 'shadow state', talking about the power gained by the 'voluntary sector'.
23. Which means, interestingly, the 'funds coming from an extensive base'. Hence the Green Book is connected by the Tibetans to the taxes they pay to their government.
24. It is interesting to note that the CTA is also publishing guidelines for projects inside Tibet: see http://tibet.net/wp-content/uploads/2013/05/guidelines.pdf
25. This plan, like the previous one, mixes practical material needs with socio-cultural and religious objectives (see Chapter 3).
26. This project was taken over eventually by the organization 'Tibet Charity', under the name 'Adopt a Grandparent' (see http://tibetcharity.in/social-program/adopt-a-grandparent/).
27. In Chapter 4, I develop further the issues surrounding this sponsorship.
28. Studied by, among others, Burman (1979) and Michael (1982).
29. My translation from the original: 'Il s'agit en l'occurrence de ce qu'on désigne par les appellations tibétaines de lugs [zung] "ordre conjugué" et lugs [gnyis] "ordre double" ou tshul [gnyis] "règle double" … autrement dit de la coordination (littéralement "syzygie") de l'ordre du Dharma ou du Sacerdoce et de l'ordre du Regnum/Imperium (chos srid zung 'brel).'
30. As identified by Ruegg (1995: 25).
31. The Dalai Lamas were not, however, the first Tibetan rulers to hold the two powers, and Ruegg (1995: 23) gives the example of Ye she 'od, who, around the year 1000, held the title of 'lha bla ma', that is, 'Majesty and Lama'.
32. This, however, was not always the case, as seen in Chapter 1.
33. This is stated in the Foreign Relations Authorisation Act 1989 of the U.S. Congress (http://www.tibetjustice.org/materials/us/us1.html).

3

The Political Agenda

This chapter describes how the Tibetans in exile, acting through their leadership, have managed to present themselves as an ideal community to the world, and especially to the Western world, thanks to their religion – a process that I call their political agenda.

'Political' has to be understood here in its original, Greek-derived meaning, namely, the management of what concerns the city or any human community. As seen already, 'politics' is intimately linked to religion in the Tibetan context. Following the *chos srid zung 'brel* model, politics and religion are inter-instrumentalized in the conduct of public affairs. Political discourses described in this chapter are hence a way to legitimize power and a means to present the community in a certain manner.

Three main discourses and actions constitute the political agenda: first, the constitution and presentation of the exiled community as a democracy; second, the creation of a generalized education system; and third, the refugees' understanding and presentation of an ideal form of development.

Democracy

When the Dalai Lama arrived in exile, he immediately took over the project of democratizing his community. Installed in a young democratic country (India), the Tibetan leader had the opportunity to push further the reforms he had hoped to implement earlier. As he recalls in his memoirs, *My Land and My People* ([1962] 1997), he had wanted to implement reforms as soon as he was enthroned in 1950. He soon created a 'Reforms Committee' composed of 'fifty members, lay and monk officials and representatives of the monasteries' (ibid.: 43). The main reforms he undertook concerned the collection of taxes, the system of land tenure on private estates, and the rights of the peasants working on them (ibid.: 43–47). But the Dalai Lama writes that he had no time to pursue all the reforms he foresaw, as the Chinese government took control of Tibet shortly after his enthronement.

In exile, the Tibetan leader had the opportunity to model his community upon the framework of democracy, understood as a normative ideal of governance by the people and for the people.[1] The idea of democratization of the Tibetan community was not only dear to the Dalai Lama, but was in any case dictated by the new contingencies of exile. Hence, Dawa Norbu (2001) remarks that India, at this time a new and proud parliamentary democracy, freed from its colonial power, would not have tolerated another form of government on its soil, and that the Dalai Lama had no other choice but to choose democracy as a principle of rule. Further, Knaus (1999: 275ff.) shows how U.S. overt and covert assistance to the refugees was contingent on their democratization. In effect, the democracy narrative adopted by the Tibetan refugees is nowadays a strong factor in the attraction of Western assistance; and different wealthy organizations committed to democracy, like the National Endowment for Democracy (NED), financed by the U.S. Congress, the German Heinrich Böll Foundation and the Friedrich Neumann Foundation, presently work with Tibetans.

The process of democratization began on 2 September 1960, when a 13-member Assembly of the Commission of Tibetan People's Deputies (later to become the Assembly of Tibetan People's Deputies, ATPD, and also called since 2006 the Tibetan Parliament in Exile, TPE), with representatives from the four Tibetan Buddhist traditions (Sakya, Gelug, Nyingma and Kagyu) and three provinces (Ü-Tsang, Kham and Amdo), took office for the first time – a day marked as Tibetan Democracy Day and still remembered every year. In 1963, the Dalai Lama adopted a Constitution of Tibet, based, according to Knaus (1999: 252), on the United States Constitution, and respecting the independence of the legislature, executive and judiciary. Interestingly, this Constitution[2] constantly refers to Buddhism, as in Article 2: 'Tibet shall be a unitary democratic State founded upon the principles laid down by the Lord Buddha'.[3] In fact, the Constitution respected the union of sacred and secular powers, as posited in the *chos srid zung 'brel.* However, Article 36 stated that the Dalai Lama was subject to impeachment by the National Assembly. This Article provoked discontent among representatives, who swore never to accept the Constitution with this provision. But the Dalai Lama stood by his decision and recalls: 'I had to explain that democracy is very much in keeping with Buddhist principles and, somewhat autocratically perhaps, insisted that the clause be left in' (Pema Thinley 1996: 12). The Buddhist origins of the Tibetan notion of democracy have been further asserted by the former prime minister in addresses to Western organizations, such as this:

The model of Tibetan democracy is fundamentally different from the modern democratic principles. Ours is based on basic principles of equality of all sentient beings on the basis of their potential of unlimited development. Such equality can be established in the day-to-day living only through cooperation and not through competition ... *Realizing this phenomenon of human behavior, the Buddha had recommended a democracy free from sense of competition.* (Department of Information and International Relations and Friedrich-Neumann Stiftung 1996: 50, emphasis added)

Beyond the mix between competition (which in the West comes from the economic system, not the political) and democracy, this quote shows that the Tibetans present their adoption of democracy as profoundly rooted in Buddhism. In this narrative, democracy is not something foreign to them but coming from their own religion. This is instrumental in their successful representation towards Western supporters, but also towards the Chinese power: they are by *nature* democratic.

Many years passed before further democratization of the Tibetan refugees was achieved. In 1990 the Dalai Lama created a commission to rewrite the 1963 Constitution. He stated that this Constitution ought to be adopted freely, by means of the votes of every Tibetan inside and outside Tibet. As this proved impossible, a Charter of the Tibetans in Exile, based on the Constitution, was adopted in 1991 by the 11th ATPD. For the first time, the assembly was empowered to elect the Council of Ministers (Kashag, *bka' shag*). Furthermore, Tibetan judicial power, known as the Supreme Justice Commission, was instituted. In 2001, the ATPD, on the advice of the Dalai Lama, amended the Charter to provide for direct election of the prime minister (Kalon Tripa, *bka' blon khri pa*) by the exile population. From then onwards, the prime minister could choose his government, subject to the approval of the assembly. In 2011, the Dalai Lama announced his formal retirement from political life and gave his temporal power to the prime minister, currently Dr Lobsang Sangay, named as Sikyong, or 'Tibetan Political Leader'.

The democratization of Tibetan society is, before all else, the Dalai Lama's personal project. In a surprising and rare top-down process, he is advancing democratization, even against criticism or dissension within his own people, a fact recognized by the ATPD itself:

[At] the present moment, with many countries experiencing an upsurge of freedom and democracy at the risk of their peoples' lives, His Holiness the Dalai Lama, the Supreme Leader of the Tibetan people, has offered the ideals of democracy to the Tibetan people, even though they have not felt the need of those ideals. All Tibetans, within Tibet and in-exile, are and remain deeply grateful to His Holiness the Dalai Lama, and rededicate themselves in establishing our faith and allegiance in the leadership of His Holiness the Dalai Lama, and fervently pray that He may remain with us forever as our supreme

Spiritual and Temporal leader. (Special Resolution passed by the ATPD on 3 July 1991; http://tibet.net/about-cta/constitution/)

The 1991 Charter and its democratic backbone created a generalization of the democracy narrative in the exiled community, among officials and within the entire population, as Frechette (2007) shows, and as I was able to confirm through my fieldwork. In Dharamsala, the seat of the so-called Tibetan government-in-exile (i.e. the Central Tibetan Administration, CTA), democracy is nowadays a strong social narrative. The claim of democracy is not only omnipresent in official discourses, but pervades the entire community. The word 'democracy' (*mang gtso*) is used as much by Tibetan politicians and administrative staff as by individuals in claiming their rights.

The emergence of the democracy narrative corresponds perfectly to the launch by the Tibetan refugees of the international campaign (ICT), seen in Chapter 1. Indeed, the democracy narrative is powerful in Western societies, where democracy is synonymous with 'good governance', and presented as the most legitimate system. A direct result of this fact is that the democratic system claimed by the Tibetans is a strong magnet for Western support. I often noticed that the claim of democracy was one of the principal motivations for those Western helpers whom I interviewed. Furthermore, the democracy narrative is also acclaimed by Western governments and parliaments. A commission of the French Senate declared the following in a report:

> Tibet in exile has adopted resolutely the path of democracy. The political functioning of the community of the exiled Tibetans prefigures what will be a Tibet that is once again master of its own destiny ... It will be a genuine democratic example for China, as it has opened itself to the world and aspires to join the community of nations. (Groupe France – Tibet 2005: 12)[4]

As this report remarks, and according also to Western politicians, Tibetan democracy is positive not only for the Tibetans, but also for China. Similarly, the Dalai Lama certainly did not choose to democratize his community purely for its own sake, nor for that of its Western supporters, but in order to prove to Chinese authorities that he did not want to maintain the old political regime. This he stated in 1991 in front of the ATPD:

> Although the Chinese have dubbed our national struggle as one aimed at reviving the old society, the steps taken by us thus far prove their accusation wrong to all those who are aware of our situation. Therefore, our efforts at democratization have had a very strong impact on Tibet also. (Bhattacharjea 1994: 13)

Finally, a civil society, constituent of a democracy, can be found in the Tibetan community. The Tibetan Youth Congress is a strong organization founded in 1970 that claims thirty thousand members and fights for the complete independence of Tibet.[5] The Tibetan Women's Association (TWA) was founded in 1984 and counts sixteen thousand members; it is dedicated to the support and assistance of women in the exile community as well as inside Tibet.[6] The Gu-chu-Sum organization was founded in 1991 to support and assist current and former political prisoners.[7] The Tibetan Centre for Human Rights and Democracy (TCHRD) was founded in 1996 and its aim is the promotion of the democratic principles in the community. It tries also to work towards the protection of human rights in Tibet.[8] A number of other Tibetan organizations as well as political parties, such as the National Democratic Party of Tibet, were also created recently, adding multiple voices to the possibilities of a democracy.

Although the structures needed for a democracy have been implemented in the Tibetan exile political system, the community is still in a phase of democratic transition, and various reservations are being expressed about further democratization. Hence, the democracy narrative often goes further than the effective political practices of the Tibetan community, as will be seen in Chapter 7.

Education

A principal transformation in the exile community has been the establishment of a successful and generalized education system. The Dalai Lama insisted, ever since his arrival in India, that an equal education for all would be imperative in exile. In Tibet, education was reserved for the clergy and some aristocrats (Dawa Norbu 1987). The Dalai Lama said shortly after his arrival in India:

> When we look back into our history we find that we have neglected many things. Our goal for now and the future should be to keep abreast with other people of the world in all aspects of educational progress and development. The education of our children, who are the future seeds of Tibet, who will carry out our national task be it political or spiritual, is vitally important. At the heart of the Tibetan educational endeavour, therefore, *lies the dual goal of preserving, strengthening and propagation Tibetan culture and tradition, and secondly, to impart and provide access to modern education.* (TCV 2000, emphasis added)

The principal task of this education system was to preserve and safeguard Tibetan culture, while allowing young refugees to broaden perspective on modernity and the new world in which they were living. Thanks to the support of Western organizations and the Indian government, the Tibetan education system has been a success in terms of infrastructure, teaching and attendance. Nowadays, the literacy rate among children born in exile is high (see below), and the consequences of this generalized education are important.

Tibetan schoolchildren in India number around thirty thousand, nearly one-third of the Tibetan population living in the country,[9] and they form a large presence in every settlement. In contrast with Indian families, I never met a Tibetan family that did not send their children to school, even in the poorest and most remote settlements, like Tezu. The Tibetan school system is efficient (in terms of accessibility, attendance, gender-equality and literacy rates) and well organized, and even the most isolated families can send their children for free to a Tibetan school, thanks to the generous system of foreign sponsorship (see Chapter 5, Portrait). In Tezu, for example, a school financed by the Indian government provides education for boys and girls from grades I to VIII. During my stay there at the end of 2006, there were 125 children attending this school (out of a total population of ca. 1,400). After grade VIII, according to the school's headmaster, most schoolchildren continue their education, and are transferred to various large schools in India, such as Shimla and Dalhousie in Himachal Pradesh, Mussoorie in Uttarakhand, and Kalimpong and Darjeeling in West Bengal. The parents of these children sometimes send them more than 2,000 km away to continue their education. In these education centres, the children, coming from Tezu but also from other small, isolated settlements, join 'newcomers' who have been sent by their parents from Tibet at great risk. In practice, the children born in India are not in the same classes as those coming from Tibet, but the boarding system is the same for both groups. One such centre is in Bir, some 80 km from Dharamsala. There, the Tibetan Children's Village (TCV),[10] called Suja, is among the largest Tibetan schools in exile, providing education for around two thousand students. It welcomes newcomers, but only from grades I to X.[11] The school is organized around 'homes', where about forty students of the same age live, study, eat and sleep together under the responsibility of a 'home mother'. Since 1998, these 'home mothers' have formed a Mothers' Training Centre, where they are taught health and hygiene rules, psychology and pedagogy, and management of a house. This organization, similar in every TCV, is a legacy of the first orphanage opened in Dharamsala in 1960. At present, every Tibetan schoolchild is educated in the same manner in the TCV's residential schools. Near TCV Bir is TCV Chauntra, which welcomes around a thousand students up to grade IX. There I was able to meet students from Tezu settlement, as the school admits pupils from all over India. These Tibetan schools are where refugees from different locations meet and learn the same culture; they are the practical apparatus of the new 'Tibetanness' constituted in exile (this chapter, and Chapter 4).

The first Tibetan school in exile was opened on 3 March 1960 in Mussoorie (Uttarakhand, India). Beginning with fifty students, the school expanded quickly with the continuing influx of refugees. Many of these students were orphans and, in May 1960, a special centre was opened for them in Dharamsala, the 'Tibetan Refugee Children's Nursery'. This nursery later became a fully fledged school, renamed the 'Tibetan Children's Village' (TCV), and has been part of the international SOS-Kinderdorf organization since 1972 (TCV 2000: 23). The TCV organization nowadays accounts for nine educational complexes, serving more than sixteen thousand students (http://www.tcv.org.in/). In 2008, the TCV received a total of 459 million Indian rupees (about 9 million USD at that time) from about a hundred organizations and donors around the world (TCV 2009: 43ff.).

In 1961, at the Dalai Lama's request, the government of India set up a committee for the education of Tibetan refugees. (In 1979 this committee became the Central Tibetan Schools Administration (CTSA), an autonomous body under the Indian Ministry of Human Resource Development.) This administration provided free education for all Tibetan students until 1975. It founded special schools for the refugees, with a curriculum designed to teach the Tibetan language and culture. Today, the CTSA manages twenty-seven schools, enrolling around ten thousand students (http://sherig.org/en/schools/ctsa-schools/). The Indian government still covers the Tibetan students' expenses for textbooks and stationery, and pays the teachers' salaries (TCV 2000: 24). In a recent move, from January 2013 onwards, the management of the schools run by the CTSA was transferred to the Central Tibetan Administration. Hence, the Indian government is giving responsibility for these schools to the Tibetan government-in-exile, while continuing to fund them.[12]

A third body of schools was founded in 1963 in Mussoorie. The Tibetan Homes Foundation (THF) schools are residential and provide the students with foster parents. Today, the THF is also part of the SOS-Kinderdorf network, and manages different schools for primary education, vocational training, and higher education, and comprises more than 2,400 students (http://www.tibhomes.org/).

The Tibetan education system has been a fine success since its earliest days, in terms of material resources and funding, and academic results. Indeed, from the early 1960s onwards, the Indian government was engaged in the financial and structural establishment of a special education system for the Tibetan refugees. At that time, the education system for Indians was poor; the best education was, and still is, to be found in schools built by the British Raj or missionaries, which are private and expensive for local people and are, as such, restricted to an elite. The Indian government was thus at the heart of a successful education system for Tibetan refugees, in contrast with that available to its own citizens. In parallel, Western donors and organizations have financed the Tibetan schools since the beginning; nowadays, the TCV and THF schools are financed entirely by sponsorship of the students and donations to the schools:[13]

The majority of the children being orphans, semi-orphans or from destitute families, TCV has the responsibility [for] helping them until they become self-supporting. Overwhelming as the task seemed it had to be tackled somehow or the other and it was in 1975 that TCV made a small, but as time was to prove, most sensible and successful beginning by starting what is called the 'Educational Reserve Fund'. Over the period of a few years the fund rose to rupees [3,630,463.91] by collecting small miscellaneous donations, and donations specially sent for the 'Fund', *and largely by diverting the surplus sponsorship money from the SOS Kinderdorf International.*

The TCV is now in a position to give scholarships on the basis of merit for further education through this fund. (Information Office of His Holiness the Dalai Lama 1981: 63, emphasis added)

The Tibetan students, particularly those from residential schools (THF and TCV), rapidly achieved successful results. In 1969, the first school, established in Mussoorie, entered its first eight students for the 'All-India Higher Secondary Examination', which they all passed (ibid.: 32). In 1973, a student from the Tibetan Central School of Darjeeling was ranked in the All-India Merit List of the top ten students in India (ibid.: 32). In 1978, eighteen students graduated from TCV and joined a college in Chandigarh (ibid.: 60). In 2006, the ratio of students passing 'grade X' was more than 72 per cent, and for 'grade XII' was more than 90 per cent (http://sherig.org/en/schools/). The survey conducted in 2009 shows that 38,060 students were enrolled in schools in India, Nepal and Bhutan, representing 94.8 per cent of the population aged from 5 to 25 years, and more than a third of the entire Tibetan population living in these three countries (Planning Commission 2010: 28 and 45). The literacy rate in 2009 among the Tibetan population in exile, aged five years and more, was 88.7 per cent (ibid.: 40).

Today, the Tibetan community presents its education system as the best example of its own success. This 'education narrative' presents the same characteristics and objectives as those on democracy. First, the education narrative attracts foreign funds. As will be seen further in Chapter 5, the sponsorship of schoolchildren is well organized and managed by the CTA, and represents a large part of the Western resources going to the refugees. In a virtuous cycle, where success breeds success, I often heard staff from the Western organizations with which I worked say that education was the refugees' biggest achievement and that they were proud to be contributing to this success. Second, as seen in Chapter 1, the education system is practically an apparatus on which the Tibetan administration can base its own legitimacy, by formatting the Tibetan culture and history according to its own vision. Nowak (1978a, 1978b) closely examines this phenomenon, and also how Tibetan youth are caught in limbo between the modern and traditional values being taught in the Tibetan schools. And third, the education narrative shows the world, and especially the Chinese authorities, how the Tibetans have developed without them, in striking contrast with what now happens in Tibet, where higher education is only provided in Mandarin Chinese (see Bangsbo 2004). Yet while the Tibetan education system is praised by the Tibetan community and its leadership, as well as by Western organizations and individuals, it presents a number of challenges (see Chapter 7).

Moral and Sustainable Development

Alongside democracy and education, the Tibetan community in exile has also adopted the concept of modern development for its future, as expressed by the long-term goals in the second (out of four) Integrated Development Plan (IDP):

> Traditionally Tibetans are a peace-loving and non-violent people who have practised non-violence with respect to all forms of life. [They wish to] *transform Tibet into a modern developed country* where all people, irrespective of caste, birth, sex and religion, can freely practise their religion, culture, thought, education and economic activities based on democratic principles. Prior to the Chinese invasion, Tibet was an unspoiled wilderness sanctuary in a unique natural environment. (Planning Council 1994: 9, emphasis added)

The Tibetan leadership, however, recently displayed the will to conduct its own form of development. Thus a conception of ideal development as moral and sustainable has developed throughout the Tibetan community, and especially the CTA's development office, the Planning Commission. During different interviews, the planning officer told me about the ideal conception of development that the Tibetans are trying to implement. This conception is largely based on Buddhist tenets like non-violence, the interdependence of all phenomena and the cyclical nature of these phenomena. He explained to me that the Tibetans were looking for a middle way of development, between materialistic development, which he identified with Chinese *and* Western development, and the purely spiritual, which could be reached only through a renunciation of the material world. Furthermore, this middle-way development should respect the environment, populations and all 'sentient beings'. Again, this middle-way development is inspired by the concept of non-violence in Buddhism (as presented by the Tibetans themselves – see next chapter) and by the Dalai Lama's policy labelled as a 'middle path'.

Having studied in Germany, the planning officer referred constantly, during our conversations, to Eric Fromm's '*haben und sein*' ('having and being', see Fromm and Funk 1995) and the need for the Tibetans to develop the '*sein*' and not the '*haben*'. In saying this, he emphasized the fact that, according to him, Tibetans do not want to fall (or should not fall) into the trap of materialism, and that all the projects the CTA manage should follow this middle way. Finally, he said that the Tibetan community has the power to implement this form of development, as the CTA receives so many project proposals that it has the ability to choose those that are most relevant (see Chapter 2).

This conception of development was formally introduced for the first time into the third IDP, published in 2004 (Planning Commission 2004), and the plan for the period 2004–2007, as follows:

> The objectives and subsequent activities of the plans are drawn upon *the need-based approach in development.* Contrary to the want-satisfying consumerist economy, the need-based approach works only *for the fulfilment of basic material needs in order to achieve moral progress of humans to live a Content life.* (Planning Commission 2004: 2, emphasis added)

The middle-way development adopted by Tibetans is illustrated in this quotation by the presence of moral concepts in the description of the development that the Tibetans want to follow. The same IDP gives four guiding principles for the development projects: '1. Non-Violence; 2. Environmental Safety; 3. Poverty Alleviation; and 4. Sustainability' (ibid.). I shall develop below the definitions of these four principles in order to understand what the Tibetans mean by them.[14]

Non-violence

The third IDP has the following to say on the subject of non-violence:

> Offending any living beings, including oneself, by negative emotion is seen as an act of violence ... *Non-violence is the essential means of understanding truth.* To the Tibetans, non-violence is the basic tenet to be practised in all its forms so as to promote peace and harmony within and without. *It can be achieved only through righteous methods and means.* Therefore, any project funded by and through the CTA should contribute to the development of a non-violent society. (Planning Commission 2004: 8, emphasis added)

Concepts such as 'non-violence', 'truth' and 'righteous methods and means' are, in fact, direct references to Buddhism.

The use of the word 'truth' is interesting because, in Tibetan, the word (*bden pa*) has two meanings, one religious and one political. The religious meaning denotes the eschatological aim of a human life, namely, to attain the ultimate truth,[15] which involves the complete liberation of a human being from worldly matters. The political meaning is to be understood as 'justice'; and the Tibetans use the word to contrast with the Chinese 'lies' and violation of human rights in Tibet, as one of my informants put it (see below on human rights). Development for the Tibetans is hence a way to follow the tenets of Buddhism and also to display a just and righteous Tibetan society to the world in general and to the Chinese authorities in particular. As the then Secretary of the CTA's Department of Information and International Relations put it in 1996, '[t]he greatest achievement of the Tibet movement is our ability to place morality, non-violence, truth and justice on the agenda of the international community' (Department of Information and International Relations and Friedrich-Neumann Stiftung 1996: 63). In a similar way, the Dalai Lama called the organizations working with the Tibetans '"the army of truth" on the political battlefront' (Department of Information and International Relations and Friedrich-Neumann Stiftung 2001: 194).

To present a non-violent image of the Tibetans, the Tibetan leadership had to delete from the history books and from the collective memory various violent episodes in their history; this included the armed Khampa resistance to the Chinese referred to in the previous chapter. As already mentioned, McGranahan talks of 'arrested histories' for these processes where the telling of past events is suspended. Ardley, in her paper 'Violent Compassion' (2000), shows how the Tibetan guerrillas justified their violent actions through Buddhist arguments and how the Tibetan authorities (not only the Dalai Lama) always denied such a justification, even if they recognized that violence could be used to defend the *Dharma* (ibid.: 1ff.).[16] Going further, Ardley remarks that, when the Tibetan population – inside or outside Tibet – shows inclinations to violence against the Chinese regime in the present context, the same Tibetan authorities oppose the Buddhist tenet of non-violence. She then describes the terrible dilemma the Dalai Lama and the prime minister faced when they were confronted in 1998 with the self-immolation of Thupten Ngodub, who wanted to denounce Chinese repression. The man, who died shouting 'Long live the Dalai Lama', had undeniably committed an extreme act of violence against himself; and the Tibetan leaders, while sympathetic to him, could not endorse his political gesture. On these dilemmas, interestingly, Ardley notes that '[they] could represent a much larger issue of the difficulty of judging a political event in religious terms – indeed, of the problems of compounding religion and politics at all' (ibid.: 20). This is even truer currently with the significant number of self-immolations in Tibet during the last four years. Actually, the Dalai Lama told an Australian journalist that self-immolations were acts of non-violence because the perpetrators could use bombs to make themselves heard, but chose instead to commit suicide.[17] As the narrative on the non-violent nature of the Tibetans demanded further elaboration, the Tibetan leadership, together with its influential Western supporters, translated this issue onto the Human Rights plane.

As seen previously, the Tibetans understand truth as justice, and are seeking this truth for their country. One of the main activities of the Tibetan government and its leader since their arrival in exile has been to denounce the treatment of their people in Tibet by the Chinese authorities. These Chinese actions in Tibet were labelled by the United Nations as violations of human rights as early as 1959:

> The General Assembly, ... [g]ravely concerned at reports, including the official statements of His Holiness the Dalai Lama, to the effect that *the fundamental human rights and freedoms of the people of Tibet have been forcibly denied them* ... [c]alls for respect for the fundamental human rights of the Tibetan people and for their distinctive cultural and religious life. (UN Resolution 1353 (XIV) on Tibet adopted 21 October 1959, in Dalai Lama [1962] 1997: 191, emphasis added)

The two other resolutions adopted on Tibet by the UN (1723 (XVI) in 1961;[18] and 2079 (XX) in 1965[19]) both concerned non-respect for human rights in Tibet. Indeed, the international political agenda adopted human rights as its main (and indeed only) criticism of the PRC; the independence issue was never formally discussed. Today, the violation of human rights and the destruction of the environment in Tibet (see below) by the Chinese authorities are the main political criticisms levelled by the CTA. The Tibetan administration is backed up in this respect by Western organizations and individuals close to the Tibet issue (the Global Tibet Movement studied in Chapter 5), who maintain activism on these two issues.

Tibetans, both inside and outside Tibet, have had to frame their fight for freedom in the international language. In addition, the concept of 'human rights' – together with the fight for their respect in Tibet – was adopted alongside the Tibetan will for independence. Schwartz (1994: 232ff.) recalls how 'human rights' were rhetorically adopted from the 1987 demonstrations onwards (see Chapter 2). Pike (2001) shows how the Tibetans, and the Global Tibet Movement, strategically adopted the fight for human rights in Tibet in order to maintain a position on the international political agenda. Pike calls this policy the 'universal rights strategy'. This strategy was instrumental in the attraction of supporters to the Tibet issue: 'Given the growing popularity of human rights and environmental issues in transnational activism, potential supporters [must no longer] be enamored of Tibetan culture before they isolate Tibet as a special human rights concern' (Pike 2001: 52).

Thanks to this strategy, the Tibet issue was no longer solely about regaining the independence of a country, but was about respect for human rights. Barnett makes the same analysis, and observes how '[i]t was the representation of Tibet as a "specialized" site of human rights violations that seems to have made the issue palatable to a broad, cross-party community' (Barnett 2001: 286). Indeed, the Tibet issue is today used in Western media as an illustration of the struggle for global human rights. Developing this further, Barnett shows how the Dalai Lama's travels to Western countries have brought the Tibet issue onto the front page. Indeed, the question for

Western politicians of whether or not to meet the Tibetan leader (at the risk of breaking diplomatic and commercial relations with China) became a test of their commitment to human rights. Hence, this coverage brought even more publicity to the Tibet cause. Barnett observes also that the adoption of this human rights strategy attracted a larger audience for the Tibet cause in the West, particularly among people with centre-left political sensibilities. Barnett's observations are still relevant today, as witnessed by the recent controversies surrounding a meeting between the U.S. president, Barack Obama, and the Dalai Lama in February 2014: the Chinese authorities denounced this meeting, as they always do, as intolerable inference in their internal affairs. However, such meetings are always popular with Western electors, who perceive their representatives showing political will in favour of human rights.

Furthermore, such a 'human rights strategy' is very effective on the political stage, as it is universal and, as such, acceptable to and adoptable by Western politicians. With this strategy, politicians can show their inclination for a general and important cause, and not a particular one such as the struggle for an independent Tibet. Interestingly, the 'human rights strategy' appeared with the launch of the International Campaign for Tibet and the abandonment of the independence claim by the Dalai Lama (see Chapter 2). From this period onwards, human rights became the international idiom of the Tibet cause, and a model for the Tibetan community in exile.

Environmentally Safe

The second concept of Tibetan development, to be 'environmentally safe', is defined as follows in the third IDP:

> *Materialism does not have self-limits while natural resources are limited.* In the past the development activities have exposed the environment to the unnatural degradation impacting all forms of life negatively ... *Each activity undertaken must be environmentally safe and at the same time, we are committed to the activities that help to restore the degraded environment as close to its pristine form as possible.*
> (Planning Commission 2004: 8, emphasis added)

In this definition, the Tibetans forge a link between materialism, identified as a Western and Chinese trend, and the destruction of natural resources. For their own concept of development, the Tibetans have chosen limitation of materialism (as seen previously) and strict respect for natural resources. Although the third IDP is the first to delimit the Tibetan ecological *ethos*, the first IDP, published in 1992, certainly mentioned that, '[p]rior to the Chinese invasion, Tibet was an unspoiled wilderness sanctuary in a unique natural environment' (Planning Council 1992: 24–25). Actually, the Tibetan ecological discourse began even earlier, in the mid-1980s, as shown by

Huber's article 'Green Tibetans' (1997). Huber shows how ecological issues became prevalent in Tibetan discourses aimed at outsiders. This discourse on ecology became prominent from the mid-1980s onwards, at a time when Western societies widely discussed ecology. In this discourse, the Tibetans presented, and still present, themselves as having lived in peace with their environment for centuries, and as being the first ecologists. As one Tibetan put it:

> [W]e Tibetans have always been aware of the interdependent nature of this world. We know that our large country, with its diverse flora and fauna, its primal forest cover, and above all the many great rivers which rise in Tibet, is a source of life to an area many times larger than Tibet itself. For most of Asia, Tibet's environment has always been of crucial importance. And so for centuries Tibet's ecosystem was kept in balance and alive out of a common concern for all humanity. (Huber 1997: 105)

Nevertheless, in 2006 I met in Dharamsala the creator of a recycling project that had been adopted for the community only in the 1990s by the Tibetan Welfare Office. While volunteering at the upper TCV, this Dutch student became worried about the amount of garbage that was not recycled. He decided to launch a recycling project, which at first seemed odd to the Tibetan locals. He told me that at this time there was no ecological awareness among the refugees. However, some while later, the project was adopted by the settlement authorities; it is still working, and is shown off as a model of the 'green' attitude of the Tibetans (who have taken credit for the project).

Huber shows further how this ontological ecological self-ascription is substantiated by Buddhist arguments. He also argues that 'folk religion' (as with Bon, see Chapter 4) and the 'ancient customs', rehabilitated by Dharamsala at the same period, are used to reinforce further the image of the Tibetans as ecologists (Huber 1997). In another article published in the same year, Huber and Pedersen (1997) show that modern scientific knowledge, such as meteorological and ecological knowledge, is used and claimed as their own by the Tibetans, who again justify these claims with reference to their centuries-old Buddhist traditions. They argue that 'these claims are anachronistic in that they are projections of ideas of nature which belong to a modern knowledge tradition unknown to the ancient Tibetans' (ibid.: 577). Indeed, Western concepts like ecology are difficult to study in a cross-cultural context, and it makes little sense to talk about defence of the environment for non-industrial societies. The idea defended by Huber in his articles, and with which I agree, is that it is not because the Tibetans lived in harmony with their environment that they were ecologists, as they claim today. These authors show that the 'greening' of the Tibetans is a strategy to achieve a closer alignment with recent Western expectations, and to distance themselves from the Chinese environmental destruction of Tibet (on this issue, see, among others, Clarke 1998). Huber shows in his 1997 article that various statements made prior to the 1980s by Tibetan leaders, among them the Dalai Lama, contradict the post-1980s discourses on ecology (1997: 107). Moreover, Huber asserts that the Dalai Lama was advised by 'various well-meaning foreign supporters to become "green" at that particular time [mid-1980s] as that would greatly add to international sympathy for their cause' (ibid.: 108). In fact, this 'greening' corresponds to the launch of the international campaign detailed in Chapter 1.[20] The Dalai Lama did not attempt to hide the fact that he became sensitive to ecological issues once in exile; in fact, he said so at the third TSGs conference: 'Of course, when I was still in Tibet, I was not aware of the environment issue. However, after meeting some specialists in this field, I realised that it is really a very critical issue' (Department of Information and International Relations and Friedrich-Neumann Stiftung 2001: 156).

This 'greening' of the Tibetan refugees has been fruitful regarding Western support. During my fieldwork in Tibetan settlements, as well as in Western organizations, I observed the power of this narrative. The Tibetans are recognized as profound environmentalists, both because they present themselves as such and also because, as a 'traditional culture', moreover Buddhist, they are automatically credited by Westerners as 'green' (see Chapter 5 on the Western reception of such presentations). But the implementation of green projects has not proceeded without challenges for the community.

During my fieldwork, I observed a pilot project that an Italian NGO had recently developed, through the CTA, for organic farming in twelve settlements, including Bylakuppe and Tezu. Only a few acres are cultivated organically in Bylakuppe for the time being, and the farmers have difficulties in marketing these organic products. There is, in fact, no market for organic products in the Indian rural areas, for economic reasons: the customers are neither ready nor able to pay more for organic products. In Tezu, a Tibetan farmer told me that, even if he liked the idea of organic farming, it was not worth the risk of losing the entire crop to pests. He argued further that there was, in any case, no market for organic food in Tezu. As in Bylakuppe, locals were unready to pay more for organic products. The CTA then had the idea of producing organic vegetables for the Tibetans, as well as non-organic crops for the local people. In Kollegal (Karnataka), the model settlement for organic farming, the main crop is maize, produced as feed for poultry and cattle. The farmers in Lugsam told me that they do not understand the benefit of growing organic vegetables for the animals. They recognize that the idea is good, coming from the West and, more importantly, from the Dalai Lama, as it is eco-friendly, sustainable and hence 'more Buddhist' (because of 'no harm to nature'); but they said they needed more advice and guidance on developing this mode of cultivation.

The discourse on ecology is also a way for Tibetans to internationalize their cause, as the environmental destruction wrought in Tibet has consequences for all Asia, and indeed the world. It is also thus a major criticism of Chinese power (China is accused by many Western organizations, as well as by the CTA's Environmental Desk, created in the 1990s, of destroying Tibet's environment), and a way of telling China that the Tibetans would have protected their environment in Tibet just as they now do in exile.

Poverty Alleviation

The third IDP gives the following definition of poverty alleviation as one of its four guiding principles:

> *Poverty is basically a critical modern construct that came with economic growth and prosperity in the 20th century.* This posited economic development as the key to [a] poverty alleviation programme where non-economic issues of the poor are more or less neglected under this assumption. *As for the Tibetan community in exile, measuring of poverty is based on socio-cultural parameters rather than just material constructs.* Under this definition of poverty, an individual or a family lacking in material and socio-cultural *capacities* to achieve individual and collective aspirations will be regarded as poor. (Planning Commission 2004: 8, emphasis added)

From this extract, it is again clear that the Tibetans are claiming their own path to development. They refer to the 'modern construct' in order to detach themselves from it.

Moreover, in referring to concepts developed by Sen (1999) – such as human development (the fact that poverty is not only material) or capabilities (referred to in this extract as 'capacities': 'the substantive freedom to achieve alternative functionings' [ibid.: 75]) – the Tibetans engage themselves in the critique of development. This stance puts them in agreement with alternative methods of development that are growing in popularity in the West, and in opposition to the classic and solely materialistic conception of development traditionally associated with both the West and China.

The same report asserts that one-fifth of the refugee community is still materially deprived. The people comprising this 20 per cent are certainly poor as far as 'material constructs' are concerned. However, using the (rather vague) definition adopted by the IDP, the entire community should be defined as poor, by virtue of its lacking 'socio-cultural capacities'. In other words, these Tibetan refugees cannot achieve their collective aspiration of returning to their home country. This statement supports the observation I made during my fieldwork concerning the adoption of a 'victim narrative'.

The Victim Narrative

It is striking when visiting Tibetan communities to see that even the poorest settlements, such as Tezu, are economically much better off than their hosts. Nevertheless, both institutional and individual Tibetan discourses on the refugee situation speak of their destitution, economic as much as political. These discourses are, as seen below, carried on by Western organizations and individuals working with Tibetan refugees.

At the institutional level, the CTA has widened its own definition of poverty in order to keep attracting foreign support. As seen before, different organizations chose to terminate their work with the Tibetans at the end of the rehabilitation phase, having made the assessment that the refugees were no longer in need. Thereafter, the CTA, which still needed material support, had no choice but to present the refugees as still poor and needy in political terms (as in, for example, their lack of capacities). The CTA strategy, in order to attract material and economic support for the refugees, has thus been to show the world that the refugees' culture and religion are in danger, as much as to show their evident poverty. This strategy I refer to as the 'victim narrative', whereby political arguments are used and sent to foreigners to improve the economic situation of the refugees.

At an individual level, the discourse that I often heard from Tibetan refugees was one of complete economic deprivation. Although it is not rare for some refugees to have more than one sponsor and to live in relative comfort, they hide their personal economic situation from their sponsors, and continue to claim total deprivation, thus abusing this 'power of the weak' in order to obtain a better socio-economic position in the community. Most often, it is the Tibetans born in exile, English-speaking and at ease with Westerners, who are able to attract multiple sponsors. By using 'impression management', these refugees adopt a 'victimized' discourse in order to attract pity and, eventually, funds. I observed the same phenomenon in an institutionalized context: many monasteries, funded by foreign organizations, claim needs that go beyond the living necessities. I recall another extreme situation: I once visited a monastery with a group of Western donors and the monk who was conducting the tour showed us a construction site for what would be, according to him, a hospital for needy people. I came back two years later and this new building was a guesthouse for foreign visitors.

The poverty assessment of the Tibetan refugees is all-pervasive among the Western organizations and individuals working with them. I observed during my fieldwork that, for these organizations and individuals, the economic argument to vindicate the existence of poverty is widespread, even though they did not always seem ready to make the same assessment of the host population, whose poverty was much more visible. I would explain such discrepancies in terms of the degree of identification between the Tibetans and their helpers (examined in the next chapters), whereby the latter compare the situation of the former with their own, which obviously makes them appear very poor. It is also evident that the Tibetans themselves, who sometimes have close contact with Westerners, tend to compare their own situation with that of these foreigners, and thus feel deprived. I would here make the comparison with what Norberg-Hodge (2000: 101) observed in Ladakh: one of her informants said in 1975, '[w]e don't have any poverty here'; in 1983 the same informant said, after eight years of many Westerners in the region, as described by the author, '[i]f you could only help us Ladakhis, we're so poor'. Norberg-Hodge wants to show by this quote the relative nature of the understanding of poverty, which can be easily redefined following foreign influences.

De Voe (1981: 88) identified another trend among Western organizations: in order to keep themselves going, these organizations cast the refugees as 'client[s] in need of assistance'. These organizations have also become institutions with economic constraints, and they therefore have every interest in perpetuating the 'victim narrative'. This is unfortunately a general trend in the development world: the NGOs from Northern countries are built on their help to people in need in the South. If these latter disappear, they will also disappear. This is equally true for individuals working in these NGOs, who have made their careers in 'development'.

Sustainability

According to the third IDP,

> [s]ustainability takes the long-term socio-economic scenarios into consideration. The current trends of changing aspirations and increasing demands/ consumerists behavior tend to increase our dependence on external factors over which we have very little control. We would like to initiate a development that draws largely on our own resources and knowledge to fulfill the needs of the people to live a Content-life [*sic*] by challenging the ones that [are] driven by wants. Such a development can only be sustainable and long lasting. … In order to have a real benefit and ownership of the projects, it is important that the projects are simple and manageable at the grass-root level. The project design should therefore be based on local and traditional knowledge. (Planning Commission 2004: 9)

This quote reflects the differing trends concerning the Tibetan community in exile. First, 'changes of aspirations' and 'consumerist'[21] trends are identified among the community and have to be counteracted. These trends oppose the ideal development defined previously in the same IDP. The planning officer told me that these trends were initiated due to two main influences: the influence of the Western and other foreign travellers who interact with Tibetans and who are, relative to them, very rich; and the influence of the way of life of the rising middle classes in large Indian cities, which many Tibetans increasingly encounter. These two models affect the Tibetans, according to the planning officer, by showing them an 'easy way of life' that they want to copy and that makes them leave the settlements for a big city or a Western country. Second, these two trends are identified as increasing the dependency on foreign assistance (i.e. the 'external factors'), which already represents up to 80 per cent of the community's total budget. In short, the IDP expresses the fact that, by adopting a consumerist way of life, the Tibetan refugees have become even more dependent on material resources. What can be read between the lines here is that foreign assistance brings in material resources, as well as consumerist behaviour – thus there is a veiled criticism of the received assistance, which is addictive for the community being increasingly assisted. The way to 'challenge' this addiction is for Tibetans to take charge of the projects, based on their 'own resources and knowledge'. This third assessment in the above quotation is identified as the only way for the community to sustain itself. During my fieldwork I identified a common discourse among different Tibetan intellectuals about the self-sufficiency of their community, and I shall describe below the ways in which this discourse is related to the will of the Tibetans to decrease their dependency on consumerist behaviour and foreign assistance.

The Self-sufficiency Narrative

The 'self-sufficiency' narrative is the Tibetan refugee discourse by which they present their community as no longer being in need of foreign economic support. This narrative, in complete opposition to the 'victim' idiom, is more discreet and difficult to identify. I see it as being directed towards 'insiders' (i.e. the refugees themselves, although it also has importance in the development world), in opposition to the 'victim' narrative that is intended mainly for the 'outsiders'.[22]

During interviews with Tibetans, including intellectuals and people working with and knowing the importance of foreign organizations for the refugees' resources, I often heard that their community was self-sufficient, as they themselves financed the expenses of the CTA. This is only true for around 20 per cent of the total CTA budget, namely its running costs. Indeed, no organizations or governments finance these costs, almost certainly for political reasons – since the Tibetan Government is not recognized internationally, it cannot be easily financed overtly. These running costs are financed by the 'voluntary tax', by the Dalai Lama himself (through the 'treasure' he brought from Tibet, the copyrights of his numerous books and other private gifts), and from the revenue of the Corpus Fund, which comprises donations managed by the CTA and traded on the stock market. However, I was allowed to gain the impression, listening to these informants, that the entire CTA budget (its running costs plus the projects' expenses) is auto-financed by the refugees. At the very least, they remain vague on this issue. A leading artist in the refugee community told me during a conversation that the Tibetans could perfectly well survive in exile on their own resources, and that it was actually the 'Westerners who needed [the Tibetans] and not the reverse'.

Indeed, a number of these informants told me that the Tibetan community does not need the support of Western organizations, but rather that 'these organizations actually need the Tibetans to survive' and that they 'cash in on the Tibetan issue'. One informant told me that, for him, '90 per cent of the Western organizations' were designed in order for their staff to 'make a career, find a livelihood and to make one's own name famous'. A director of an old people's home told me that 'Western organizations need my old and disabled people because they need target groups'.

These statements make the link with the 'victim narrative' by framing the refugees as clients. In the end, while these Tibetans are well aware that the refugee community needs the organizations if it is to survive, they tend to minimize the help received from this quarter, ignoring, willingly or otherwise, the reality that up to 80 per cent of the community's budget is financed by foreign help.[23] It is also important to note that this narrative is never officially expressed by any Tibetan authority, as this could jeopardize the success of the Tibetan community. On the contrary, the authorities glorify the funds that Westerners are providing (see Chapter 4).

I have tried to understand the reasons for foreign assistance being overlooked in this way. I believe that the Tibetans want to stay masters of their own development and destiny (as expressed by the third IDP), that they have a certain pride in thinking of themselves as independent and unassisted, and that, finally, the CTA can, thanks to such a discourse, extend its influence and importance by exhibiting good management of the situation in exile. I have also wondered how the Western organizations could accept such a discourse, which denies their own assistance. It seems that they are either unaware of this discourse, or they choose not to protest. In the latter case, this could be because their relations with Tibetans are strong, or because they derive a certain power from the Tibetans (see below). It is surely a rare situation where the beneficiary population can get away with claiming that it does not need its helpers, and yet keeps receiving the help. The practical characteristics of such a discourse, implemented in the IDPs as the 'exit policy' (i.e. a policy to lessen assistance – see, for example, Planning Commission 2004: 17), is a requirement of modern development: according to the famous image, the organizations have to teach the helped populations how to fish, and not merely give them fish. On the Tibetan side, the self-sufficiency narrative is further fuelled by the religious agenda, which is the main source of power in the relationship with Westerners (see Chapter 4).

Summary

The Tibetan leadership in exile – the Dalai Lama and the CTA – has taken great care to transform and present the exiled society by means of an ideal 'middle-way' approach. This approach allows Tibetans to accommodate what are recognized as global values, and negotiate their own position vis-à-vis these values. Their religion is the ultimate legitimation of this position, and this chapter has detailed how they instrumentalize the religion for political aims. The 'middle-way' approach consists of normative discourses (on democracy, education and development), which are not always followed through in practice by the exile population. Moreover, the Tibetans put their political agenda on the same level as their first objective of regaining freedom for their country, as expressed in their Charter:

> Achievement of the Common Goal and the Social Welfare of the Tibetans-in-Exile – Article 15.
>
> The primary aim of the Tibetan Administration-in-Exile shall be to endeavor to *maintain a just policy for the achievement of the common goal of Tibet*, and in addition, at the present moment, to protect Tibetans in Tibet from present hardships and danger; and shall *formulate a policy to secure just and equal opportunities for the economic development of Tibetans-in-Exile*. Furthermore, it shall endeavor to provide reasonable opportunities to all Tibetan youth for the procurement of a modern education and the derivation of the ancient cultural heritage of Tibet; and in particular, shall also strive to provide adequate health services for sound mental and physical development. (http://www.tibetjustice.org/materials/tibet/tibet6.3.html, emphasis added)

This (certainly rare) presentation of refugees has a sound strategic importance, because it guarantees the survival of the Tibetan refugees and their cause, and also distances them from the Chinese authorities' policy in Tibet.

Western organizations and individuals have become very sensitive to the Tibetans presenting themselves as an ideal society (see Chapter 4).[24] Such presentations involve Western values, yet at the same time criticize or diminish them, and thus appeal to many Westerners. Thanks to this Tibetan depiction of an ideal community, Westerners are able to project their own fantasies of the ideal society. These projections are further fuelled by the Tibetan religious agenda, described in the next chapter. As a result, the Tibetans attract support in different forms, which guarantees their survival in exile and also fosters an international awareness of their situation. The deployment of the political agenda in the West is of primary importance for the Tibetan leadership, as shown by the representative offices opened by the CTA in capital cities in Europe, the United States, Japan, Australia and South Africa; management costs for these offices account for more than half of the CTA's operational budget.

Moreover, the Tibetan political agenda is also a way for the Tibetans to distance themselves from what the Chinese authorities are doing in Tibet. By presenting ideal policies for themselves, the Tibetans show the world, including the PRC, how they could have developed without the Chinese occupation and, at the same time, answer Chinese accusations about the feudal and autocratic power of the Dalai Lama.

Finally, while the political agenda derives from accommodation with foreign values, the next chapter will show how the Tibetans have used their own religion to reinterpret and negotiate their relationship with their supporters, in a process that I call the 'religious strategy'.

Notes

1. Frechette (2007: 115) shows how the term 'democracy' is derived in Tibetan from *dmangs gtso*, the rule of the people, even the socially lowest, which, by extension, has taken on the sense of 'power to the vulgar', *mang gtso*, the rule of the majority. I will not elaborate on the perspectives on democracy in Asian and Buddhist countries, but instead refer the reader to works that summarize the issues about this perspective, including Wood (2004) and Inoguchi and Carlson (2006).
2. Knaus (1999) asserts that the Constitution was written by an American citizen, Ernest Gross.
3. The Preamble of the Constitution states that: 'Whereas it has become increasingly evident that the system of government which has hitherto prevailed in Tibet has not proved sufficiently responsive to the present needs and future development of the people; *And whereas it is deemed desirable and necessary that the principle of justice, equality and democracy laid down by the Lord Buddha should be reinforced and strengthened in the government of Tibet*; And whereas it is deemed essential that the people of Tibet should have a more effective voice in shaping their destiny; Now, therefore, His Holiness the Dalai Lama has been pleased to ordain, and it is hereby ordained as follows: [...]' (http://www.tibetjustice.org/materials/tibet/tibet2.html, emphasis added).
4. My translation from French from the original: 'Le Tibet en exil s'est résolument mis à l'école de la démocratie. Le fonctionnement politique de la communauté des Tibétains exilés préfigure ce que serait un Tibet à nouveau maître de son destin ... Ce serait un véritable ferment démocratique pour une Chine qui s'ouvre au monde et aspire à rejoindre la communauté des nations.'
5. See http://tibetanyouthcongress.org
6. See http://tibetanwomen.org/aims-objectives/
7. See http://www.gu-chu-sum.org/
8. See http://www.tchrd.org/
9. These are figures from the second survey of the refugee community, made in 2009 (Planning Commission 2010).
10. See below for further details on the TCV network of Tibetan schools.

11. The 'newcomers' have a special curriculum that gives them the opportunity to fill their educational gap if they did not previously attend a school in Tibet.

12. See the official statement: http://ctsa.nic.in/writereaddata/CircularFilePath/82e41595-Transfer%20of%20CTSA%20Schools%20to%20Department%20of%20Education%20,CTA%20Dharamsala.pdf.

13. See: The Information Office of His Holiness the Dalai Lama (1981: 72) for a list of donors of the THF in 1980; TCV (1980: 4) for the donors of TCV in 1980; and TCV (2006: 32–39) for an exhaustive list of donors in 2006.

14. It will become apparent that different Western concepts are developed according to these definitions, which I attribute to the fact that the planning officer responsible for the third IDP received his higher education in Germany.

15. I shall not enter into the details of the two natures of truth, absolute and relative. For one of several treatments of this complex topic, see, for example, Newland (1992).

16. Actually, in a later study, Ardley (2003) shows that non-violence is well understood by the Dalai Lama, who in fact goes further on the subject than did Gandhi. Gandhi, Ardley remarks, 'thought violence was sometimes acceptable; he preferred it to inaction where the honour of a country was at risk' (ibid.: 168).

17. See http://www.abc.net.au/7.30/content/2013/s3781436.htm

18. See http://www.tibetjustice.org/materials/un/un5.html

19. See http://www.tibetjustice.org/materials/un/un6.html

20. Cantwell published a response to Huber and Pedersen in 2001 (Cantwell 2001). Her argument is that the 'greening' of the Tibetans is in no way a strategy to attract Western supporters. Moreover, according to her, this ecological behaviour does not come from Buddhism but from local rituals like the earth ritual (*sa'i cho ga*). She argues that, if the Tibetans were truly ecologists for centuries, then it was only out of fear of angering local divinities connected to these rituals. I think that this argument does not contradict Huber and Pedersen, who are not talking about the practices but instead the knowledge and discourses on the environment. Moreover, the concept of ecology is so contextualized within modern Western society that it is hardly transposable.

21. The planning officer told me that 'changes of aspirations' were the reason why many refugees were increasingly thinking about their own material improvement and becoming 'consumerists', and were no longer community-driven or focused on the ultimate goal of returning to their liberated country (personal communication).

22. For outsiders, the discourse is sometimes the opposite of the 'self-sufficiency' narrative: the third IDP remarks that, '[d]uring the past 45 years ... there has been a gradual attitudinal shift towards dependency rather than self-reliance' (Planning Commission 2004: 3).

23. Some of my informants even rejected this figure of 80 per cent, which has been confirmed to me by the planning officer. Importantly, the planning officer told me that people who cited other figures were ill informed about the CTA's budget.

24. In a similar manner, Bhutan, another Himalayan Buddhist culture with Tibetan roots, one of the poorest countries in the world, has developed ideal presentations of its society. An excellent example is the invention of a 'Gross

National Happiness' index, which categorizes Bhutan among the happiest (although economically poor) societies, and has had huge media and popular success in the West. This totally subjective index is appealing to adherents of existing trends in the West towards an alternative development model (see Chapter 5).

4

The Religious Agenda

The Gift Exchange in Tibetan Culture

Gift exchange in Tibetan culture is an essential soteriological dimension of both Buddhism and Tibetan Buddhism. I will develop here two important forms of this religious exchange relevant to my argument: one links a priest to an individual patron, known as *sbyin bdag*; and the other, on a grander scale, links a political hierarch with a religious figure – the *mchod yon* relationship.

The sbyin bdag *Form of Exchange*

A very important relationship in Buddhism is the link between the *danapati* (Skt.; *sbyin bdag* in Tibetan), who is the 'generous donor, loyal and lay head of the household (*khyim bdag*)' (Ruegg 1995: 56), and the cleric (Skt. *bhiksu*, Tib. *dge slong*), who belongs to the monastic community (Skt. *Sangha* or *Samgha*, Tib. *dge 'dun*). This relationship goes back as far as the Buddha himself, who was sponsored by a rich merchant. Hence, every head of a household should be able to assume this socio-religious role of donor.

The notion of voluntary giving on the religious side of this exchange is very important: the cleric gives his teaching, or 'the gift of the Dharma', not in return for material alms, but voluntarily. He is not linked to the gift by a reciprocal counter-gift in a Maussian understanding (Mauss 1954; Godelier 1996); and indeed this gift can be considered as free, with no expectation of return. On the other side, the donor, the *sbyin bdag*, gains religious merit by the very fact of giving. Hence, in this exchange, the recipient is empowered and placed in a position at least as high as that of the donor.

Ortner, who studies the social implications of sponsoring, remarks upon two interesting facts. First, the sponsor must give without any demand or expectation of any return. In that sense, his gift is not aimed at creating a relationship that will bind him to the recipient, and 'does not contain, in other words, a tendency toward social bonding but rather tends in the opposite direction' (Ortner 1978: 38). Actually, the charity[1] gift is not aimed at the recipient at all, but at the Sacred. This relationship becomes social again with the ultimate aim of *Mahayana*, which is the salvation of every sentient being. The second fact, which Ortner details elsewhere, is the social status that one can gain by giving to religious institutions, which is certainly an additional motivation for this giving. These two facts, which can seem contradictory, actually show how the religious is entwined with the social.

The mchod yon *Relationship*

In order to understand the *mchod yon* dyad, often rendered as the 'patron–priest' relationship,[2] which has been prominent in the history of interaction between Tibetans and their neighbours, it is important to describe its origins.

At the beginning of the thirteenth century, Genghis Khan extended his Mongol Empire, and arrived at the threshold of Tibet. In 1207, a Tibetan delegation was sent to meet the Khan and establish friendly relations. It was a success and Tibet was not invaded, having instead to pay a yearly tribute to the Khan (Shakabpa 1967: 61ff.). When Genghis Khan died in 1227, the Tibetans stopped paying the tribute and, in 1240, Genghis's grandson, Godan, sent his troops into Tibet, where they looted and destroyed several villages and monasteries. Godan then asked his officers to give him the names of outstanding Tibetan religious leaders. On the list appeared the name of Kunga Gyaltsen, also known as Sakya Pandita, the ruler of the Sakya monastery, whom Godan asked to come to instruct him. In 1244, Sakya Pandita left for Godan's camp with his nephew Phagpa (*'Phags pa*). There he began the Buddhist instruction of the Khan, and was soon writing to different Tibetan leaders to enjoin them to cease any resistance against the Mongols and to resume the payment of their tribute. Before his death, he wrote this message for them:

> The Prince has told me that *if we Tibetans help the Mongols in matters of religion, they in turn will support us in temporal matters.* In this way, we will be able to spread our religion far and wide. (Shakabpa 1967: 63, emphasis added)

Sakya Pandita died in 1251, after empowering his nephew Phagpa, and Godan died soon afterwards. Godan's successor, Kublai, founder of the Mongol Yuan Dynasty, which would rule China from 1271 to 1368, then invited Phagpa, aged 19, to instruct him.[3] Phagpa accepted on the condition of being given temporal power over Tibet, and Kublai agreed. As such, Phagpa became the first temporal and religious leader of Tibet. His power was recognized in Tibet and he gained both authority and the respect of the other Tibetan leaders when he declined Kublai's proposal to forbid and destroy every other Buddhist tradition in Tibet. Phagpa actually delegated his power to a temporal ruler, based in Sakya, known as the Ponchen (*dpon chen* or 'Great Chief') (Cassinelli and Ekvall 1969: 18–19). These two Tibetan rulers were linked by a dual relationship, called *bla dpon* or 'lama and officer' (Ruegg 1995: 73), which was integrated into the *chos srid zung 'brel* concept (as seen in Chapter 2). Ruegg writes:

> It is this couple, composed of a religious sovereign member and of an executive lay member, which had the mission to protect Tibet by means of the 'two sciences' (*gtsug lag gnyis ka*), the spiritual and the temporal (ibid.; my translation).[4]

In 1254, Kublai gave Phagpa a letter of credence conferring on the Tibetan ruler all power in Tibet.[5] In this letter, Kublai tells Phagpa how much he esteems Buddhism, and writes:

> As I have elected to be your patron, you must make it your duty to carry out the teachings of the Lord Buddha. By this letter, I have taken upon myself the sponsorship of your religion. (Shakabpa 1967: 66)

In 1260, Kublai was enthroned as the new Khan. Phagpa conducted the enthronement ceremony, and the relationship between the two was like the 'sun and the moon in the sky' (ibid.: 67). This relationship was now, for the first time, described in Tibetan historical annals as a *mchod yon* (or *yon mchod*, which means the same thing) relationship.

'*Mchod yon*' is the grammatical contraction of two terms representing the two actors of the relation: on one side, the *mchod gnas* (contracted to *mchod*), the beneficiary, who is the donor's spiritual superior as his preceptor, and, on the other side, the *yon bdag* (contracted to *yon*), who is the donor, 'the one who makes an offering, such as wealth, land, people, or power' (Cassinelli and Ekvall 1969: 15). The *mchod yon* relationship thus implies a political and material protection from the *yon bdag* side, and religious service from the *mchod gnas* side. Ruegg recalls that the naming of *yon bdag* and *mchod gnas* had been a fact seen since the time of the Tibetan king Tride Songsten (*Khri lde srong brtsan*, c.800–815), but that the term *mchod yon* had only appeared with the relationship between Phagpa and Kublai, and is also best exemplified by them. This arrangement of a temporal king receiving religious education from a preceptor, to whom he offers material protection, was to be continued with the Dalai Lamas and their Chinese (during the Ming dynasty, 1378–1644) and Manchu (during the Qing dynasty, 1644–1912) *yon bdag* (Ruegg 1995: 29).

It is important to note that *yon bdag* is a more formal formulation of *sbyin bdag*, and that hence these two forms of exchange are linked. It could be said that one is political or institutional, and the other individual or social. In the *mchod yon* relationship, as in the *sbyin bdag* system, both parties have power and can rule their own domains, which means that one is not enfeoffed to the other. The power issues embedded in these two Buddhist sets of relations are central to the relationship between the Tibetan refugees and their Western donors, as will be seen later on.

The *mchod yon* association is far from being formalized, as '[n]o written bond sealed this relationship and no other basis was recognised for the connection between the two countries' (Snellgrove and Richardson [1968] 2003: 148). It is, nevertheless, central to the relations between China and Tibet and their claims of authority over the High Plateau. Their respective readings and understandings of the historic relationship between Phagpa and Kublai, and the subsequent relationship between successive Dalai Lamas and the Chinese and Manchu emperors, are entirely opposed.[6]

Reorganization of the Religion

The reorganization of the religion by the Tibetan leadership is a dynamic process. After crystallizing Tibetan culture around its religion, the religious leadership unified it, before proceeding to essentialize it. The main consequence of this process was that people came to recognize Tibetan Buddhism as a universal religion, and the world was presented with the claim that Tibetan religion (that is, Tibetan culture) was a jewel worth saving.

Crystallization of the Culture

Tibetan Buddhism is constitutive of the Tibetan collective and individual identity. Nevertheless, after 1959 the Tibetan leadership used religion as a strong element of unification for the refugee community and for the internationalization of its cause. As a result, religion became the marker, almost exclusively, of Tibetan culture. During the fieldwork conducted for this book, I devised different sets of questions, and my informants were surprised that I was neither interested only in Tibetan Buddhism, nor a Buddhist myself. It was difficult for many to understand that I had an interest in their society distinct from their religion. Many told me that, in order to understand them, I needed to understand their Buddhism. This statement shows the vital assimilation of culture and religion in the Tibetan context. As religion is omnipresent in the daily life of Tibetans, from morning rituals to evening prayers, it is natural that they should consider their culture to be one with their religion. Moreover, the political context, for refugees and Tibetans inside Tibet, has helped to crystallize the culture around the religion, which is treated as the symbol of the nation.

McLagan (1996: 11) identifies a 'culture strategy', that is, the propensity of the Tibetan leadership to insist on culture, especially Tibetan Buddhism, in its political fight and its communication on the international stage. I agree with her argument, but will transform it into a 'religious strategy', given that the culture presented by the Tibetans is almost entirely religious. The cultural performances presented outside the Tibetan communities are mostly linked to religious rituals (as McLagan herself points out in a later article: McLagan 1997): religious dances (*'cham*), construction of mandalas, exhibitions of *thangkas*, and more (see below).

This reduction of culture to religion has been formalized by Tibetan leaders during public talks and political statements. In 1991, the Dalai Lama said in New York that there was no difference 'between Tibetan Buddhism, Tibetan politics, and Tibetan culture. They [are] all the same' (McLagan 1996: 483). He went further than that, and said that Tibetan Buddhism was what the Tibetans had to offer the world, and asked what would be the use of saving the culture were it not for Tibetan Buddhism (ibid.). Similarly, Samdhong Rinpoche, former prime minister of the Tibetan government-in-exile, said that the Tibetan cause was all about its spirituality (Thubten Samdup 2004: 15).

By reducing Tibetan culture to Tibetan Buddhism, the leadership transformed their supporters de facto into *sbyin bdag*, or sponsors. Furthermore, the emphasis on Tibetan religion in the culture was only possible thanks to a reorganization of the religion itself, which transformed itself into a 'world religion', exportable to the Western religious market.

Unification of the Religion

After the collapse of the Tibetan Empire in the ninth century, Tibet was divided into principalities, which supported different schools or sects of Buddhism, and also Bon (Karmay 1998), which Tibetans regard as the original faith of the country. Some of these principalities managed to assert their power over others by establishing relations with the secular power, as in the case of the *mchod yon* relationship between the Sakya master Phagpa and the Mongol Khan. Similarly, successive Dalai Lamas perpetuated the supremacy of their Buddhist sect, the Yellow Hats (Gelugpa, *dge lugs pa*), through relations with China's rulers. These contacts between foreign powers and Tibetan masters guaranteed the power of their sect in Tibet. This created tensions between the different sects in their competition for power, and battles between monasteries even occurred. Snellgrove and Richardson describe these events at the time of Phagpa (thirteenth century). Such intrigues continued long thereafter with power struggles during the reigns of the Dalai Lamas: 'It was a period of bitter, bloody deeds and unscrupulous intrigue, in which men of religion played the leading parts and monks fought in the battles, for fighting seemed already to have become the responsibility of one class of monastic inmates' (Snellgrove and Richardson

[1968] 2003: 148). The Tibetan religious hierarchs were not all sectarians, and the fifth Dalai Lama is recognized for his great tolerance and interest in other sects. This tolerance was limited, however, as Karmay illustrates: '[The Fifth Dalai Lama] included Bon in his edict as an official religion of Tibet, but he was merciless, when the Bonpos in certain regions were at one time suspected of allying with the Karma-pa. The celebrated religious tolerance in Tibet was only true so long as one school did not interfere [with] the political sphere of another dominant one' (Karmay 1998: 533).

At the time of the fifth Dalai Lama (seventeenth century), a cult to the deity Dorje Shugden (*rdo rje shugs ldan*) arose. The origins of the deity are unclear, but the story, as reported by Nebesky-Wojkowitz (1975: 134–44), tells that a Gelug monk opposed to the fifth Dalai Lama was murdered in mysterious circumstances. He then returned to this world as a wrathful spirit, seeking revenge. The spirit's power became so strong that the fifth Dalai Lama and his government were forced to seek reconciliation, and finally to accept him as a protector deity (*chos skyong srung ma*) of the Gelug order. From this time onwards, the deity Dorje Shugden, as he was now known, became a powerful guardian of the purity of the Gelug order, and threatened people who failed to strictly follow the rules of the school or who mixed religious practices with rituals from other schools. However, as Dreyfus (1998) remarks, the fifth Dalai Lama began to legitimize his spiritual and political power over Tibet by claiming to re-establish the power of the early Tibetan Empire. To this end, he adopted rituals from other schools, and particularly from the first one, the Nyingma, to form links with the old empire. He could thus extend his political and religious leadership by rooting his power in Tibet's history and by showing openness towards these schools. His successors returned to more strict Gelug practices, until the installation of the thirteenth Dalai Lama (b. 1876), who had the same vision for his country as the fifth.

The current, fourteenth Dalai Lama was raised by his tutors under the practices of the Gelug ritual system. But, growing in maturity, '[h]e felt a strong appreciation for the Fifth's political project, which he has described as a master plan for building Tibet into a nation able to take part in the history of the region rather than a marginal state governed by religious hierarchs mostly preoccupied with the power of their monasteries and estates' (Dreyfus 1998: 252). To follow the example of the fifth, the incumbent Dalai Lama also began to adopt rituals from other schools. In the mid-1970s, he abandoned his Shugden practice as incompatible with his new vision of a non-sect-driven religion.

In 1975, a book was published in Tibetan by a Gelug Rinpoche (*rin po che*, lit. 'the precious one': a respected religious master) follower of Shugden. In this book, the author wrote the story of different religious hierarchs and monks whose lives were shortened by Shugden because they did not follow a pure Gelug path. The fifth Panchen Lama was one of them, as he followed

Nyingma rituals (Dreyfus 1998). Shocked by this book, the Dalai Lama decided to end the cult of Shugden, and thus in 1978 he 'spoke out publicly against the use of the deity as an *institutional* protector, although maintaining that *individuals* should decide for themselves in terms of private practice' (Mills 2003: 56). Dreyfus recounts how the Dalai Lama progressively restricted the Shugden practices. But only in 1996 did he answer positively to Nyingma deputies who threatened to leave the Tibetan Parliament if the Shugden practices continued to encourage Gelug domination (ibid.: 63). The Dalai Lama denounced Shugden publicly as an 'evil spirit', able to harm the Tibetan fight for freedom and its cause. Consequently, the Dalai Lama announced that he would halt tantric initiations to Shugden worshippers. On the Dalai Lama's official website, three reasons are given for this ban, which can all be summarized in the sectarian nature of Shugden worship, which leads to disunity in the Tibetan community and is therefore harmful not only to the cause in general but also to the life of the Dalai Lama himself.[7] Two months after this public denunciation of Shugden, in May 1996, the Cabinet (*bka' shag*) published a statement explaining that the government would enforce the ban:

> It is the duty of the Tibetan Government-in-exile to encourage compliance with any advice given out of concern for the cause of Tibet, the security of its head of state and the honor of all Tibetan Buddhist traditions including the Geluk tradition ... Most people with connections to Dolgyal [Shugden] have come to understand that propitiating him undermines the cause of Tibet, compromises the personal security of His Holiness the Dalai Lama and brings harm to the individual propitiator himself or herself ... We consider this an acceptance of responsibility for the greater good of Tibet. (http://tibet.net/dolgyal-shugden/)

In June 1996, the Tibetan Parliament (Assembly of Tibetan People's Deputies, ATPD) passed a resolution formalizing the ban on Shugden, commanding the 'departments, their branches and subsidiaries, monasteries and their branches ... functioning under the administrative control of the Tibetan Government-in-Exile ... not to indulge in the propitiation of Shugden' (ibid.). As for individuals, the resolution stated that: 'it is up to ... themselves to decide as they like. We cannot force anyone to do anything against his or her wishes. However, we would like to emphatically plead to the Shugden-worshippers that they should stop taking tantric initiations and teachings from His Holiness the Dalai Lama' (ibid.). Further, the CTA published a booklet entitled *The Worship of Shugden: Documents Related to a Tibetan Controversy* (Department of Religion and Culture 1998). In this booklet, the Shugden propitiation is presented as harmful, not only for religious reasons, as a threat to the Dalai Lama's life and as a cause of religious sectarianism, but also for political reasons, namely, the disunity of the Tibetan community and the weakening of the Tibetan cause on the international stage because of this disunity and the allegations against the Tibetan leader. Finally, the CTA accused the Shugden groups of being supported and used by the PRC to harm the national cause. Essentially, the religious ban expressed by the Tibetan leader was, from now on, enforced by the Tibetan political system, a mix epitomizing the *chos srid zung 'brel*.

The ban fostered profound disunity within the Tibetan community, which reached its nadir in February 1997 when the principal of the Tibetan Institute of Buddhist Dialectics (based in Dharamsala) and two of his disciples were found stabbed to death. The principal was known for his anti-Shugden activities, and the investigation was quickly directed at the Shugden followers. Indeed, two out of the six suspects were directly linked to the Shugden society based in the Tibetan settlement of Majnu-Ka-Tilla in Delhi.[8] My first visit to this settlement took place in August 1998, more than a year after these events, and I remember clearly that Majnu was physically divided between the area occupied by the Shugden society and its members, and the rest of the camp. For many of my informants and friends, this area was a no-go zone. The Shugden issue still divides the Tibetan community, even if the banned deity's Tibetan worshippers are nowadays much more discreet.[9]

Today, the Dalai Lama and his government continue to promote unity between the different schools by encouraging ecumenical movements like Rime (*ris med*, literally, non-partisan or non-sectarian). The Rime movement was initiated at the end of the nineteenth century by religious masters who wanted to benefit from the practices and rituals of different schools without melding all Tibetan Buddhist schools into one. This movement, which has gained increasing popularity since the 1960s, works for better understanding between the schools. The present Dalai Lama promotes this movement and shares its ecumenical vision, as expressed by Ringu Tulku:

> His Holiness, the 14th Dalai Lama, has been strongly influenced by some great Rime teachers such as Khunu Lama Tenzin Gyatso, Dilgo Khentse Rinpoche and the 3rd Dodrupchen Tenpe Nyima. Due to their efforts in recent years, there has been more interchange of teachings amongst different Schools of Tibetan Buddhism than ever before. Following the traditions of Rime, the Dalai Lama has been receiving and giving teachings of all schools in their respective traditions and lineages. (Ringu Tulku 1997: 821)

Finally, the Dalai Lama gave a place to the Bon tradition in the Tibetan religious sphere. This recognition took a long time. The Constitution adopted in 1963 does not specify anything about Bon, and although respect for all religions is advocated, the preamble expresses its Buddhist inspiration. It was only at the end of the 1970s, as Karmay (1998: 535) recounts, that Bon was recognized in the refugee political and religious organs. From then on, Bon was in effect displayed as a 'fifth school' of Tibetan religion, and represented in the Tibetan Assembly. Karmay writes that it was a 'tardy gesture, but better than none, and essential if Tibetan unity [was] to be maintained at all' (ibid.). Representing only 1 per cent of the refugees, the Bonpo acknowledge this recognition as a success; one of them told Skorupski that, '[f]or the first time in the history of Tibet, we have been recognised as a valid religion and our traditions are respected' (Skorupski 1981: 41).

Over time, I became conscious of reduced divisions between the different schools: monks take religious degrees from other schools, and therefore stay in monasteries from different traditions. The inevitable question of which schools they belong to – and that no Westerner hesitates to ask – seems to them increasingly odd, and the official discourse that I heard at the CTA's Department of Religion and Culture was that there were no more differences between the schools, since they were celebrating the 'entente cordiale'. The reality is more nuanced than this, but certainly the context of exile and the new challenges that it has posed to religious identity have blurred the differences between the schools; these differences are still mostly emphasized in the claims of 'authenticity' alleged by Western Dharma followers (see Chapter 5).

The removal of anything that could cause religious disunity within the refugee community has been paralleled by an evolution of practices and rituals themselves, generated by the exigencies of exile. As the Dalai Lama puts it:

> We divided our culture into two types [after having arrived in exile] … In the first category we placed that which, we determined, needed to be retained only in books as past history. The second category included whatever could bring actual benefit in the present. These things, we resolved, must be kept alive. Therefore, many of our old ceremonial traditions I discarded – no matter, I decided, let them go. (Avedon 1994: 92)

That leads him to say:

> it's much better now in India [in exile, than in present Tibet] trying to learn about Buddhism; a purified form of Tibetan culture will be found in India and not in Tibet. (Dalai Lama 1995: 104)

These changes to Tibetan religious practices also affected the way in which they have been presented, and created a dynamic of essentialization.

Essentialization of the Religion

Regarding the religious identity of Tibetan refugees, I was struck by the homogeneity in the answers of my informants about their definition of Tibetan Buddhism. For them, it was about 'praying to Buddhist gods', and showing 'compassion to all sentient beings'. To that they add different rituals that they follow strictly. The clerics gave me the same types of answers, adding thereto only the study of their texts, which they called 'wisdom'. Indeed, the notions of 'wisdom' (Skt. *prajna*, Tib. *shes rab*) and 'compassion'[10] (Skt. *karuna*, Tib. *snying rje*) were represented as the principal characteristics of Tibetan religion, not only in the English-language literature intended for international readership, but also in tourist souvenirs of the Tibetan religion (T-shirts and mugs printed with religious sentences or texts). Actually, I at first thought that this essentialization of religion was only meant for the 'frontstage', as Goffman (1959) puts it, but, from my own research and observations, it became clear that this was not the case. People presented religion in these terms not only to outsiders but amongst themselves as well. I was struck at that time by the difference between the 'high theories' of Tibetan Buddhism, propounded in books, with philosophical concepts difficult to understand, and my informants' answers.[11] They all phrased the importance of the two concepts of wisdom and compassion in essentializing their religion, emphasizing the fact that one without the other was nothing.

Interestingly, this dualism appeals to the Western mode of structuralist functioning and it explains, among other factors, why Westerners are attracted by Tibetan religion and Tibet's cause. Lopez (1998: 130) records the same fact, noting that the Dalai Lama explains the famous Tibetan mantra '*Om mani padme hum*' in terms of the union of wisdom and compassion. My Tibetan informants projected this dichotomy of 'wisdom' and 'compassion' onto religious liturgy and objects: hence the yellow colour worn by the monks symbolizes 'wisdom' and the red 'compassion'; the ritual sceptre (*rdo rje*) represents 'compassion' while the bell (*dril bu*), always joined to it, represents 'wisdom'; and so on. The display of Tibetan Buddhism as something essentialized in these two notions may not be new, but it is certainly strongly emphasized in exile. This essentialization of Buddhism around its core notions has permitted Tibetan religious leaders to condense and simplify the religion that they have been presenting to the world, and also to avoid the internal 'asperities' (like sectarian incompatibilities) that could have arisen from a broader theoretical presentation.

Moreover, this essentialization has not only characterized the leaders' discourse, but has also pervaded the lay population, and has, furthermore, become the dominant idiom for the conceptualization of Tibetan Buddhism in the West. The Tibetan Buddhist literature directed at the West is full of examples of essays and religious masters' teachings on 'wisdom' and 'compassion'.[12] Similarly, according to Lopez (1998), different Tibetan religious treatises, like the 'Tibetan Book of the Dead', were reinterpreted into Western understandings and conceptions. The 'Dharma Brokers' (as Ström [2001: 270] calls the Tibetan religious masters installed in the West) popularized this simplified view of Tibetan Buddhism in their Dharma centres in the West. This simplified dyadic structure facilitated the adoption of Tibetan Buddhism as a universal religion in a new religious market.

Universalization of the Religion

The reorganization of Tibetan Buddhism around notions that can be seen as universal values, like 'wisdom' and 'compassion' – and which resonate with a Western Christian ethos – permitted a universalization of this religion and its presentation as a 'world religion' concerning all humankind, or at least Western society (Lopez [1998: 199ff.] makes a similar observation).

In the late 1960s, a new 'religious market' appeared in Western societies, the fruit of a reconfiguration of different beliefs, as detailed in Chapter 5. Thanks to its unification and essentialization in exile, the Tibetan religion has a strong position in this market, where, as a result, it has been commodified. At present, the Tibetan religion represents a 'brand' in this religious market; it is recognizable not only by its stress on 'wisdom' and 'compassion', but also thanks to perceptions of Tibet in the West. Its values, like non-violence, gender equality, eco-friendliness and more, have been declared as universal attributes and developed by the Tibetan political agenda.[13]

This commodification of Tibet in the religious market runs parallel with its presence in the commodities market in the West – a state of affairs that has been discussed by Bishop (1989), Lopez (1998) and Korom (2001). Congdon's thesis on Tibetan music in the United States describes how Tibet became a brand in the West and remains relevant for the Western religious market:

> While 'Tibet' still means cultures, people, places, and has connotations of nation or political space, it has also come to represent the trendy, somewhat spiritual, or supernatural. The word carries all of these connotations as a brand name in the marketing of a wide variety of products. For marketers, the word Tibet has become a key word or slogan (brand) and is used to evoke images of wealth (through association with Hollywood, the rich, and premium product), salvation, morality, and a spiritual lifestyle directly related to representations of Tibet and their place in contemporary Western culture. (Congdon 2007: 77)

This massive presence of Tibet in Western markets has created the conditions for an appropriation of the *mchod yon* relationship by the community of helpers of Tibet in the West. The ultimate commodification occurs when the consumer becomes the brand itself, and this has happened increasingly with the recognition of Westerners as Tibetan *sprul sku* (traditional lineages of reincarnated masters). As Lopez remarks, this is nothing new for the Tibetans, who instrumentalize their religion, but it is certainly new for Westerners: 'In this way [Tibetans recognizing Western *sprul sku* like they did for the Fourth Dalai Lama who was Altan Khan's grand nephew] Tibetans have quite literally incorporated foreigners into their patronage sphere through their own version of colonialism, what might be termed a *spiritual colonialism*' (Lopez 1998: 206; emphasis added). This spiritual colonialism, the power of the Tibet brand on the religious market, has permitted the Tibetans to show the world that their religion, and hence their culture, and with it their entire cause, is worth saving as a part of the world's heritage. The universalization of the Tibetan religion has guaranteed that the Tibetans will attract followers and supporters, and not be forgotten on the international stage.

The West in Need

Tibetans tend to represent Western societies as spiritually weak and, as such, willing to receive the religious teachings of Tibetans. This idea is reinforced by the fact that a large proportion of Westerners seen in the Tibetan settlements feel a – sometimes very strong – connection with Tibetan Buddhism. This representation of Westerners as weak and in search of spirituality provided by the Tibetans gives the latter an important position in the relationship. One Tibetan told me as much, quite directly: 'The Westerners are helping us because they need us. They are suffering from mental diseases and are lost. They need spiritual guidance and can find it only with us, Tibetans. We developed through centuries special methods able to cure the mind. We are here to help the Westerners' (Personal communication #31 2006).

This conception is widely diffused in the settlements and even commodified. The following words, supposedly from the Dalai Lama, can be found on any number of t-shirts, tea cups, calendars and such like sold to Westerners: Never give up / No matter what is going on / Never give up / Develop the heart / *Too much energy in your country is spent developing the mind instead of the heart* / Develop the heart / Be compassionate … (emphasis added). This message of the spiritual weakness of the West, a message reproduced on a large scale and commodified for the Westerners themselves, shows that the Tibetans have something to offer in their relations with Westerners, namely, their religion. The Tibetans emphasize that they are spiritually rich, as in statements made by the Dalai Lama at the third Tibet Support Groups (TSG) conference: 'Tibet is materially backward. Of course, spiritually we are quite rich, but materially we are backward. … Tibet is a land-locked country and materially backward. We need material development, though spiritually we are very well developed' (Department of Information and International Relations and Friedrich-Neumann Stiftung 2001: 156).

The Dalai Lama's addresses to Western audiences have become emblematic of such trends: he elaborates the dichotomization of the material and spiritual; the former represents the strength of Western society and the latter the strength of Tibetan society. As a result, the Dalai Lama's speeches on the limits of material development resonate in Western ears:

> It is natural that India should strive to improve its people's standard of living by promoting science and technology. At the same time we cannot allow our

profound and vast philosophy to wane. Its strength is related to developing mental peace, while science and technology are related to material progress. *But a combination of these two can provide the complete conditions for obtaining real human happiness.* (Dalai Lama 1995: 176; emphasis added)

In this statement, the terms of the exchange are clear: the Tibetans bring mental peace, and the Westerners science and technology.

Moreover, according to the Dalai Lama, the Tibetans also have something to offer to the West regarding science. As Obadia (1999: 159ff.) shows, the Dalai Lama proposes his religion as a solution to the problems left unanswered by science, and, at the same time, explains the relevance of his religion by its similarities with science. His discourse is double-stranded: science does not explain everything, and Tibetan Buddhism can make up for its shortcomings; yet at the same time, Tibetan Buddhism is compatible with science in its explanation of the world. A French doctor in genetics, Matthieu Ricard, became a monk many decades ago. He is well known in Europe and internationally, and is a translator for the Dalai Lama in French. He began a few years ago a series of conferences where he invokes the scientific method to test Tibetan Buddhist meditation and other religious practices.[14] According to him, the test findings are clear: these religious practices can change the brain and mind of the practitioners, leading to more compassion and happiness, like a new science of the mind. The link between science and Tibetan Buddhism is in this example totally affirmed. And indeed, Tibetan Buddhism is often compared in the West to a science, either as a medical science able to perform cures, or as a technical science. In the context of development, this is particularly significant because development intends to cure the living conditions of people; thus to cure their minds can be attractive for different developers.

Going further, the former government was identifying Tibetan problems with a 'modern malady':

We do not perceive the problem of Tibet as an isolated problem for the Tibetan people alone or a struggle between just two nations, namely China and Tibet … The present problem, as we see it, is *a symptom of a large human malady which [is] perpetuated in the modern world* … therefore we shall have to search the remedy also at a larger plan, at the level of all human societies. (Samdhong Rinpoche 2005: 11, emphasis added)[15]

The former prime minister explained further the origin of this 'malady':

In the 20th century situation, China changed as a result of changes the world over, particularly changes in the West. This change was caused by the so-called Industrial Revolution that led to *the creation of the Capitalism, which further gave birth to the Marxism and Communism.* (Office of Planning Commission and SARD 2005: 11, emphasis added)

By conflating communism (which caused Tibet's fall directly) and the West, the former government indirectly locates the fault for the Tibetan plight in the West. By adopting the discourse of an ex-colony, something that Tibet never was, the government thus mobilized anti-colonialist forces in the West, which cover the entire range of Western organizations, from governments to civil and alternative society.

With such discourse and instrumentalization of their religion towards the West, the Tibetans have been able to frame Westerners as their 'clients', in need of their religion, in a process symmetrical to that described by De Voe (1981), whereby Tibetan refugees are represented as clients of the relief organizations. This process resonates with the 'self-sufficiency' narrative, which, on a political level, places the Tibetans as independent from their donors. The main consequence of this dynamic is that Tibetans do not feel like passive recipients of Western assistance, but rather participants in a form of *mchod yon* relationship, which empowers them, and where they exchange 'wisdom' for 'compassion' (see Chapter 5).

Spiritualization of Assistance

Tibetan refugees looked for new forms of assistance during the 1980s and consequently launched the previously mentioned 'International Campaign for Tibet'. At this time the Tibetan leadership began to instrumentalize its religion in a movement that I will call the 'spiritualization' of the received support. The Dalai Lama, carrying his country's cause, became omnipresent on the Western stage, undertaking multiple religious and political speeches and acts. By showing the West everything that could be gained by support of Tibet, he placed this support within the *mchod yon* relation framework.

Meaning of Spiritualization

In the Durkheimian dialectic between the sacred and the profane, sacralization is the opposite process to that of secularization; it is the transformation of a profane element into a sacred one, the passage from one world to another (Durkheim [1912] 1995: 36ff.). As Durkheim puts it, the sacred and the profane principles alternate constantly, and, 'now as in the past, we see that society never stops creating new sacred things' (ibid.: 215). Durkheim gives various examples, such as the cult of authority: 'Moreover, the routine deference that men invested with high social position receive is not qualitatively different from religious respect', or the cult of the nation or values such as reason, liberty, and progress (ibid.).

Contrary to the Weberian analysis of secularization and sacralization, Durkheim is concerned not with the decline of the sacred, but with change in its different manifestations. Giving the example of the French Revolution, Durkheim remarks that '[i]n a specific case, we saw society and its fundamental ideas becoming the object of a genuine cult directly – and without transfiguration of any kind' (Durkheim [1912] 1995: 216). The Tibetan context seems to be outside the Durkheimian model: as seen previously, there is no dichotomization of the sacred and the profane; the two are linked, and there is no clear distinction between them. The fact that the Tibetan refugees framed the assistance received within a religious discourse is, then, a normal process of instrumentalization of their religion, and not, properly speaking, a sacralization. In this case, I will use the term 'spiritualization', which expresses the fact that the Tibetans display and present their religion in a politically instrumentalized form towards the assistance they receive, rather than sacralizing the assistance itself. This spiritualization operated by the Tibetans nonetheless takes on the features of sacralization (or, more properly, re-sacralization) *for Westerners* – whose assistance has lost its sacred value, as described and analysed in Chapter 5.

Internationalization through Religion

Through the universalization of their religion, the Tibetan refugees have been able to emphasize different religious concepts and use them to mobilize support for their cause on the international stage, in a dynamic of spiritualization.

The idea of interdependence derives directly from Buddhist theology: given the concepts of reincarnation and karma (*las*), all sentient beings are linked, and the actions of some have consequences for others. From this basis, the Tibetan religious leadership formulated the notion of the 'global family' and 'universal responsibility',[16] which must lead to 'compassion' among people.

This tenet is the foundation for the internationalization of support for Tibet. In following this narrative, to help Tibet helps not only the Tibetans but the entire world. As the Dalai Lama puts it:

> Belief in rebirth should engender a universal love, for all living beings and creatures, in the course of their numberless lives and our own, have been our beloved parents, children, brothers, sisters, friends. And the virtues our creed encourages are those which arise from this universal love – tolerance, forbearance, charity, kindness, compassion. (Dalai Lama [1962] 1997: 29)

These virtues can be practised through support for Tibet, as the Dalai Lama has further expressed it:

> Human compassion forms one of the basic qualities of human beings. ... *As a Buddhist monk I can say that the understanding and compassion you show to*

the Tibetans is in a way the work of Dharma. As I said before I think, if you compare the Tibetans with other people, the Tibetans are by nature kind and they believe in moral ethics and therefore form a good community. *Therefore I think that by helping the Tibetans you do not only contribute to the achievement of happiness of the Tibetans but I also think that it is relevant to the happiness of the world at large.* (http://tibet.net/important-issues/worldwide-tibet-movement/tsgs-conferences/first-international-conference-of-tsgs-dharamshala-8-9-march-1990/; emphasis added)

Following this logic, the Tibetans fighting for the Tibet issue have a global responsibility, as they have part of the destiny of the world in their hands. Samdhong Rinpoche, the former Tibetan prime minister, explains that '[d]ealing with [the People's Republic of China] leadership is for us a humane responsibility that must be performed' (Office of Planning Commission and SARD 2005: 13). This argument of human responsibility to save Tibet is strong and popular among people from the Tibet Movement. Bob Brown, an Australian senator, said at the third TSG conference:

> I am standing here because I am not just an Australian, I am a world citizen, and that means I am a Tibetan. And until Tibet is free I am not free, none of us is free, and I will work towards the freedom of Tibet so long as I draw breath. (Department of Information and International Relations and Friedrich-Neumann Stiftung 2001: 198)[17]

Another religious concept described by Tibetans and linked to their religion is non-violence. This non-violence should lead to universal peace, and thus here, once again, the Tibet issue is internationalized. The Dalai Lama developed the idea that the Tibetans were totally pacified by the arrival of Buddhism in Tibet:[18]

> Before Buddhism flourished [in Tibet], the people's nature was quite violent. Then Buddhism came and flourished in this area, and the whole of that area's people eventually become more peaceful in nature, of a more compassionate nature, generally speaking. (Dalai Lama 1995: 160)

Thanks to this non-violence, the Tibetans are worthy of receiving international support. As the Dalai Lama puts it:

> Friends, as you all know the Tibetan people are generally strong believers in peace and we try our best to practise peace. Tibetan people by nature are gentle and the Tibetan people are also profoundly religious. Now there is every danger that these people are swept completely from the face of this earth. Yet we are very encouraged that people who believe in truth, people who support justice, come to the support of the Tibetan people, and it is because of this kind of feeling that you have all gathered here. (http://tibet.net/important-issues/worldwide-tibet-movement/tsgs-conferences/first-international-conference-of-tsgs-dharamshala-8-9-march-1990/)

The non-violent nature of the Tibet cause was ultimately recognized in 1989 with the award of the Nobel Peace Prize to the Dalai Lama. Nowadays, the Tibetan leader is often compared to Gandhi on account of his peaceful struggle, and publications edited in Dharamsala emphasize this comparison.[19]

Sometimes, the instrumentalization of the religion ultimately draws on universal values such as happiness, truth[20] and justice. These are part of the mainstream religious discourses presented by the Tibetan leader, and are what Magnusson (2002) calls 'soft issues'. Magnusson studied the titles and subjects of the Dalai Lama's public talks. He concluded that these articulated four 'soft issues', terminology that he coined from Nye's definition of soft power resources (such as cultural attraction, ideology and international institutions) (ibid.: 205). These four 'soft issues', which give the Tibet issue soft power, are 'Human Ethics', 'Global Peace', 'Environmental Issues' and 'Tibet'. 'The first two categories amounted to about 75 per cent of the lectures, and environmental issues to about 17 per cent' (ibid.: 206). Finally, only 13 per cent of the lectures had Tibet as their main subject. In the context of assistance to Tibetans, the 'soft issues' of justice and non-violence are particularly emphasized. As Samdhong Rinpoche emphatically puts it:

> The ever-increasing goodwill and sympathy for the Tibetan people and our cause found everywhere among the people of the world, is the result of the selfless efforts of these [Tibet support groups]. This is not an ordinary achievement. The efforts of our supporters must be termed as 'selfless' because no economic or political gain is involved in it. They are not serving their own interests. By raising their voice against violence, oppression, torture and wanton destruction, they are securing the noble cause of justice, and non-violence. They stand for truth and goodness, which are today being rendered feebler and feebler by the onslaught of the force of untruth and evil. (Department of Information and International Relations and Friedrich-Neumann Stiftung 2001: 27)

Finally, the ideal of the *Bodhisattva*,[21] epitomized by the Dalai Lama himself, holds that salvation is not sought for the individual alone, but for the sake of 'all sentient beings'. Two levels of development and eschatological salvation, individual and collective, can hence be found in this tradition. A speech by the Dalai Lama in France summarizes this point: 'Inner Peace and External Peace' (Tincq 2008; translated from French). It is this dual integration of the individual and the universal that allows the reinvigoration of the development partnership between the Tibetans and the Westerners, as shown in Chapter 5.

To summarize, the internationalization of the Tibetan religion is the religious legitimation and accreditation of the different values described in this section, as well as the political agenda described in the previous chapter. This religious legitimation was made possible thanks to subtle transformations of the religion itself, which, as seen in the previous sections, led to a new form of Tibetan Buddhism. With the internationalization of their religion, the Tibetans followed a strategy described by Bob:

> [The local movements] simplify and universalize their conflicts … embrace voguish rhetoric, and appeal to the self-interest, as well as the sympathy, of distant audiences … At a deeper level, movements tap into cultural motifs having wide and perhaps universal appeal, such as good guy versus bad guy or underdog versus bully. (Bob 2005: 30)

In the Tibetan case, one more 'cultural motif' must, however, be added: religious values, as recognized by the Tibetans themselves and expressed by the secretary of the CTA's Department of Information and International Relations (DIIR): 'The greatest achievement of the Tibet movement is our ability to place morality, non-violence, truth and justice on the agenda of the international community' (Department of Information and International Relations and Friedrich-Neumann Stiftung 1996: 63). How this religion is practically brought to foreign countries, and especially Western countries, is described below.

Monks on Tour

Performances by Tibetan monks in Western countries are an increasing trend.[22] Since the end of the 1980s and the deployment of the international campaign, cultural performances by Tibetans in the West have increased greatly, with monks presenting religious rituals and forms of art like *'cham* (religious dances), *mandala*[23] and *thangka* (religious paintings). These monks come principally to raise funds for their monasteries, and they perform in temples and also in institutions like museums. Their visibility is important, and they attract attention to Tibetan culture and Tibet's fate. In doing so, they recreate a temporary form of patron–priest relationship, which can nevertheless lead to long-term bonds and inspire vocations to serve Tibet's cause. I met several people involved in activism or developmental projects for Tibet who had discovered Tibetan culture through these religious performances.

Calkowski (1997), McLagan (1997) and Schrempf (1997) have studied (in the same book: *Tibetan Culture in the Diaspora*) the method of staging these art forms in foreign countries. They suggest that these performed arts have become 'secularized' (Calkowski 1997) and have lost their profound meaning. McLagan (1997: 82) asks what the significance of such performances is: 'art, religion, or entertainment?' At the same time, however secularized these performances may be, they are almost always introduced for a general non-specialist audience and, replaced in their context, they contribute to the Western familiarization of Tibetan religion and are thus a vector of its internationalization.

One result of such appearances by Tibetan monks in the West is that many Westerners identify Tibetans with monks. Many informants told me about their bitterness in the face of the narrow interest shown in non-monks by Westerners who visit Tibetan settlements. Moreover, many refugees feel that Tibetan religion is being misused for worldly purposes. This was bluntly summarized by Tenzin Lodoe, the Dalai Lama's nephew:

> There are some aspects [to the promotion of Tibetan culture] which are cancerous aspects. I call it the 'prostitution of our religion'. Lamas who, reluctantly or didn't know what they were getting into, go to the West and then promote Buddhism, promising instant awakenings to followers just to get their money, pimping around, you know – the West is full of that … There's a very thin line of using our culture to promote our freedom struggle, and abusing it. What we are seeing today, particularly in the West, is *using* our culture to promote independence or our freedom struggle turning into *abusing* our culture. Why I say this is because at meetings, at these festivals, Tibetans who are there are treated as *tokens*. 'Wow, that's a Tibetan, that's a Tibetan monk, look at the dress, look at those things, they're so beautiful. OK, let's go back.' (Pike 2001: 53)

Ultimate performances are the religious initiations by Tibetan monks launched in the West. An increase in the number of *Kalachakra*[24] initiations bestowed by the Dalai Lama (see Lopez 1998: 206ff.; and Lenoir 1999b: 342ff.) is representative of this phenomenon. Obadia (1999) observes that, through these initiations, the Dalai Lama wants to empower people for the eschatological fight at the end of the world, which will happen in the Kingdom of Shambala (linked to Shangri-La and described in the next chapter). In this case, Obadia talks of missionary activities by Tibetan monks (ibid.: 116–18): these initiations ultimately join Westerners to the fate of Tibet through a religious ritual.

If these religious performances are not aimed principally at raising support for the entire Tibetan community and its cause, then they are certainly meant to spread Tibetan values in the West. Moreover, it is not only religious groups in the West, such as Dharma centres and their followers, who sponsor and finance Tibetan religious institutions in exile. Different organizations, non-religious in nature, also contribute – and these organizations are then thanked in a religious manner.

Thanks and Praise to the Donors

A common subject of discussion among Tibetan refugees is the *sbyin bdag*, or sponsors. As seen at the beginning of this chapter, the term *sbyin bdag* concerns the religious relationship between a cleric and a lay person. In tourist settlements like Dharamsala, Bylakuppe or even Darjeeling, foreigners are constantly approached by lay or religious Tibetans suggesting that they establish a relationship of sponsorship. Such a relationship involving a lay Tibetan is obviously not religious, but, when I was approached (frequently), it was always linked somehow to a religious argument, such as the need to save the religion, or giving the recipient the opportunity to be more useful to the community and thereby save the culture.

As Prost notices, the sponsor in such a relationship invariably receives 'religious blessings like ritual threads (*srung mdud*) or blessed medical pills (*rin chen ril bu*)' (Prost 2006: 240). The term *sbyin bdag* is used nowadays by Tibetan refugees to refer to their foreign sponsors. This fact is not new: De Voe noticed it in the early 1980s (De Voe 1983: 63). The refugees do not apply the term *sbyin bdag* to the sponsors of religion only, but also to any foreigners (usually Westerners) who finance them or their family or any social institution. One day I bought a new battery for my friend's motorcycle. We had known each other for a long time and had no relationship involving money. Nonetheless, among his friends he referred to me to as *sbyin bdag* when they asked him where he had obtained the battery.[25] Thus the term '*sbyin bdag*' is used in a general sense, but has not totally lost its religious meaning.

Monks in particular use the religious argument to obtain sponsorship, and do so openly. It is more than common in Dharamsala to meet monks talking to Westerners in the streets or cafes, and it is common knowledge that most of them try to establish a financial bond with their new acquaintance. They can also be seen in the cyber-cafes, exchanging mail or 'chatting' with their *sbyin bdag*. While visiting a monastic college (*grwa tshang*) in Bylakuppe, a monk, speaking a dialect of Tibetan that I did not fully understand, asked me for something, which, after a complex exchange using hands, appeared to be my e-mail address. I gave this to him because, as a scientist on a mission, one should not refuse any experience. After some days I received an e-mail written in excellent English asking me for a donation for this monk, in return for Buddhist merit and his personal prayers for my happiness and long life. He obviously did not write this message himself, as a few days before he could not speak English. I had similar experiences in Dharamsala, where every second day different monks were knocking on my door, showing me a text, sometimes with pictures, to ask me for donations and offering me an opportunity 'to accumulate merit'. This was always to the delight of my Tibetans flatmates, who were never asked and always recalled my quality as an *inji* (*dbyin ji* or Westerner) to be a good *sbyin bdag*. In the Tibetan community, some of these monks are called, pejoratively, 'fishermen' (*nya pa*), as they angle for sponsors; and many stories circulate about them. Some people say they are just fake monks, taking the robe to attract sponsors, as it is well known that Westerners have a special attraction to Tibetan monks.

Others say that these monks collect sponsorship and have rooms filled with the latest technological gadgets, meaning that they are rich, contrary to what they claim.

In fact, these individual practices reflect institutionalized ones. At the end of the 1970s, when the Tibetan leadership had to find new sources of funds, it found them in Western spiritual expectations, which it answered through the spiritualization of the help received. The leadership developed the kind of relationships that already existed between Tibetan monasteries and their foreign patrons. Indeed, every monastery in exile has links with foreign patrons, these being either Dharma centres installed in the West to finance them, or individuals.

Staying for several months in the guesthouse of a monastery in Dharamsala allowed me to observe the links between the monastery and its sponsors. These relationships fell within the religious framework of the *mchod yon*, an exchange of material for spiritual protection. Thus, the monastery organized regular prayers for the benefit of its sponsors. Their names were also displayed visibly at the entrance to the main temple, with a sentence explaining their compassion and the merit they earned through their sponsorship. When some of these sponsors came to visit the monastery, they were received with the greatest respect, and thanked in religious terms. As an extreme example, I will quote the thanks a French NGO received from a monastery:

> With most of humble regards, the [name] Monastery is most pleased to offer the certificate of appreciation to [name of the director] for the long-term support in the field of education by sponsoring.[26] We regard these activities as those of the Bodhisattva. As expounded in this verse on the Bodhisattva's way of life:
>
> For as long as space endures
> And for as long as living beings remain,
> Until then may I too abide
> To dispel the misery in the world.
> As does the Bodhisattva dedicating all his or her effort for the sake of all sentient beings.

Similarly, the Tibetan Children's Villages pose a question on their website: 'What does it mean to sponsor a child or help TCV?' They then propose an answer, one of which states: 'It will promote love and universal responsibility' (http://www.tcv.org.in/content/sponsor-child). This shows the connection to the universal responsibility as a Buddhist concept described earlier.

As stated above, the Tibetan leadership developed this religious relationship to thank its principal donors. When these donors visit a settlement, they are welcomed and officially received. Depending on the importance of the *sbyin bdag*, he or she is taken on a tour of a family house, an institution, or the entire settlement, the climax being a meeting with the Dalai Lama himself. These tours, which are always almost identical,[27] re-enact the *mchod yon* relationship of Tibetan spiritual culture, greeting its benefactor. In these tours, the donor is shown what has been realized thanks to his support, his value is reiterated, and he is honoured with white ceremonial scarves (*kha btags*). I will develop further below the formulae of religious gratitude on the part of the Tibetan leadership.

The Tibetan settlements are dotted with commemorative plaques, which thank the different donors for financing schools, monasteries, hospitals, and so on. 'With love from Spain and Holland' is written in giant letters on one of the buildings of the TCV School in Chauntra (Himachal Pradesh) (see Figure 9). I asked someone why it was written so big – without even the name of the donor agencies, which is normally the case – and his answer was that 'we don't want to forget that God gave us such fantastic *sbyin bdag* from these two countries'.

I came to read letters that the sponsored schoolchildren have to write regularly, in English, to their sponsors. Indeed, schools that function thanks to the system of sponsorship from abroad (almost all schools) require their children to write regularly to the sponsors, as institutionalized thanks, and this duty is transformed into a pedagogical exercise in English classes. That means that each sponsor of the same school receives essentially the same letters. In addition, the letters to the sponsors are very similar from one school to another, which leads to the conclusion that the exercise is coordinated between the different schools in exile.[28] Again, I was struck by the references to 'God' in these letters, and was able to read representative statements like this one:

> If you haven't help me, then my willingness to study and capability to be successful in studies will be just gone in waste. But you save me from this. *So that I can even compare you with the God. You are like the god's angel from the good heaven.* Thank you very much from the inner core of my heart. And I pray for the unbreakable coordination between us as the parents and child. (Emphasis added, and grammar respected)

The use of 'God' (in English) – generalized among Tibetan refugees born in exile – shows that the relation to the *sbyin bdag* is still seen in a religious way, no matter how it is expressed.

The Tibet Support Group (TSG) conferences are also good places to observe the spiritualization of support operated by the Tibetans. The first TSG conference was organized and launched in 1990 by the CTA. As will be described in the next chapter, the TSG conferences, held regularly ever since, bring together the CTA and organizations from the Global Tibet Movement. In Berlin, in 2000, Kesang Takla, the Secretary of the CTA's Department of Information and International Relations (DIIR), compared the international community to a fourth refuge for Tibetan Buddhists:

His Holiness the Dalai Lama once said that when we Tibetans prayed, we prayed to the three refuges: the Buddha, his teachings, and the community of monks who preserve and hand down his teachings. *Now*, because of Tibet's tragic political fate and our non-violent struggle, *we pray to a fourth refuge, that of the international community.* (DIIR 2001: 52; emphasis added)

This meaningful comparison of the supporters of Tibet to a religious refuge, beside the Buddha, the Dharma and the Sangha, the 'three jewels' of Buddhism, is not an isolated statement by an individual, but is representative of the kind of discourses found throughout these conferences. The values of the supporters, such as compassion, love and good-heartedness, are strongly emphasized by the Tibetans, and are linked to the fate of the entire world, as in this declaration by Samdhong Rinpoche:

Your *pure and humanitarian love and compassion* helped us and in fact rescued us. And today, we are in a position to think for the future, and also trying to contribute something *for the betterment of the world and future of the entire humanity.* (Office of Planning Commission and SARD 2005: 10; emphasis added)

This community of supporters is nevertheless presented as active and ready to defend their objectives, as Kesang Takla puts it: 'Elsewhere and in the past, movements for liberation were led by a band of soldiers armed with guns. *The Tibet movement consists of an army of NGOs equipped with belief in truth and justice*' (DIIR 2001: 55; emphasis added).

This 'army', which the Chinese authorities call the 'hostile Western forces' (DIIR 2001: 194), is led by the CTA, as described in the next chapter. This labelling as an army is not meaningless: this army of supporters can be seen as being parallel to the army of believers who, according to Vajrayana eschatology, will fight at the end of times against the enemies of the Dharma, and are recruited by the Kalachakra initiations that are increasingly being organized in the West by the Dalai Lama (see previous section).[29] Hence, in these different discourses, the army, armed with 'truth and justice', fighting with love and compassion, is the fourth refuge of the Tibetans: the spiritualization is complete.

Furthermore, to enhance the religious framework, each TSG conference begins with prayers and invocations recited by Tibetan monks (the third one was launched with prayers from the Venerable Geshe Thubten Ngawang of the 'Tibetan Centre'; Department of Information and International Relations and Friedrich-Neumann Stiftung 2001: 4), and the first 'donors conference' launched by the CTA in 2005 was organized in an ashram (a place of religious retreat) with no electricity or modern facilities. The location was justified by Samdhong Rinpoche in the following terms: 'I feel the place has its own significance for the kind of a vision Tibetan society in exile has' (Office of Planning Commission and SARD 2005: 8).

This gratitude shown by the Tibetans to their supporters, whether individual or institutional, and expressed in religious terms, is a practical deployment of spiritualization. In doing so, the Tibetans present their supporters as patrons of their culture – that is, of their religion, in a new generalized form of *mchod yon*. Moreover, this spiritualization also ties in to the fact that the Tibetans are generally perceived as very religious by their donors (see Chapter 5).

Summary

As they have done for centuries, the Tibetans have used their religion to survive as a society and a culture in the face of different political and economic realities. In exile, they have developed the ability to present themselves as religious tutors to their supporters. They have achieved this thanks to what I call a religious strategy composed of different transformations of their religion, the *sociodicy* of their socio-political system and the spiritualization of the support they receive. In doing so, the Tibetans have vindicated Richardson, who wrote:

> If the Tibetans themselves and especially the religious teachers can make a synthesis of their own beliefs and ideas with the learning of the outside world, a distinctive and valuable Tibetan community may survive in the foothills of the Himalaya. (Richardson [1962] 1984: 243)

It is interesting, however, to remark that the understanding of a religious concept is always uneven in different social contexts. Indeed, the comprehension of a term like 'compassion'[30] is very different in Tibetan and Western societies. From my own observations, compassion is often understood by Westerners as 'charity', in the sense of the Christian value. Hence, the organizations working with Tibetans propose that their members put their 'compassion into action'.[31] I am not sure, however, that the Tibetan sense of compassion is proactive in the same way as Christian *caritas*, and I will return to this subject in Chapter 5. In Tibetan thought, every 'sentient being' arrives in this world with capital earned through actions in past lives, and this is called *karma* (Skt.; *las* in Tibetan). It is not possible to change the *karma* of someone directly, and hence, in a way, compassion is more about understanding and having empathy for that person than it is helping them to change their situation in a practical sense.

Finally, whatever the understandings of their religious discourse may be, the Tibetans have been successful in applying such a discourse to their fate and the assistance they receive, which resonates with Western expectations, as we will see in the next chapter. Indeed, both partners have something to gain, which guarantees the perpetuation of a mutually beneficial relationship.

Notes

1. Ortner uses 'charity', which is a Judaeo-Christian concept that has been subtly integrated into modern Buddhist practice.
2. As referred to by Snellgrove and Richardson ([1968] 2003: 148), it is also called the 'patron–priest' relationship by Klieger (1978). It is also interesting to note that Ishihama (2003: 539) labels the two parties in the relationship as 'donor and donee'.
3. For a detailed history of the Sakya rulers and the Mongols, see Petech 2003.
4. From: 'C'est ce couple composé d'un membre religieux souverain et d'un membre laïc exécutif qui avait pour mission de protéger le Tibet au moyen des "deux sciences" (*gtsug lag gnyis ka*), la spirituelle et la temporelle.'
5. Phagpa received the title of 'Teacher of the Emperor (Ti-shih)' (Stein [1962] 1972: 78).
6. I will not enter into greater detail on this debate, and shall instead refer the reader to the work of Powers, who addresses the issue in *History as Propaganda* (Powers 2004: 48ff.). The Chinese version of the historical relationship of *mchod yon* can be found in Shan (2001: 143ff.), and the Tibetan version in *Mongols and Tibet* (Department of Information and International Relations 1996).
7. See http://www.dalailama.com/messages/dolgyal-shugden
8. See http://tibet.net/dolgyal-shugden/
9. There is actually a very active community of Shugden worshippers in Western countries, which is accusing the Dalai Lama of 'religious repression' (see, for example, Western Shugden Society 2008).
10. We will see below, and again in Chapter 6, the understanding of 'compassion' from a Western perspective, which is important in the context of this research.
11. This dichotomy between popular Tibetan Buddhism and the intellectual variety is actually what Samuel (1993) shows in another context.
12. See, amongst hundreds of others, *Virtue and Reality: Method and Wisdom in the Practice of Dharma* by Thubten Zopa and Nicholas Ribush (1998); *Universal Compassion: Inspiring Solutions for Difficult Times* by Geshe Kelsang Gyatso (2002); and *Uniting Wisdom and Compassion*, by Thub bstan chos kyi grags pa and H.I. Köppl (2004).
13. Values that are ultimately connected to the religion by the Tibetan leadership, as seen in the previous chapter.
14. See, for example, Evin 2013. And see the Foundation 'Mind and Life' co-founded by the Dalai Lama: http://www.mindandlife.org.
15. Samdhong Rinpoche gives a name to this malady: 'The present major problems of humanity, including problems facing the PRC, are "violence". Unless the violence is eradicated, none of the human problems, national or international, can be resolved on a sustainable basis. Keeping in view the objectives and the methods mentioned above, our struggle is a struggle between truth and falsehood, justice and injustice, violence and non-violence' (Samdhong Rinpoche 2005). The remedy for this malady can be found in the Tibetan religion, and the government therefore aligns its discourse closely with that of the Dalai Lama.

16. The expression of 'universal responsibility' has become a leitmotif in the Dalai Lama's speeches since the beginning of the 1990s: it can also be found in each of his books (one compilation of his speeches even has it for a title: Dalai Lama 2002), and the Foundation established with his Nobel Peace Prize allowance is called the Foundation for Universal Responsibility of His Holiness the Dalai Lama (http://www.furhhdl.org/). See also the page on that subject on the Dalai Lama's website: http://www.dalailama.com/messages/world-peace/the-global-community.

17. As I will show in the next chapter, the embodiment of the Tibetan cause by its Western supporters is very important.

18. This point is discussed and supported by different historians and Tibetologists: see, amongst others, Goldstein and Kapstein 1998.

19. See, for example, Inamdar 2005. Ardley (2003) studies the influence of Gandhi on the Dalai Lama and Tibetan activists. She does this through the Dalai Lama's own writings, although without explaining why the Dalai Lama came to use such a reference point, or how he is using it. Since it only describes the references to Gandhi made by the Dalai Lama, this book does not explain when the Dalai Lama began to recognize the Gandhian influence on himself, or the importance or nature of this influence. A perspective on the effect of Gandhi on the Dalai Lama is thus lacking in Ardley's study.

20. Described in Chapter 3.

21. A Bodhisattva (*byang chub sems dpa'i*) has reached the ultimate ideal of Mahayana Buddhism: he is a person who has reached enlightenment but decides to return to the phenomenological world until all 'sentient beings' have reached the same state.

22. In Asian countries such as Japan and Taiwan, too.

23. Two- or three-dimensional 'psycho-cosmogram' of the Buddhist universe (see Tucci 1969).

24. The *Kalachakra* tantra, or wheel of time, is a ritual of high tantrism. The first initiation ever performed outside Tibet and India by the Dalai Lama took place in 1981 (Magnusson 2002: 205).

25. When I asked him why he said *sbyin bdag* and not simply friend, he said that in this special case I acted like a *sbyin bdag*.

26. Many NGOs do not fund projects linked directly to Dharma but rather social projects like education of the clerics, health installations, and so on.

27. I participated in various tours, as I was officially received in different settlements during my final fieldwork because I had a letter of introduction from the CTA detailing my research and asking for any support needed.

28. I cannot yet say definitively whether a model for such a letter is sent to the schools by the CTA, say from its Department of Education, or whether these letters are copied from one school to another, which is certainly possible given that they are networked (as seen in Chapter 2, there are only four managing bodies for the schools in exile).

29. Powers recalls that Robert Thurman writes in his book *Essential Tibetan Buddhism* that the Buddha Vajrapani chose to incarnate himself as Mao Zedong, as he knew that China would invade Tibet. He did so for different reasons: to take on himself the bad consequences of this act, to force the Tibetans to live

closer to their religion of 'detachment, compassion and wisdom', and to spread Buddhism in the world. 'Thus he hoped to better prepare the world for the coming apocalypse foretold in the Kalacakra-tantra' (Powers 2004: 236).

30. Which, as seen, is at the heart of the essentialized Tibetan Buddhism.

31. For example, the Tibet Relief Fund, based in London, exhorts donors to 'Put Compassion into action and help us help Tibet' (http://www.enlightenedgifts. org).

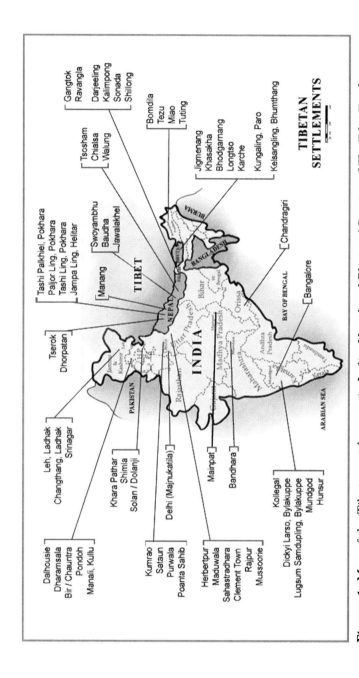

Figure 1. Map of the Tibetan settlements in India, Nepal and Bhutan (*Courtesy of The Tibet Fund*)

Figure 2. Tibetan refugees arriving at Missamari Camp in India in 1959 (See Chapter 1 – *Courtesy of The Tibet Relief Fund*)

Figure 3. The road works at the early stage of exile (See Chapter 1 – Date and location unknown – *Courtesy of The Tibet Museum*)

2006

2001

2014

Figures 4–6. Transformations of the main road of Dharamsala (McLeod Ganj) in 2001, 2006 and 2014 (See Chapter 1 – Picture from 2014 from Wangchuk)

Figure 7. Reconstruction of Monasteries in exile (Chauntra 2006 – See Chapter 4)

Figure 8. Reconstruction of Monasteries in exile (The Golden Temple in Bylakuppe 2006 – See Chapter 4)

Figure 9. Thanking the donors (Chauntra 2006 – See Chapter 4)

AGRICULTURAL RURAL SERVICE CENTRE
(Funded by Norwegian Church Aid Norway)
TOL Tractor — cum — Workshop Section

THIS SITE OF 3,0060 ACRES
IS THE GIFT OF
The AMERICAN EMERGENCY COMMITTEE
FOR TIBETAN REFUGEES
SEPTEMBER 1964

SAVE TIBET

DONATED BY MR. BERNARD FORSTER & MRS EDITH FORSTER,
SAKYA KUNGA TSCHOLING, GERMANY

Figures 10–13. Thanking the donors (Bylakuppe and Darjeeling 2006 – See Chapter 4)

Figure 14. The Global Tibet Movement: The Dalai Lama at an International Tibet Support Groups Meeting (Dharamsala – 2012 – *Courtesy of Tibet Sun/ Lobsang Wangyal* – See Chapter 5)

Figure 15. A house in camp 4 of Bylakuppe settlement (2006 – See Chapter 7)

Figure 16. A house in Bir settlement (2006 – See Chapter 7)

Figure 17. A house in Tezu settlement (2006 – See Chapter 7)

5

Reception of the Tibetan Agendas in the West

Constitution of the Global Tibet Movement

Portrait: Two Organizations

This chapter describes the success of Tibetans in the West. To introduce this, I first present fieldwork findings and personal experiences in organizations working with Tibetans. I dwell mostly on the two organizations where I completed internships. I do not name these bodies, since the objective is not an assessment of their work but a description of it, with a view to understanding the dynamics that operate between such organizations and the communities they ostensibly serve. One organization is among the largest in France that works with Tibetan refugees and Nepalese. The second, one of the most important, and oldest, in the UK, works with Tibetans inside and outside Tibet.

The Organizations

The main activities of these two organizations are to establish and maintain sponsorship relations throughout the Tibetan refugee settlements in India and Nepal, and to manage different development projects. For example, the French organization launches every year different 'volunteer construction camps' in Tibetan settlements and Nepalese villages.[1] These camps enjoy increasing success, and the organization has to conduct a rigorous selection of candidates. Successful ones stay for a month in a local community, where they develop projects such as the construction and restoration of buildings and roads. These organizations also fund projects through the Central Tibetan Administration (CTA). The French organization manages around two thousand sponsorships, and the British around twelve hundred. They both support lay and religious people, old and young, without distinction, although the sponsorship of schoolchildren represents the largest component.

The selection for sponsorship is conducted by the Tibetans themselves. A selection committee is part of a school, a hospital or a nursing home, or, in the case of individuals, part of the Settlement Office, the executive body of the settlement. The committee's task is to check whether the claimant is really in need of the sponsorship and has no other sponsor. The sponsorship can vary from simply paying an institution's fees to a monthly stipend for daily expenses. The two organizations do not double-check this information in the same manner: the French one is very strict with every beneficiary, who must sign (or leave a fingerprint) when receiving the grant; the British one places greater trust in its local partners.

The relationships between the sponsor and his or her beneficiary are important, especially regarding schoolchildren. Both organizations send a complete file to the sponsor with the personal details of the sponsored person and, usually, his or her picture. Normally nobody can choose whom he or she wants to sponsor, but there are infringements of this rule.

The sponsored person assumes a moral obligation to begin a correspondence with the sponsor. This exchange of letters is organized by the schools, and the letters are ritualized and follow the same schedule: the sponsor receives a card for Christmas and Easter, as well as for the Western and Tibetan New Year. This correspondence is managed by the organizations and the local partners: the letters are forwarded from one side to the other. As a result there is a kind of control on this exchange. Sponsors are asked not to send money to their pupils, and their beneficiaries are not allowed to ask for money, so the sponsorship relationship is kept within the institutions. A Tibetan friend told me that, after graduating from school, he asked for the address of his sponsor, but the school did not want to give it to him. When the scholarship ends, the sponsor is asked if he would consider financing another student.

These organizations perpetuate the Western mainstream discourses on Tibetans, described in the previous chapters and in the next one. Tibetans are hence seen and described as deprived and poor, but also hard working, honest (their reports or statements are hardly questioned) and spiritual: it seems that the Tibetan culture is dominated by its religion. The British organization published this statement on Tibetan culture:

> The ancient Tibetan culture has developed along very different lines from others in high Asia. Saving this unique culture essentially comes down to the issue of religious freedom, because Tibet's cultural identity is tied in with its religion, and the Chinese do not respect that religion. (2008, Source withheld)

The deprivation of the Tibetans in exile, their situation as refugees and the extinction of Tibetan culture in their country are the principal subjects on which these organizations communicate. The archives of a third important international organization that has worked with the refugees since the 1960s revealed that communications have always operated along similar lines to those that are currently in place. However, the stress is now on the religious and human rights issues, and the destruction of Tibetan culture on its own soil. Recently, the wave of self-immolations[2] in Tibet received attention in their main communications. Importance is also given to the fact that the Tibetans in exile are democratically organized, and that they are environmentalists. The Tibetan agendas are thus absorbed by these organizations. Moreover, many organizations have the Dalai Lama as their 'patron' because they work under the 'guidance of the Dalai Lama',[3] and they all collaborate with the CTA.

In Tibet, where I interviewed staff of Western organizations, I found that they do not have access to Dharamsala's discourses, and thus do not take them up. They, too, recognize the considerable spirituality of the Tibetans, but do not elaborate on their hard work, environmental awareness or gender equality, as do their counterparts working in exile. For obvious reasons, the political agenda of the Tibetan refugees is not reproduced in Tibet, but this is also because the socio-economic context is extremely different. In Tibet, the Tibetans are economically weak, underemployed and politically powerless. As a consequence, the discourse on Tibetans that I heard from the organizations working with the refugees differed greatly from those working in Tibet.[4]

In exile, however, the economic success of Tibetans tends to be overlooked by the organizations. I showed pictures of the Tibetan settlements to staff of the organizations, who were surprised, if not shocked, to see houses corresponding more to an Indian middle-class standard than to their image of refugee housing (see Figures 15 and 16). Some of them are well aware of the situation, but choose not to communicate on it in order not to lose support. The members of these organizations sometimes reassess their positions, as expressed in this email sent to the director of the French organization by a disenchanted sponsor:

> Does [name of the organization] really have the opportunity to witness the economic reality of the [refugees]? What is the attitude of the local leaders? Don't they have an interest in blackening the situation in order to attract support?

> During the Christmas vacation, I met [name's] sister and her husband in Paris. I did not really understand the purpose of their visit, but I did not get the feeling of being confronted by poor people. They can afford a trip to Paris for two persons; even if they stayed with friends, they had to pay for the flight ticket from Kathmandu, which is very costly. Moreover they were equipped with the latest technology: a digital camera, for example … It is your task to put pressure [on the local leaders] for solidarity to be developed horizontally first of all, before they start asking the French middle classes, who would probably be happy to go to Kathmandu to visit their godsons and goddaughters but do not

have the necessary money. Moreover, I consider that our participation in the support of this community is not intended to pay for luxuries, but for essentials: survival and education. (2008, translated from French)

The same French organization has a difficult relationship with the Tibetan leadership, even though it has to work with the CTA as a local partner. Its director explained to me that the Tibetans are 'spoiled' by the excessive material support that they receive. He said that not only are there more and more organizations financing the refugees, often acting unprofessionally and just 'distributing the money and pouring it into Tibetan communities', but that many individuals, while visiting settlements, just give out large sums of money from 'hand to hand' without asking for any accounting or justification. As a result, organizations like his tend to be ignored in favour of the ones that are not too particular about where the money goes. Such direct financial transactions are increasing, according to him, even in Tibet, and 'spoil the Tibetans'. After that statement, the director also told me about power relations with the Tibetan administration, which are 'more and more demanding' and 'less willing to compromise' with received support – a direct consequence of their success in attracting increasing amounts of assistance. He told me that he wanted to maintain the focus of his organization's projects, but that the CTA had often had conflicting ideas, and thus he took the decision to terminate them. The director added that control by the Tibetan administration goes so far as to obscure the origin of different projects and institutions in the community. Hence, he said, the Tibetan Homes Foundation (THF) and the Tibetan Children's Villages (TCV), built and financed by major NGOs, barely recognize their indebtedness on their websites.[5] Moreover, according to him, his organization's ideas of developing vocational training centres in the settlements, or launching workshops for the settlement officers and the cooperatives presidents, were all adopted by the CTA without giving due credit to the French NGO. If these claims say something about relations between the CTA and this particular organization, they also illustrate the fact that many organizations working with Tibetans consent to be guided, and sometimes even led, by the Tibetan administration.

The French organization decided to work with other populations in Nepal. When the director informed his Tibetan partners of this, they were 'shattered', thinking that 'this could not be possible'. But the motivation to work with other populations was due not merely to bad relations with the CTA and a wish to shock them, but also because the director assessed that there would soon be few Tibetans to help, as so many were leaving for the West and, with the growth of organizations working with Tibetans, there was less to be done in the settlements. When I asked him why he chose not to work with Indians, he said that they were 'lazy and not trustworthy, the exact opposite of the Tibetans'. He was willing to work inside Tibet, yet lacked the contacts and knowledge to realize this. Finally, even if the organization's relations with the CTA were not perfect, the director knew that working with Tibetans guaranteed success for the perpetuation of the organization.

These two organizations are indeed businesses, employing four people in the French case, and three in the British one, and finance is a delicate issue. To ensure its perpetuation, the French organization changed its name and activities: its initial name accorded with its mission to free Tibet, and it engaged only in political activism. Over time, its goals changed to sponsorship and development projects, and it changed its name in order to remain eligible for French government funds. The British organization has two branches with different names, one for political activism and the other for relief. To remain economically viable, the organizations have thus to follow contingencies dictated by the political context.

The Staff

Staffs working in these two organizations do not come exclusively from the world of the Tibetan cause (the 'Global Tibet Movement'); many are from the development sector, or have worked in an NGO as their primary vocation. Their knowledge of Tibet and Tibetans has thus been acquired during their time with the organization, and I noticed that most became closer to the Tibetan cause, or were even participating in it on a private level. In 2005 I interviewed the project officer for Tibet in the Asia-Pacific Bureau of a major intergovernmental organization based in Geneva. She told me that she had discovered the Tibetans during her work, and that they were 'absolutely unique thanks to their aura'. She told me also, 'off the record':

> For myself, having worked in many countries, [Tibet] is certainly the most beautiful society I know, the most beautiful people on Earth thanks to their Tibetan religion, the Buddhist philosophy I mean; they are the ones who have studied it in its purest form. The rest of Asia has developed variants of Buddhism, but the Tibetans respect it so much that they have it in its purest and deepest form. [Tibet] is the only place on the planet I know that has had such an effect on human beings.
>
> ...
>
> For me, the Dalai Lama is the last great philosopher on the planet. He has done remarkable work for twenty years, visiting all the Western governments. Everybody succumbs to his charisma; he is such an enlightened, complete being. Frankly, for me, Tibet is certainly the most evolved culture, [and the Tibetans] are surely the most complete people, who went farthest into Buddhism and this philosophy of life unique to them, and they made this enormous work which dates back seven hundred years or even more. This culture is a jewel of the world. To lose it would be to lose a unique culture that the world needs. We

[Westerners] have to prevent that from happening. (Personal communication #03 2005, translated from French)

As seen in this example, the staff working in these organizations carry the knowledge and discourses elaborated in the Global Tibet Movement. These employees feel they are working both for a noble cause, assistance and development, and for a unique population, the Tibetans.

The founders of these organizations were, nevertheless, connected primarily with the Tibet cause rather than with development in general, and have a special link to Tibet. As such, their discourses on Tibet go further than those of their staff, and are sometimes very close to the myth of Tibet, described below. Their first motivation to work with Tibetans was induced directly by Tibet and not by working in an NGO.

Donors and Members

The members and donors of these organizations are involved in the organizations' activities to varying degrees. As with the staff, I first thought that anyone sponsoring a Tibetan refugee was connected to the Tibet cause, but according to my informants in the organizations, this is not the case. Indeed, many are looking to sponsor someone (especially a child),[6] whether Tibetan or otherwise. Most Westerners sponsoring a child develop a strong bond with him or her – 'a very intimate or emotional relationship', as the French director told me – and many want to visit the child, see how he or she is living, and increase contact. In many cases, there is a kind of 'appropriation' of the child, who becomes like a member of the family. The director of a foundation based in London and working with Tibetans told me something similar when he explained to me the failure of the projects in remote settlements: 'The Westerners want to call something 'mine', and as such they want to 'have' Tibet and Tibetans, so that it becomes theirs. As a result, the places where Westerners do not go [in remote settlements] are underdeveloped' (personal communication #5 2006).[7] Actually, as the director told me, if most people involved in activism or connected with the Tibet cause sponsor a Tibetan, the opposite is not true: the sponsors are not all engaged in the Tibet cause but they feel close to either Tibet or Buddhism.

Other activities like developmental projects, through volunteer camps as in the French example, also attract people for differing reasons: some help Tibetans specifically, while others think of helping a population in need. But, as my informants told me, these activities pull people towards the Tibet cause, and most of them, once involved, want to know more about and become committed to Tibet.

During general meetings, where committed members and donors represent the core of the Tibet movement, one sees political activists, Dharma followers and those attracted by the religious nature of Tibetan culture; all share similar images and discourses on Tibet. Broadly speaking, these people come from similar socio-economic backgrounds: an educated middle-class[8] in search of new ways in their lives. High value is placed on action, or a new model of development or new forms of spirituality – all encompassed in their representations of Tibet and the Tibetans.

Undeniably, the Tibet cause attracts people with different motivations, but it succeeds in crystallizing these different vocations thanks to its multidimensional representations in the West (examined below). Hence the organizations receive regular proposals of commitment, as this message received by the French organization illustrates:

> I perused your website with interest, and immediately began to love this country, this people, this culture that you defend. I would like to know how I could register with your organization. I also would like to send you some money, but I cannot. I am, however, really eager to help you physically and want to be committed to the cause. (2007, translated from French)

For people committed to the Tibet cause, the pilgrimage to Dharamsala or another settlement in exile represents a journey to 'authentic Tibet'. Indeed, a journey to Tibet, even if it is a must, is more problematic, as it presupposes a relation with the Chinese government and population,[9] who are accused of being the source of the Tibetan plight. Moreover, Tibet is seen here as the opposite, in terms of politics and authenticity, of 'Tibet-in-exile' (especially Dharamsala), and so will be sought instead for its immutable characteristics (see below).

The Global Tibet Movement

The success of the Tibetan cause in the West is primarily to be found in the existence of a large network of sympathizers who constitute a transnational community. I refer to this network indiscriminately as the Global Tibet Movement (as the CTA calls it) or the 'transnational community'.

Constitution and Composition of the Global Tibet Movement
Constitution

The number of different groups helping Tibetans mushroomed in the late 1980s and early 1990s. These groups were brought together by the CTA, which organized the first conference of the so-called Tibet Support Groups

(TSGs) in Dharamsala in 1990. This conference, considered a great success, has been followed by six more, the last in India in November 2012, with increasing numbers of participants every time.

McLagan (1996: 343) observed that at the first Tibet Support Group Conference, 'activists began to refer to themselves as part of a "movement", and recognized themselves as sharing the same political goal (though not necessarily the same strategies)'. These TSG conferences certainly created for these groups the sense of belonging to a special cause, and in 2000 they decided to launch a coordinating organ called the International Tibet Support Network (ITSN). The initiative to create the ITSN was taken by two Tibetans, Lobsang Gyalpo, living in Austria, and Thupten Samdup, former North American representative to the Assembly of Tibetan People's Deputies (ATPD) and former director of the Tibetan Institute of Performing Arts (TIPA) in Dharamsala. The ITSN, recently renamed the International Tibet Network, now includes more than two hundred organizations, with over one hundred thousand members (as numerous as Tibetan refugees living in India and Nepal).[10] This exceptional mobilization of individuals and organizations for the Tibet cause has not slackened and is still growing. A sense of belonging to a community with similar objectives – the Global Tibet Movement – has been generated and sustained by the CTA, its twin agendas and its presentation as an ideal society.

Keck and Sikkink (1998) describe a 'transnational advocacy network' (TAN), made up of 'networks of activists, distinguishable largely by the centrality of principled ideas or values in motivating their formation' (ibid.: 1). The authors insist on the influence of these TANs, which I will describe below for the Global Tibet Movement. Hence, '[they] refer to transnational networks (rather than coalitions, movements or civil society) to evoke the structured and structuring dimension in the actions of these complex agents, who not only participate in new areas of politics but also shape them' (ibid.: 4). The same authors observe that there are 'three different traditions justifying actions by individuals or groups outside the borders of their own state: religious beliefs, solidarity, and liberal internationalism' (ibid.: 81), and they include within this latter tradition the defence of human rights.

One dimension Keck and Sikkink do not develop for their TAN, and which can be found in the Global Tibet Movement, is the strong embodiment of and identification with the Tibetan cause and culture. There is a strong romanticization of the Tibetans and their culture by participants of the Tibet movement, who feel they are members of a potential new world, able to touch the 'lost paradise', with the possibility of *becoming* Tibetan, because this is the way that their commitment is presented by the Tibetans themselves.[11] To illustrate this point, I recall different TSG meetings that both Westerners and Tibetans attended and where the first person plural ('we') was always used in a formative and inclusive way, thereby forming new mixed identities. In short, the Tibet movement is an 'imagined community' as theorized by Anderson (1991), with political dimensions (the birth of a 'national conscience' [ibid.: chapter 3]) and also religious and cultural dimensions. In fact, this transnational 'imagined community' can identify itself with the Tibetan 'imagined community', created in exile and described in Chapter 2.

The Global Tibet Movement, as an 'imagined community', did not adopt a symmetrical construction of its identities. If Westerners can embody Tibetan identities, the opposite is not really true, since the refugees have to maintain a clear discourse on their identity as 'authentic' Tibetans and will not compromise on that – indeed both Tibetans and Westerners want to defend this identity. Adams (1996b: 235ff.) writes that there is a kind of 'mimesis' of identity between Sherpas (as trekking guides for tourists in Nepal) and Westerners in a process she describes as a 'mirroring of identities'. But in the Tibetan context, for the Tibetans and their Western 'friends', I would rather talk of a 'mirroring of norms and values': identities must be frozen[12] because the Tibetan one has to be safeguarded. Hence, the two communities share a common corpus of norms and values such as human rights, the safeguarding of an endangered and authentic culture, and the respect of traditional beliefs. Finally, the Global Tibet Movement is solidified and led by Tibetan religious discourses and reference to its ultimate catalyst, the Dalai Lama.

Composition

Given that a central criterion for belonging to the Global Tibet Movement is subscription to a common view and discourse on Tibet, the spectrum of its members is large. It ranges from members of TSGs to individual donors who feel a special link to the Tibetans, from staff working in intergovernmental organizations to members of Parliament, from political activists to Dharma followers, and also from travellers to journalists, including academic researchers. The Tibet movement is thus constituted by individuals as well as organizations from the five categories described in Chapter 2.

During my fieldwork in Europe and India, I encountered members of this movement who could be quite different from one another in terms of culture, motivation, or social origin, but who shared the same interest in and discourses on Tibet. Crucially, this movement is composed of foreign supporters of Tibet (not only Westerners) and by Tibetans themselves, especially the young generation who were born in exile and share representations of Tibet with Westerners.

Clifford Bob (2005: 18ff.), who has studied the 'marketing' and strategies of the TANs, defines the power relations inside these networks. He calls the leading organizations 'gatekeepers', who identify and validate the cause to be helped, but also '[validate the] actors, their performances, and their claims' (ibid.: 18). The 'followers' are all the other organizations that are led by these 'gatekeepers' (ibid.). In the Tibetan context, the gatekeeper is clearly the CTA itself. For example, the CTA organizes the TSG conferences, and these orient the transnational community by validating its discourses. A few years ago the CTA asked Western political activists not to jeopardize its renewed dialogue with the Chinese authorities by demonstrating against Chinese interests. Many organizations felt frustrated by such a demand, but nonetheless accepted it and suspended their actions against China. The CTA has this power and is followed by the Global Tibet Movement. The leadership of the CTA was indeed formally recognized by the Global Tibet Movement, as expressed in the concluding remarks of the second TSG conference:

> One of the messages which has been clearly brought out during the discussions is the uniqueness of the Tibetan movement, uniqueness in the fact that it is *the only non-violent movement for liberation which has a State and a government of its own*. This point of view was also highlighted by His Holiness the Dalai Lama. The uniqueness and the strength of the Tibetan movement [is] that it is actually a state-in-exile or a government-in-exile. We should not forget this important point, especially in the light of the fact that *we have all agreed to convince other governments, the UN organizations and other bodies to recognize Tibet and the Tibetan Government as the legitimate representative of the Tibetan People*.
>
> We also have to find the right road, as Tibet Support Groups, between the essential elements of Tibet Support Groups being independent in the sense they are not part of the government establishment and do not represent the government, and at the same time being a part of the movement which supports the recognized leadership of the Tibetans. (http://tibet.net/important-issues/worldwide-tibet-movement/tsgs-conferences/second-international-conference-of-tsgs-bonn-14-17-june-1996/, emphasis added)

This long quotation shows the argumentation for the different TSGs to recognize the Tibetan leadership as theirs, while remaining independent. Clifford Bob (2005: 18ff.) describes how influential and charismatic individuals can also be instrumental in the networks, and he calls them 'matchmakers'. In the Global Tibet Movement, such a matchmaker is, unsurprisingly, the Dalai Lama himself, who is almost as respected by Westerners as by Tibetans. The figure of the Dalai Lama is central to the Tibet movement, and his charisma is a leading cause of the constitution of the community.

Actions and Discourses of the Global Tibet Movement

Actions

The Global Tibet Movement forms the basis of success for Tibetans; it is a platform in the West for Tibetan aspirations. The community not only finances projects for the refugees directly, such as the welfare state and developmental projects, but also campaigns for different causes linked to Tibet, and publicizes – through various media – the refugees' fate, and their actions to save their culture and regain their country. The community actually provides three types of assistance, as described in Chapter 2.

The Global Tibet Movement also shares a common history of success in influencing national politics and private companies, which strengthens its cohesion and shows its power. One of these successes is the termination of a dam project in Qinghai province (Tibetan region in China), which was planned by the World Bank and would have required the resettlement of thousands of Tibetans (Pike 2001: 113). Another success is the release of Tibetan political prisoners in China under pressure from the transnational community, which advocates internationally on their behalf. A nun, Ngawang Sangdrol, was freed after a campaign and the publication of a book telling her story (Laeng and Broussard 2001). While it is difficult to assess the community's real influence on international decisions, these examples are victories for the people involved.

Discourses

The Global Tibet Movement is the main outlet in the West for the diffusion of knowledge on Tibet. Such discourses on Tibet, importantly, attract funds and commitments to the Tibetan cause. It is thus imperative to study these discourses in order to understand the Tibetan success in attracting support in the West. Moreover, an analysis of these discourses leads to an understanding of power issues in the partnership between Westerners and Tibetans.

As will be shown, the narrative on Tibet is still constructed around the 'myth of Tibet' – that is, the vision of Tibet (before the Chinese invasion) as a lost paradise – and its related stereotypes. It is striking how the knowledge on Tibet carried by the Global Tibet Movement still follows pure elements of these fantasized visions, how Tibet is essentialized around core stereotypes (marking a real 'suspension of disbelief') and how Tibet became a 'brand' in the West, a label directly recognizable and easy to remember.

The West still considers Tibet to be a land of mystics and magicians, guardians of authentic secret knowledge and practices that are able to solve the 'crisis of modern times', as an informant put it to me. During my fieldwork in Tibetan settlements and with Western organizations, I encountered the same ubiquitous knowledge about Tibet and Tibetans. The Tibetans, through their religious and political leaders, initiate or propagate stereotypes for the Western world, presenting themselves in an idealistic conceptual framework, following political and religious agendas, as peaceful environmentalists, gender equal, democratic, and, moreover, very religious. The discourses elaborated by the CTA are taken over by the Global Tibet

Movement and thus penetrate Western societies. This strategy is important for the CTA, with its Department of Information and International Relations and an office called the 'TSG Desk' created specially for contacts between the CTA and the TSGs.[13] The discourses generated by the CTA are even more easily accepted by people from the Global Tibet Movement because these discourses already existed in the Western imagination[14] and because most of the members of this movement have only an indirect knowledge of Tibet and its culture.

These stereotypes have penetrated deeply. For example, a member of the Swedish Parliament delivered this message during a conference of TSGs, showing the semiotic power of Tibet:

> High up, just beneath the sky, lies the fairy-tale country Tibet, the most beautiful country in the world. The Tibetans are friendly and peaceful ... No doubt, in many cases the Tibetans have different values compared to us in the Western world where ownership and materialistic values predominate. (Department of Information and International Relations and Friedrich-Neumann Stiftung 1996: 35)

The discourse on Tibet and Tibetans issued by the transnational community, and that permeates Western societies, can be divided into three linked themes. First, Tibetan culture is precious, ideal and endangered; second, the 'authentic' Tibet is now located in exile; and third, spiritual Tibet can save a 'decadent West'. These themes dichotomize the contexts, stereotyping and sometimes over-simplifying the situation, but they function nonetheless as a rich metaphor for the transnational community and the Tibet cause. Moreover, all these discourses are pervaded with a sense of urgency: Tibet and its culture must be saved now (in exile)[15] or they will be lost forever under Chinese rule.

A Precious and Ideal Culture

As the CTA continuously states, to lose Tibetan culture would be, for the world, like losing a jewel, one able to cure modern problems. The loss of Tibet is thus put on a par with other major problems that the world faces, like global warming or the extinction of natural species (elements of the current Western narrative on a generalized decline). The Tibet issue is thus relocated in the world: it has a global dimension. A statement by the American actor Richard Gere, chairman of the board of the International Campaign for Tibet, summarizes this vision:

> Tibet is a human rights issue as well as a civil and political rights issue. But there's something else too – Tibet has a precious culture based on principles

of wisdom and compassion. This culture addresses what we lack in the world today; a very real sense of inter-connectedness. We need to protect it for the Tibetan people, but also for ourselves and our children. (ICT: http://www. savetibet.org/resource-center/all-about-tibet)

An important characteristic of Tibetan refugees stressed by the Global Tibet Movement is that, thanks to their unique culture and religion, they do not suffer from collective depression like other refugee communities.[16] The Tibetan refugees did not thus succumb to collective intoxication, suicide or apathy. As one American woman volunteering in Dharamsala wrote to me:

All Tibetans, even the Dalai Lama, are of 'refugee' status in India (most extremely poor) living in a poor country, [with] no legal status, no passports, no country, little opportunity for work and little hope. It is a desperate situation for many of them. But at least they are free and safe and they can practice their religion openly. *In spite of their hardships which they tend to keep to themselves, they are the most lovely, dignified, kind, gentle, generous, sweet people I know. They are always polite and welcoming and they smile a lot.* They are very happy to be near the Dalai Lama. I feel very fortunate to live alongside them. (Personal communication #82 2006, emphasis added)

For people using this argument, the ability of Tibetan refugees to face their destiny positively is a response to the present Western pessimism about the world's future (which I could identify inescapably in discourses elaborated by members of the transnational community). Given such skill of the Tibetan refugees, it is thus even more important to save their culture.

This argument can be observed and summarized. In the Western media and documentation by support organizations, the Tibetans rarely suffer, even if their plight is described as terrible. (The recent self-immolations by Tibetans are exceptions, though these are presented as individual history and destiny and not collectively.) Thus, in the communication of the Global Tibet Movement over the past fifty years, it is difficult to find images that contravene the rule of Tibetans as strong and happy. Browsing through the archives of an organization based in the UK, which has helped Tibetan refugees from the outset, I noticed this trend began as early as the 1960s. At that time, one could already see clichéd pictures of Africans, Indians and other populations suffering from disease or famine, photographed in postures of despair and need – in striking contrast with the Tibetans, who were also described as needy and desperate[17] but were never shown as such. Instead, Tibetans were shown in active postures, working hard in their fields, constructing their houses, and more. Now, more than fifty years later, this pictorial trend has changed little: one still finds pictures of desperate Africans crushed under their destiny, but happy Tibetans facing their fate courageously.[18] Actually, unlike the African populations, the main argument used to attract funds for Tibetans is not based on pity, but rather on the urgency of providing assistance to an endangered spiritual resource – 'help them before we lose this treasure'. A slogan of the Tibet Relief Fund of the UK sums up this fact: 'Help us to put compassion into action'.[19] This visual representation of the Tibetans is even respected by the refugees themselves. In Dharamsala, the Tibet Museum retraces the early years of exile.[20] The terrible hardships that the refugees had to face are described exhaustively, but there are few pictures of *people* illustrating these difficulties; most depictions are of the material conditions of the refugees.

The message that emerges clearly from this representation is that the Tibetans have kept their faith despite all hardships, thanks to their culture and religion, and also by following the religious strategy described in Chapter 4. This is seen in the West as an inspirational message of hope and a model to follow. These organizations know that, in working with Tibetans, they appeal to specific archetypes in the Western Judaeo-Christian tradition: respect for an ancient culture; keeping the faith whatever happens; and working hard to change one's fate. These discourses are intrinsic to the Western development relationship described in the next chapter.

Organizations that help Tibetans know that they must follow and respect these common clichés if they want to attract funds and resources to survive. The director of the French NGO cited at the beginning of this chapter told me that he was aware of the stereotyped message that his organization was delivering, but could not change it without risking 'killing the goose that lays the golden egg'. Hence, the stereotypes of Tibet and Tibetans are inescapable, sustained and spread by the different constituents of the Global Tibet Movement. Moreover, Tibetan society in exile is inevitably represented as ideal, both spiritual and evolved. In a kind of holistic movement, Tibetan society is not only 'authentic' and spiritual but also 'modern', because it has developed the values praised in the West.

'Authentic' Tibet vs 'Sinicized' Tibet

For the Tibet Movement, Tibet has been relocated in exile: by a remarkable inversion the 'copy' has become the 'original'. This was quite predictable given the discourse of Dharamsala, which states that the refugees are the only Tibetans able to save Tibetan culture and preserve its authenticity. Following this inversion, and according to the Tibetan refugees and the transnational community, exile has become the home of Tibetan culture. This is even truer today, and is confirmed by the Tibetans who committed self-immolations to proclaim that their cultural identity has been violated in Tibet under Chinese rule.

In the same way, it is considered that the exile community has preserved the authenticity[21] that the Chinese authorities have killed in Tibet by modernizing it or introducing Chinese influences. As such, the refugee community is renamed 'little Tibet' with its capital 'little Lhasa' (i.e. Dharamsala; see Anand 2002). More importantly, the present refugee discourse is accepted and integrated as the only authentic and traditional one, and the evolution of the community in exile is considered to be a model of what would have happened in Tibet itself if the Chinese invasion had not occurred. Thus, one of my informants, volunteering in a TSG told me:

> Look at what [the Tibetans] did in exile. Look at their achievement, the way they could keep their culture and religion, intact, untouched, and at the same time develop a democracy based on love and compassion. They would have done that inevitably had they not been invaded by the Chinese. (Personal communication #11 2006)

When Westerners travel to Tibet or to 'little Tibet', they rarely reassess their stereotypes against the reality they see, but rather attribute any contradictory elements to sinicization (in China) or modernity (in exile). On this subject, Adams writes about the 'karaoke' fashion in Lhasa:

> For many Westerners visiting Tibet, but particularly for those involved in the movement to free Tibet who have come to Lhasa to validate their time-consuming intentions and efforts, karaoke is usually discussed as a sign of the 'decline' of Lhasa and the 'loss' of an authentic Tibet at the hands of the Chinese. (Adams 1996a: 514)[22]

Indeed, some of the Tibetans to whom I spoke in Lhasa told me candidly: 'Why shouldn't we like modern things like mobile phones, satellite TV, or cars?' Modernity in Lhasa is perceived as Chinese aggression by many Westerners, but these same Westerners do not consider it evil in exile, as long as the Tibetans maintain a stereotyped and cultural discourse that is seen as 'authentic'.

Most of the time, Western media or organizations describe the Tibetan plight in a dichotomous way: the Tibetans are innocent victims of invasion by an evil force. According to this narrative, a pure and authentic culture was raped by China, but fortunately this culture was reconstructed and has even been ameliorated in exile – with the introduction of democracy and the other developments. The depictions of 'little Tibet' and its model illustrate this dichotomization. 'Little Tibet' is represented as both 'authentic' and traditional, and also modern and up to date. Refugees and Westerners adopt this representation: the former because they can thus show what they would have become in Tibet without the Chinese invasion; and the latter because they do not want to support what could be seen as a medieval society. The refugees are therefore represented, visually and narratively, in their daily religious routine, but also learning foreign languages and computer skills, and communicating with the world with the help of new technologies, and more.

For the transnational community, Tibetans embody a perfect balance between high spirituality and modern materialism, this latter being the main disjunction of Western culture. In such a view, Tibetans can show the way to the integration of a modern dilemma (between spirituality and materialism, between tradition and modernity), and to support their cause is to follow their model.

On the other hand, everything modern in Tibet itself is seen as a loss of 'authenticity' initiated by the Chinese authorities. Tibet itself is not seen as a real country populated by living inhabitants, but merely as a 'lost paradise' that was raped by the evil twins of the West and China. Tibet 'lost its reality' when invaded by the People's Republic of China, and entered forever 'the mind's Tibet' described by Hugh Richardson to Patrick French (2003: 266).

At present, Tibet *and* Tibetans living inside Tibet have become a landscape, an ideal and a fantasized perfection: it is the reification of the 'ethnoscape' as defined by Appadurai (1996). This struck me while in Tibet, observing Western tourists and their photographic habitus. I saw countless tourists pointing their huge lenses unashamedly close to Tibetans praying in front of the Jokhang, Lhasa's central temple, sometimes even asking their 'subjects' to assume different postures or to move to more photogenic places. The same phenomenon occurred in front of other tourist sites. In the grasslands, Western tourists complained to me about the nomads' satellite dishes, as these ruined their perfect photos of the grasslands *with* the nomads. This is again the world of the stereotype, visual stereotypes, where Tibetans are *part* of a perfect landscape. Back in the West, the imagery of Tibet is composed almost solely of these perfect landscapes that merge nature and human portraits.[23] In such a view, Tibetans in Tibet are as removed from time as is their natural environment. This may constitute a catharsis regarding the political situation in Tibet, but a consequence of it is that Tibet is no longer considered on the political stage in the West. Even the recent self-immolations are presented by organizations and the Dalai Lama himself as very Buddhist in the way that they do not harm anybody else, as terrorism does. Again, a religious and ideal analysis of this issue eclipses the political violence of such acts.

Apart from the discussion on 'authenticity', Tibet is seen in the West as a spiritual culture, and this is important in the attraction of support, as I shall argue in the following section.

'Spiritual' Tibet vs 'Decadent' West

A major preconception of Tibet in the West is its strong spirituality, an attribute capable of solving the world's problems, and especially those of the 'decadent' West (the expression is from one of my informants). In this line of argument, Tibet is relocated in the West because the former can save the latter.

In the West, the central paradigm of the spiritual nature of the Tibetan cause is the Dalai Lama himself. The Dalai Lama epitomizes the plight of his people and is, moreover, a symbol of peace.[24] He gained huge international recognition in 1989 upon winning the Nobel Peace Prize. The presentation speech stated this Tibetan spirituality – quasi surreal:

> This year's laureate will also be able to celebrate a significant jubilee, as it is now fifty years since he was solemnly installed as H.H. the Fourteenth Dalai Lama of the Tibetan people, when he was four years old. Pursuing the process of selection that resulted in the choice of him in particular would involve *trespassing on what, to a Westerner, is* terra incognita, *where belief, thought and action exist in a dimension of existence of which we are ignorant or maybe have merely forgotten.* (http://nobelprize.org/nobel_prizes/peace/laureates/1989/presentation-speech.html, emphasis added)

During my stay in Dharamsala, I encountered and spoke to dozens of Westerners who were committed to the Tibet cause. Some of them are long-term residents of 'little Tibet', and some have taken religious vows. They are involved in the Tibetan fight for cultural survival or freedom, and they all share the positive and quite idealistic view of Tibet and Tibetans. It is common there to meet Western people who literally want to *embody* 'Tibetanness': they dress like Tibetans (especially women, wearing the Tibetan traditional robe, the chuba [*phyu pa*]), learn the Tibetan language (many courses for different levels are organized at the library), and have a strong feeling of being part of a special community. Moreover, everything happens as though the Westerners could in fact finally 'own' their own fragment of Shangri-La or 'Tibetanness'. Hence, there is a strong materialization of assistance: sponsors receive regular letters from their pupils (organized by Tibetan institutions), projects in the settlements are shown and visited, donors are thanked through commemorative plaques and invited to official ceremonies of thanks, and more. The members of the Tibet movement who visit the settlements and who are formally or informally received by Tibetans, thanks to their special bonds, are no longer common tourists, but have attained the distinction (in the sense of Bourdieu 1979) of being part of the Tibetan global family, part of the Shangri-La. For centuries the concept of Shangri-La (which carried different names) was only a dream in the West, and it is now reified through the refugees.

The main discourse used by the different volunteer organizations in Dharamsala is that of a community, a global village, where people from all over the world gather and meet to help one another. A flyer from one such organization states that '[v]olunteering [with us, in Dharamsala] is a way to connect with another culture, become part of a *small closely knit community*, build new friendships, and discover more about yourself and *the world we all share*' (source withheld 2006, emphasis added).

I noticed that a common lexique Westerners use regarding Tibet is linked to home and nostalgia: they express the fact that belonging to the Tibetan community is like 'coming back home', 'feeling at home again' or 'longing for home'. In this way, they feel they have come back to their 'origin', back to a form of 'life and knowledge, we [the Westerners] have forgotten and destroyed'.[25] These statements encompass the theme of lost innocence, of the symbolic return to childhood; and I was struck during my fieldwork observations by the obvious behaviour of many Westerners who act among the Tibetans as children do with their parents (and not only amongst the Dharma followers in their relationship with their lama). In such cases, it is as if Westerners were liberated from responsibilities and were leaving their fate in the hands of Tibetans. These statements are strongly linked to the vision of the Tibetans and their culture as authentic, genuine, unspoiled by modernity and, as such, are able to communicate to Westerners what they have lost – namely, a form of spirituality.

Back in the West, I encountered the same kind of perceptions in the Global Tibet Movement. Some of these people had experienced a life crisis and had been seeking answers before discovering Tibetan culture. The founder of a TSG told me that one of his children was born with a severe handicap, and that this had changed his life. He was then looking for answers about life, which he had found in Tibetan culture, especially its religion. From this he wanted to help the Tibetans, and he now runs a successful TSG, sponsoring several hundred Tibetan refugees. Other people told me about their 'mid-life crisis', which remained unanswered by Western spirituality, and how they had discovered that 'Buddhist philosophy' (meaning Tibetan Buddhism) was able to help them. In their gratitude, they wanted to help the Tibetans materially, and so became involved with the refugees. Hence, many donors and people committed to the Tibet cause come to it via religion.

In a word, Westerners in the transnational community have adopted the Tibetan construction of Western societies as being spiritually weak and in need of a special spirituality. This illustrates the integration by the transnational community of Tibetan conceptions, and in this sense one can argue that these Westerners are also 'prisoners of Shangri-La' (a point articulated especially by Lopez 1998).

Notes

1. Volunteering while travelling is a very fast-increasing trend. A word was coined for this trend: 'voluntourism'. See http://www.travelandleisure.com/articles/going-the-distance-february-2004

2. In May 2015, 146 Tibetans had found death through self-immolation. Most of them from inner Tibet (139) and mostly since March 2011 (see http://www.savetibet.org/resources/fact-sheets/self-immolations-by-tibetans/).

3. Personal communication #5 2006.

4. I shall not elaborate further on this issue as it is beyond my main subject. However, the comparison of the two contexts, inside and outside Tibet, is very interesting, as the socio-economic situation of the two groups of Tibetans differs greatly. The interested reader may consult the works of Yeh (2003, 2013), Fischer (2005, 2013), Kolas and Thowsen (2005) and Barnett (2006) for the present situation in Tibet. The situation in exile is described in this book.

5. See http://tibhomes.org/history/ for the history of the THF and http://www.tcv.org.in/content/historical-background for the TCV.

6. Certain categories of people are more likely to be sponsored than others, according to my informants. Children are the first category, followed by the elderly. However, some are 'unsponsorable' (translated from the French neologism '*imparrainable*'), such as destitute adults, and the organizations then have to find finances for them elsewhere. There is an undeniable dimension of image and perception in the sponsorship relationship. See, on this subject, Smith's (2004) article, which analyses a flyer designed to generate sponsorship.

7. See below on the 'embodiment' of the Tibet cause.

8. With an over-representation of middle-aged women: many whom I interviewed about their motivations told me that they came to help Tibet after personal troubles, often a 'mid-life crisis' (many women because they felt 'empty after having educated their children'; personal communication #31 2007), and that they had found answers in the Tibetan culture. See later in this chapter for more coverage on this.

9. Chinese people are almost always represented in the Global Tibet Movement as evil. I heard so many first-hand stories from people who had travelled in Tibet and sometimes represented the Chinese in a totally absurd and caricatural manner. But the members of the Global Tibet Movement are as ready to believe improbably negative things about Chinese as they are ready to believe improbably positive things about Tibetans (as detailed below).

10. See http://www.tibetnetwork.org/home.

11. See the previous chapter on the spiritualization of assistance.

12. At least in what Goffman describes as the 'frontstage', that is, the displayed identity (Goffman 1959: 44ff.).

13. The tasks of this desk are described as such on the CTA's official website: 'The main functions of the TSG Desk at the Department of Information and International Relations of Central Tibetan Administration based in Dharamshala, North India, are to: Inform TSGs about the policies and initiatives of the CTA; Inform TSGs about Tibet and the Tibetan communities in exile; Interact with members of TSGs, and coordinate their programme during their visit to Dharamshala; Act as an observer to the ITSN Steering Committee; Facilitate international conferences of TSGs; Keep records of campaigns and activities of TSGs, and present annual reports on the state of the worldwide Tibet movement' (http://tibet.net/important-issues/worldwide-tibet-movement/#4).

14. These discourses represent what Olivier de Sardan (1995: 105) calls 'ideological populism': the projection onto a population of ancestral values (or values identified as such) and of qualities that have a stereotypical nature.

15. The message 'Time is running up. Save Tibet' can be read everywhere in the settlements, printed on tourist souvenirs.

16. Like refugees from South East Asia, for example. Different studies (of varying quality) show this fact. See, amongst others, Miller (1978); Holtz (1998); Jacobson (2002).

17. See Chapter 3 for the victimization discourses adopted by the CTA.

18. The photographs used to raise funds for African disasters are highly stereotyped, and often represent emotional scenes, like mothers with their emaciated children. They are also often taken from above, with the subject looking up at the camera, and hence giving the impression of being dominated (see the post-modern analysis of development) and crushed under their fate.

19. 'Compassion' is indeed the key word in the definition of Tibetan Buddhism in the West. See Chapter 4 for the Tibetan construction of this discourse.

20. Clare Harris (2012) studies extensively the different kinds of museums devoted to Tibetans in the West, in Exile and in China. Her Chapter 5 analyses the Tibet Museum in Dharamsala.

21. I use 'authenticity' here, in line with my informants, to mean the ideal state of a culture, untouched by anything modern. Even if the anthropologist knows that 'authenticity' is a myth, the concept is still strong in the West and acts as a catalyser of the collective imagination. In the context of Tibet in the West, authenticity is a powerful narrative, as will be seen in Chapter 6.

22. In the same way, see Barnett (2003) for a description of the olfactory impressions of Western tourists visiting Lhasa.

23. See the best-selling photos of Olivier Follmi, the self-styled 'humanity photographer', in which Tibetans look totally unreal and out of time (http://www.follmispirit.com/).

24. The Western vision of the Dalai Lama has not always been so apologetic, as Miller has observed. This author studied the popular perceptions of Tibetans in the Western news. She found out that in the 1920s and 1930s, '[t]he Dalai Lama was described as a Machiavelli who had been responsible for the massacre of the Chinese in 1912, while the Panchen Lama was a gentle dream' (Miller 1988: 10). At that time, the Dalai Lama was considered as the Buddhist alter ego of the Pope, and as such was not well considered by the 'American White Anglo-Saxon Protestant' (ibid.). This perception was inverted after 1959, since the Panchen Lama was 'collaborating' with the Chinese government until just before his death (ibid.: 19). It is also noticeable that the Dalai Lama is now often considered the anti-Pope: when the former is declared 'modern' (appearing in a computer advertisement, for example), open-minded and non-dogmatic, the latter seems exactly the opposite. One can observe that the perception of the Dalai Lama in the West follows the conception of the Tibetans, and his present position as a global spiritual figure shows how Tibetans are now received in the West.

25. These are all statements I heard during interviews.

6

A New Model of Partnership and its Adaptability

Tibet in the West

To understand the special relationship between Tibet and the West, it is important to investigate the construction of Tibet in the Western imagination. It will then become apparent that this construction has not only Orientalist characteristics, but also a redemptive dimension through the re-enactment of lost traditions and rituals. These spiritual elements have come to be integrated into the religious market that has sprung up amidst the quest for new spirituality.

Tibet in the West before 1959

Contact between Western countries and Tibet dates back to the sixteenth century. When travellers first discovered Tibet they were dazzled by the religion that they observed. Many thought that it might be a degeneration of Catholicism, since the rituals were comparable (incense, colours, monasteries, one absolute leader, and more). The first myth of Tibet to appear was the legend of Prester John, a priest who left Europe to Christianize Asia and never returned. The story was that he had found a lost 'Paradise on Earth', and had reigned over it ever since. Lopez (1998: 16ff.) describes further how, in the nineteenth century, the Tibetan religion was seen as a reverse of Christianity, following the Orientalist movement of comparison and separation (Said 1979: 1). After these first encounters, knowledge of Buddhism and its different schools evolved in the West, and Tibet became popular again in the nineteenth century with the emergence of esoteric movements. These movements, mostly deriving from Christianity, were connected to the medieval 'irrational' traditions, and they show how, along with science, a certain freedom of thought was emerging from the religious dogma, a process that had begun in Europe as far back as the Middle Ages (Obadia 1999: 64ff.).

One of these movements, the Theosophical Society, founded by Henry Olcott and Helena Blavatsky in 1875, was connected directly to Tibet. The society presented itself as a syncretism of every existing religion and, as such, in possession of ultimate Truth. A certain emphasis was, nevertheless, given to Buddhism, and society members were the first Westerners to call themselves Buddhists, even if they did not convert to this religion (Obadia 1999). Moreover, Blavatsky, a Russian medium, claimed to be in psychic contact with spiritual masters in Tibet, who chose her to receive their teachings about a 'secret doctrine', the essence of all known religions, called 'Theosophy'. The theosophical credo is not about Tibetan Buddhism, which could be taught by Tibetans, but about a secret knowledge, key to an ultimate Truth, which had been lost in the West but kept intact in Tibet. Hence Tibetans were not held in high regard by the society for their peculiar religion or culture, but rather as the guardians of lost Western treasures. The Theosophical Society, popular in Western bourgeois milieu, reinvigorated a fascination with Tibet in the West. From then on, Tibet was considered as a secret country possessing spiritual treasures lost in the West. Alexandra David-Néel, a French explorer and member of the Theosophical Society, perpetuated Western fantasies about Tibet with her books on Tibet and its mysteries and extraordinary events. Her books, like *Magic and Mystery in Tibet* (1971, first published in 1929), remain best-sellers. At the same time, a psychological reading of Buddhism was developed, and, in 1927, W.Y. Evens-Wentz published his translation of *The Tibetan Book of the Dead*, with a preface by the Swiss psychiatrist, Carl Gustav Jung (1875–1961), founder of analytical psychology.

In 1933, James Hilton published a novel called *Lost Horizon* (1933), in which a group of Westerners make the chance discovery that other Westerners have been living in a monastery hidden in Tibet – called Shangri-La – for centuries, protecting fabulous treasures such as immortality and wisdom. This successful novel defined Tibet as a fabulous, secret country, paving the way for other fantasies, including a number of specious books written by a Briton with the pen-name Lobsang Rampa. The author claimed to be the reincarnation of a Tibetan monk, and as such to possess magical powers. These fantasies, often centred on Westerners and not Tibetans, entered the collective imagination.[1]

Bishop (1989: viii) shows that these representations were constructed not only by spiritual agendas, but also by political concerns, changing aesthetics and scholastic constructs. Different groups of people in the West with different interests in Tibet created as many 'Tibets' (ibid.) as their agendas. Bishop gives the example of British explorers who described Tibetans as lazy and thus deserving of conquest (something that occurred in 1904, with the Younghusband mission to Lhasa) (ibid.: 121). A powerful Victorian era narrative saw mountains as aesthetic natural constructions. Mountains represented strength, idealism and 'freedom from materialism through a simplified lifestyle', as well as a source of salvation thanks to their purity (ibid.: 117ff.). As Tibet was located on the highest plateau in the world, it excited these imaginings and became, like other mountainous places, a source of spiritual gain worth conquering. Bishop describes how this quasi-surreal representation of Tibet was totally deprived of its inhabitants and their daily life experiences: Tibet was seen purely as a sublime and magnificent landscape with an exotic religion (ibid.: Chapter 4).

After the Second World War this vision became inverted, with the decline of the conquest narrative and the rise in spirituality: Tibet became represented in the West as having a rich religion within an exotic landscape (Bishop 1989: 244). Similarly, Ortner analyses Western mountaineering in these regions as a critique of modernity: '[t]he earliest climbers seemed to view climbing as embodying a spirituality that was lacking in modern life' (Ortner 1999: 36). Bishop (2000) further notes that the protean myth of Tibet continues to evolve as Western needs dictate. Shangri-La has now been transformed into a 'cyber-la'. Tibetan culture, and especially Tibetan religion, is now entering the high-tech Western imagination: it is regularly compared with modern science and with new technologies.[2]

These ever-changing forms of the myth of Tibet maintain the idea of a lost paradise where anyone can go back to their origins and find what they are looking for. This paradise is filled with images, or stereotypes, such as salvation, idealism, freedom from materialism, lost and secret knowledge, authenticity, purity – images that are still developed in different forms of art or in the media in the West.

The formation of these representations is linked to the construction of an oriental 'Other'. Edward Said, in *Orientalism* (1979), describes how the West has always defined its 'Self' through the 'Oriental Other'. This is created on the basis of various stereotypes or fantasies. As Said puts it, '[t]he Orient was almost a European invention, and had been since antiquity a place of romance, exotic beings, haunting memories and landscapes, remarkable experience' (ibid.: 1). To these characteristics could also be added 'wisdom' and 'Buddhism'[3] for Tibet, which epitomizes the entire Orientalist trend.

The myth of Tibet colonized the Western mind and touches almost every level of Western societies. The ethereal, oneiric visions of Tibet are hard to escape, and at the extreme the 'mind's Tibet' (French 2003: 266) is totally disconnected from practical reality. Tibet, as a land inhabited by a population with a culture and a history, is, in fact, 'deterritorialized' (Appadurai 1996: 54) in the myth. As such, Tibet becomes in these Western representations ethereal, unreal and ultimately Utopian. Masuzawa (1999: 541) calls Tibet a 'virtual nation', and a 'hyper-nation', because, unlike other nations, it is perceived as a political entity based on spirituality and not material power.

Tibet in the West since 1959 and the Quest for New Spirituality

The arrival of Tibetans in exile represented a new opportunity for Westerners to meet Tibetans. For the first time, Westerners could easily encounter the culture they were imagining. In the 1960s and 1970s, with the development of the hippie and countercultural movements, and the growth of so-called New Age philosophy, which attracted thousands of young Western travellers to the roads of India and Nepal, the contacts with Tibetan refugees greatly increased. The first relationships were established with Tibetan religious masters, who were invited to open Dharma centres in the West. The first Tibetans who arrived in exile and later came to Western countries could discover a Western dynamic spiritual and religious stage where ancient beliefs were reformed and replaced by new forms of religiosity.

Today, sociologists[4] describe how Western 'secularization' is not the disappearance of religion as forecast by positivism, but a reconfiguration of beliefs: secularization did not extinguish religious beliefs but rearranged them. This metamorphosis engendered a religious *bricolage* and reintroduced a 'magical thinking' into modern societies. As a consequence, a religious 'market' appeared, in which different beliefs were borrowed synchronically and diachronically (Hervieu-Léger 1993: 233ff.). Religious norms and values became commodified, as predicted by Marx (1994: 137ff.), and freed from their referents: a characteristic of this new market has been the liberation from traditional religious institutions and their attached constraints (Hervieu-Léger 1993: 247). In the West, Tibet's beliefs and religion – labelled as a philosophy – are interpreted as non-dogmatic and free from institutional obligations, and thus have a visible and important place in such a market.

The conceptualization of a religious market where social actors can find and create their own beliefs 'à la carte' has been criticized for its 'post-modernist' conception of a total freedom for these individuals, freed from social constraints.[5] Indeed, as in the economic market, the social actors cannot produce the goods they are consuming in the religious market; they are dependent on the supply. Touraine (1992) observed that organizational cores appear in such markets, capable of answering and anticipating the needs of the actors as consumers. Obadia (1999: 128) argues that the growth of Tibetan institutions in the West since the 1960s constitute such a core, able to respond to the increasing spiritual needs. The same author remarks that representations of Buddhism – and I would add, of Tibetan Buddhism – can now be used in the same way as other symbolic resources by social actors in the religious market. These stereotyped representations are loaded exclusively with positive connotations, and as such enjoy a legitimacy that can explain the steady increase of Western interest in anything connected to Tibetan spirituality.

Tibetan Buddhism is seen in the West as perfectly compatible with modernity and Western values. There are thus no Western dilemmas in encountering Tibetan culture and its religion; on the contrary, where traditional beliefs have failed to address modernity, and where Christianity especially has dug its own grave, Buddhism, and especially Tibetan Buddhism, is seen as a path for the rebalancing of modernity.

The reception of Buddhism in the West follows the same rule that governs the religious market: an evolution and fluctuation of values, of the organizational cores, which are indexed on the needs of the actors. Zen Buddhism, coming into the West from Japan through spiritual masters like D.T. Suzuki, which was dominant in the West in the 1980s (Lenoir 1999b), has ceded its place to Tibetan Buddhism, which is seen as more 'magical' and mysterious, and which now dominates Western representations of the religion. Indeed, the 'cold' Zen, deprived of any magical or esoteric elements, has given way in the contemporary religious market to Tibetan Buddhism, with its rich and 'warm' rituals that are more in accordance with contemporary spiritual needs. More generally, Obadia (1999: 74–75) notes, interpreting Weber, that the Mahayana form of Buddhism, of which Zen and Tibetan Buddhism are part, had always known greater success in the West than the Hinayana, because of its collective and compassionate dimension (less present in Hinayana) that resonates with Judaeo-Christian societies.

From these new beliefs were born different emblematic movements, especially the New Age on a spiritual level. The contestation or resistance to settled values led to the formation of new movements on a *praxis* level, such as the hippie movement, which would eventually constitute different 'alternative movements' (see Hanegraaff 1996). These movements were ready to integrate Tibet and its culture as presented in the West, but also as presented by the refugees and their agendas.

The New Age and Other Alternative Movements

The New Age movement, emblematic of the spiritual market described previously, is difficult to define because it is polymorphic and atemporal. Nevertheless, New Age can be delimited as a form of transcendence-less spiritual syncretism that has the ability to ingest and integrate different elements of Western representations of 'authentic spirituality' (Vernette 1992: iv). Its history is connected directly to Western representations of Tibet as a lost paradise, and rooted in the Theosophical Society and its first attempts to connect different forms of (especially Tibetan) spirituality. The myth of Tibet archetypically constitutes the backbone of the New Age movement, and McLagan (1996: 413) speaks of 'New Age Orientalism' as the actual form of the myth (see also Korom 2001).

Vernette (1992) shows that the New Age movement concerns developing physical and mental aptitudes in order to improve one's life. The movement is not eschatological, but rather is rooted in its followers' daily lives and their ways to better control it. Lenoir worked on the main motivations of French followers of Buddhism, and found that a majority mentioned the pragmatic and efficacious nature of Buddhism for a 'psycho-corporal support' (Lenoir 1999a: 141). The same author notices that this reason is also mentioned for Tibetan Buddhism.

The perception of Tibet and its culture cannot be reduced to its New Age dimension, as the myth and Western representations involve more than that: the eschatological and redemptive dimension of Tibetan Buddhism is very strong in the West, and Tibet is seen as both a spirituality and a repository of values. But the relationship between New Age and Tibet is important to understanding the Western construction of knowledge on Tibet, a construction labelled by Jamyang Norbu (1998: 21) as 'New Age colonialism'.

The reconfiguration of beliefs in the West parallels the redefinition of norms and values, and the emergence of the movements that carry them. The 'hippie' or countercultural movement that arose at the end of the 1960s in Western countries, and continues today in alternative movements, was loaded with values such as a denial of materialism, a communitarian and cooperative way of life, the notion of global citizenship (Bishop 1989: 99), ecology and the defence of the environment. These movements are mixed in the New Age, which encompasses conceptions on new values and norms. Tibet has an important place in these movements because the values defended by these groups correspond to the representations of Tibetan culture in the West, and to Tibetan refugees' presentations developed through their two agendas.

Upon their arrival in exile, Tibetans faced Western representations of their country and culture. The refugees arrived in exile at a moment when Western societies were experiencing a reconfiguration of their own religious beliefs and a redefinition of norms and values. These societies could find what they were looking for in their representations of Tibet. Moreover, they had the chance to meet this culture for the first time. The Tibetans could then use these expectations and the myth about them to develop their agendas, and this helps to explain the successful reception of the 'religious strategy' (described in Chapter 4) by the Global Tibet Movement.

The next section shows how the redefinition of values in the West touched not only spirituality but development itself, and how these two phenomena have been instrumental to the success of Tibetans in the West.

The Development Relationship in the West

The exchange of gifts has been studied in many prominent works, such as those by Mauss ([1924] 1950), Weber ([1905] 1964), Lévi-Strauss ([1949] 1967) and Godelier (1996). My aim here is not to detail these works, but rather to describe the form of exchange between Western organizations and individuals with Tibetan refugees. To do this, I look at the wider context of the development relationship, which concerns donor and receiver countries, organizations and individuals. The most trenchant analysis of such a relationship is to be found in the anthropological critique of development. I will focus on two relevant areas of this analysis: first, the articulation of the relationship in terms of power and negotiation of power; and second, the values inherent in and exchanged through the relationship. With such an analytical framework, the nature of the power relations between the Tibetan refugees and their supporters, and the nature of the norms and values exchanged, which are instrumental in the refugees' success, will become clear.

The Relationship in Terms of Power

In the 1990s, with the growing power of development and its discourses, an anthropological critique of the field emerged, together with a critique of development anthropology, seen as the 'evil twin' of the discipline (Ferguson 2005). These critiques were born from the observation that, after five decades of development, even its primary objectives had not been achieved and, even worse, it had generated its own range of new problems.[6]

The anthropological critique of development, dating back to the mid-1990s, first analysed the discourses and construction of knowledge of the development apparatus. This Foucauldian deconstruction, also labelled 'post-modern', came naturally with the observation of failure of the development methods that had been applied up to that time. Works that follow this trend share a critical analysis of the history of development and the failure of its aims,[7] a Foucauldian analysis of development and developers' discourse, and a critical analysis of development's aims.

In his study *Encountering Development: The Making and Unmaking of the Third World* (1995),[8] Arturo Escobar embarks upon, among other things, a 'discursive critique of development'. Applying Foucault's concepts, he studies the articulation of power and knowledge in development discourse. He first shows (ibid.: 9ff) that the Orientalist projections initiated by Western countries are the corollary of the development discourse. He then argues that the discourse of development created the objects and subjects of its competency:

> The development discourse was constituted not by the array of possible objects under its domain but by the way in which ... it was able to form systematically the objects of which it spoke, to group them and arrange them in certain ways, and to give them a unity of their own. (ibid.: 40)

Escobar sums up this idea by saying that the reality 'had been colonized by the development discourse' (ibid.: 5).

Ferguson (1994: 55ff.) demonstrates the 'violence' of this discourse: it is purposely generated by the West. For this author, Western governments and organizations want the 'developing countries' to adjust to their own categories, even if this distorts the reality of the field. In a similar vein, Crush (1995: 5) argues that the purpose of the discourse is to 'convince, to persuade, that this (and not that) is the way the world is and ought to be amended'. The result of such an unbalanced relationship, according to Ferguson, is that development becomes an 'anti-politics machine':

> By uncompromisingly reducing poverty to a technical problem, and by promising technical solutions to the sufferings of powerless and oppressed people, *the hegemonic problematic of 'development' is the principal means through which the question of poverty is de-politicized in the world today.* (Ferguson 1994: 256, emphasis added)

Ironically, if development is an 'anti-politics machine' in poor countries that are attempting to develop, then in Western countries it has evolved in the opposite direction, very much into a form of politics (Maillard 2007). The power relations inherent in the principles of development remain highly conspicuous.

Hobart (1993) writes that the field of development contains a confrontation between 'local knowledge' and 'Western knowledge'. Olivier de Sardan (1995: 174ff.) studies the same fact, and talks of an 'arena'[9] wherein local and global knowledge are in conflict, with the latter being the inevitable winner. This confrontation creates a 'growth of ignorance' (Hobart 1993), leading to the collapse of development projects. These authors, even if not systematically referring to it, conceptualize development as a form of neocolonialism: the Western world still uses its influence and power to subject the rest of the world to its own will and interests. This exercise of power explains the failure of the whole idea of development, in that the target populations are powerless and left without agency.

Such a critique of these authors was formulated by Grillo and Stirrat (1997), who, after presenting the works of Escobar, Ferguson and Hobart, attacked them on the grounds that they were blinded by the 'myth of development': 'Rather as those engaged in anti-racist training sometimes argued that there are "racists" and there are "victims of racism" (Donald and Rattansi 1992; Gilroy 1993), the development myth proposes that there are "developers" and '"victims of development"' (ibid.: 21). Indeed, the argument continues, the authors under criticism do not allow any possibility of agency or response to the 'developed' countries on the part of the 'victims'.

The authors cited so far observe development on a grand scale, and a limited number of other authors have examined the power relations between the developers and the people they help on a micro-level – that is, at the level of the projects and the organizations and individuals involved. Crewe and Harrison (1998) describe the developers' sense of superiority: 'As one radical ecologist colleague put it: "It is very difficult to shake off the idea that we know more than them and accept that we might even learn from them"' (ibid.: 30).

According to Crewe and Harrison, these populations are well aware of the expectations of their developers, and respond to these expectations in order to shift the balance of power within the relationship in their favour. The populations have different methods of transforming their identities in order to please their developers, the most important of these being the 'invention of tradition' (Hobsbawm and Ranger 1992). In *The Paternalism of Partnership* (2005), Baaz observes that the power relations are inherently unbalanced because there is more at stake for the assisted population (which she refers to as the 'partner') than there is for the donors. The partners are willing to address and share the donors' expectations, but, due to conflicting and different interests, the partnership is often brought to an end and the blame for its failure is laid at the donors' door (ibid.: 74–75). These authors still see an unbalanced power relationship between the donors and their partners, but they accord (albeit limited) agency to the latter, in contrast with the authors cited earlier, who represent them as powerless.

The Relationship in Terms of Values

The critical analyses presented so far too often fail to account for the moral and ethical aspects of development – that is, the practical aims, motivations and value systems of the people *conducting* development. Such approaches have been advanced in *A Moral Critique of Development* (Quarles van Ufford and Giri 2003). The main argument developed by the authors is that critics of development do not take morality, the ethic of development agencies and their staff, into consideration. This ethic has two dimensions: first, an ethical 'care for the other'; and second, an 'aesthetic "care for the self"'[10] (ibid.: xii).

It is the loss of these dimensions that has, according to these authors, led to 'alienation and domination, the picture of which has been movingly portrayed for us by James Ferguson (1990) and Arturo Escobar (1995)' (ibid.: 270). In this sense, they agree with the post-modern analysis of the field, and describe how these organizations have lost their moral engagement during their process of becoming 'market friendly':

> Earlier development organizations had the primary self-understanding of themselves as partners in people's struggle against the unequal and unjust systems, and for a more dignified life and society. But now more and more development organizations have the self-understanding of themselves as entrepreneurs. (Escobar 1995: 270)

In other words, they describe how organizations have lost their 'soul', and appeal, as 'scholar-activists' (Giri 2005), for a return to morality in the engagement's relationship.

In his own publications, Giri (Giri, Harskamp and Salemink 2004; Giri 2005) goes a step further and appeals for consideration of the vertical dimension of development, or what he sees as the relationship with the metaphysical, of 'nature and the divine' (2005: 348). In *The Development of Religion, the Religion of Development* (Giri, Harskamp and Salemink 2004: 4), Giri writes: 'The role of religion and religious sentiments in the practice and theory of development is usually played down'.

Development is nevertheless recognized by different authors as originating from Christian values and as having become a 'secularized mission' (Giri, Harskamp and Salemink: 2). Similarly, Nederveen Pieterse (2001: 25) re-contextualizes development as a secular form of Christianity, which is able to link positivist determinism and Christian Utopianism: '[In development, the] basic scenario of the Scripture, Paradise–Fall–Redemption, comes replicated in evolutionary schemes'.

Moreover, according to the same author, development has retained epistemological, if not practical, elements of the Christian missions, because it is also a philosophy, almost a dogma, projected onto populations who have to be converted to an appreciation of the relevance and efficacy of development. The concept is also based on Christian or Judaeo-Christian notions, such as the linearity of history (Tenbruck, quoted in Featherstone 1990: 198): here, the theory of development asserts the transitivity of the conditions that led to the socio-economic prosperity of capitalist nations to different social, cultural and historical contexts. Indeed, a basic topos of development is that 'Europe shows the rest of the world the image of its own future' (Crush 1995: 9). Progress itself is inherently linked to Christianity: 'the Western notion of progress ... is a secularised and technicised translation of the Christian longing for a new heaven and a new earth' (Buijs 2004: 104). As the same author remarks, '[t]racing th[e] religious depth of the development practice makes one aware that undeniably this is a missionary practice' (ibid.).

Going further, Quarles van Ufford and Shoffeleers (1988) note how development and religion have experienced changes in their discourses since the end of the Second World War. They also show that development can be studied as a quasi-religious phenomenon, given that both theories are articulated around two worlds (a chthonian one and a transcendent one).

Development is the link between the world in the process of development and the world that has achieved this 'transcendent', developed state, which serves as a paradise-like model for Christians. Thus, 'the development experts are the 'priests' ... who mediate between the two worlds' (ibid.: 19ff.). Salemink (2008) expressed the idea that the principle of development is the reproduction of Self in the Other, in much the same way as, in the Bible, God created Man in His image.

The study of the development relationship in the West has shown that, in the Tibetan context, issues of power – seen by post-modern critics of development as the main reasons for the failure of development – are redefined in the relation between the Global Tibet Movement and the Tibetan refugees. The former adopted the leadership and the discourses of the latter. Moreover, this special relation also encompasses what the moral critics of development are calling for: a notion of self-development and the reintegration of values into the development relationship. Hence the context studied here demonstrates, by contradiction, the claims of these two forms of criticism – the integration of political and spiritual dimensions into the development relationship can save it.

Unions of Utopias

It is remarkable to see the parallel between the development of the Tibetan agendas and Western needs, in spirituality and in a reformation of the development relationship. The Tibetans could answer Western expectations thanks to their leadership and agendas. By developing their concept of *chos srid zung 'brel* ('religion and politics combined'; see Chapter 2), they could relocate their claims within the framework of two significant Utopias in the West: a 'lost spiritual paradise' (i.e. Tibet) and 'development'. The assistance to Tibetans in general and Tibetans in exile in particular is the fusion in a single cause of these two Utopias: two eschatological pursuits of a better world and a better future. Tibetans arrived in exile at a time when these pursuits were at their height, and the refugees could and did model their agendas on these Utopias.

The union of these two Utopias created the perfect conditions for what the critics of development are advocating: a re-spiritualization of development with a moral system and the integration of the care for the self,[11] as much as the care for the other, in development. Since Tibet's spirituality is seen as ontologically redemptive for the individual and for the world (see the Global Tibet Movement's discourse on precious, ideal Tibetan culture), the conditions for a moral development are created.

If the success of such a 'practical spirituality' (see Kauffmann 2007) is perpetuated, it is also because the Tibetans are successful in the management and realization of the projects given to them; and this situation, where success breeds success, could be called a 're-enchantment' of development. By this I mean the inversion of the Weberian concept of disenchantment, where Weber observed that the ('modern') world is disenchanted because religion has lost features such as magic and charisma (Weber et al. 1989). The same observation could be made with development, as we have seen previously. Re-enchantment here would mean the restoration of these features to the relationship.

Indeed, the transnational community can find its motivations in different concepts, norms and values proposed by the Tibetan refugees through their agendas: for example, sponsorship (very popular with donors because it is emotionally loaded); ecology (with an apocalyptic vision; see Chapter 3); culture and religion that need to be saved before it is too late, with the religion containing compassion and salvation. The dichotomy between the two worlds, secular and religious, is solvable in the *chos srid zung 'brel*, 'religion and politics combined'. Hence it makes no difference whether members of the Global Tibet Movement have different motivations – political or religious – for supporting the Tibetans, because these motivations are interconnected and joined in the *chos srid zung 'brel*. Some are interested in sponsoring, others in liberating Tibet from Chinese rule. Some organizations work with the Tibetan refugees because the latter have a reputation for being hard working and successful in the implementation of developmental projects, and because fund-raising will be easy thanks to the positive representation of Tibetans in the West. In answering the needs of development like empowerment, capacity building, and other concepts seen throughout this book, and in putting assistance in a religious framework, the Tibetans could perpetuate their success in attracting Western support.

For the transnational community the Tibetan refugees form an ideal indigenous population, one that has had the capacity to transform itself to Western expectations without losing an identity that is recognized in the West as 'authentic' (a major discourse of the Global Tibet Movement). In doing so, the refugees have transcended the one-way power relations inherent in development, and have acted as leaders in the Global Tibet Movement, showing the way and offering a model for the integration of religion and politics. This fact created a total shift of the distribution of power in the relationship between donor and recipient.

Reconstruction of Temporalities

A Western identification with the Tibetan plight is linked to the refugees' broken 'temporal triangle', as described by Zetter (1999).[12] This author analyses two theories that are relevant to migration studies: (1) the myth of home, and (2) the refugees' transition to their new environment. The author brings together 'transition' and 'return' theories, which he sees as being complementary rather than antithetical. He observes that it is 'the present' that links these two theories. Within a framework called the 'temporal triangle' (the relationship between past, present and future), the context of 'the present' mediates the refugees' perspective of the past (existing through the 'myth of return home') and the future (adaptation and transition of the refugees to their new environment) (ibid.: 8). If any one element of the triangle collapses and the triangle is 'fragmented', a common situation for refugees, the population endures a crisis of identity because a fall of one temporal element provokes the fall of the others.

As seen in Chapter 1, the Tibetan refugees were able to reconstitute their religious institutions in exile. Moreover, they could re-establish, in the new context, their traditional lineages of reincarnated masters (*sprul sku*, lit. 'emanation bodies'). As such, their past remained unbroken because they had *it* with them; the *sprul sku* are the embodiment of past lineages. The Tibetan could thus avoid the total dismantlement of the 'temporal triangle' that usually characterizes refugee populations.

Western societies experienced a fragmentation of their temporal triangle with the crisis of norms and values that they experienced from the end of the 1960s onwards. These societies are still experiencing a discontinuity with, or a fragmentation of, their 'past', according to the assessments of post-modernist thinkers (Lyotard 1979; Jameson 1991) and sociologists of religion (Touraine 1992; Hervieu-Léger 1993). In the same way, Hervieu-Léger (1993) describes religion as the memory per se of a population. Religion, according to her, carries symbols, norms and values constitutive of a society, and thus represents a collective memory. Hervieu-Léger further observed how secularization breaks this collective memory (ibid.: 183), which is a fragmentation of the 'temporal triangle' in Zetter's conceptualization.

Time is indeed an important notion in the post-modern analysis of Western societies. Not only have these societies lost a connection with their time in the past, but also with their present: the main analysis of present Western societies shows that people suffer from a lack of time, and feel its acceleration (as stated by the analysts of post-modernism cited above). What Buddhism, and especially Tibetan Buddhism, proposes is based on the notion of time: its epistemology recreates the temporal triangle, and techniques like meditation improve the participant's life. Meditation is indeed directly connoted with time in the West, and is a way to regain it. In such a view, temporality is a powerful marker of Tibetan culture and religion.

Westerners committed to the 'Tibet cause' can entwine their fate with that of the refugees, thus projecting themselves into the Tibetan temporal triangle. Accordingly, they do not appear to suffer from a disconnection with their past, and hence are guaranteed to share the Tibetan eschatological destiny. For Western support groups, to be committed to Tibet's destiny is not mere benevolence, but an asset for the betterment of their own existential condition, a further reason for the success of Tibetans in the West; hence the previously studied discourse about the spirituality of the Tibetans, the will of members of the Global Tibet Movement to embody 'Tibetanness', and the 'nostalgia' and 'longing for home' that they experience in their contacts with Tibetans.

A Model of Partnership

The Tibetans arrived in exile with their traditional model of the 'priest–patron' relationship (*mchod yon*), and they developed it with their new Western benefactors.[13] As this entailed joining two powerful Western expectations, two Utopias, the transnational community integrated it by accepting the role of patron. It is unique in development interaction that Western organizations should integrate an indigenous relationship. Clifford Bob describes the power relations in a partnership:

> [T]he relative power of each party [donors and receivers] to the exchange hinges on two factors: the value of each party to the other reduced by the need of each party for the other. Value means the extent to which one party benefits from establishing a relationship with the other ... *In most cases, value and need considerations heavily favor NGOs* ... Faced with a plethora of suffering in the world, NGOs select among potential clients and choose the one that best suits their own requirements ... In rare instances, NGOs may flock to an indigent insurgent that enjoys high value, perhaps because of spectacular mobilizations or a celebrity leader. (Bob 2005: 20, emphasis added)

The last sentence of this quotation refers directly to the Tibet issue and the Global Tibet Movement.[14] The value and need of Tibetans for the transnational community are very important, as shown through its discourses: Tibet is presented to the world as a jewel that it would be catastrophic to lose.[15]

The integration of *mchod yon* by the transnational community reconfigured the power issue observable in the common partnership: the donors are no longer the leaders in the partnership. According to the Tibetans, with the *mchod yon*, the donor is indebted to the recipient, because he can gain merit only through the acceptance of his gift (see Chapter 4). This is exactly where the relationship takes on a new dimension, whose description is lacking in the existing literature.[16] In short, Frechette's 'entitlement model' (2002), where the international assistance shapes the Tibetan identity, is completed by the Tibetan agendas that shape Western support. Tibetans create the conditions of their own success in attracting support; the developmental relationship is no longer about giving to a deprived and powerless population, but rather the exchange is bilateral and balanced, and every party gains something. This is a form of ideal relationship desired by the moral critique of development.

Obviously, not every member of the transnational community integrates the Buddhist notions involved in the *mchod yon*, but the relationship empowers the Tibetans, who do not feel indebted to their patrons and even have the ability to choose them: the refugees often have to refuse projects, as they are offered too many to manage (see Chapter 2). Moreover, there is a strong integration of essentialized Buddhist values such as karma (which is fundamental to the *mchod yon*) in the Global Tibet Movement, and not only by its Buddhist members, as seen in Chapter 4 on the spiritualization by the Tibetans of the received assistance. The values, Buddhist and otherwise, accorded to Tibetan culture by the New Age movement and its different vectors are also crucial to this constitution of the *mchod yon* relationship. The redistribution of power in the partnership is also strengthened by the charismatic figure of the Dalai Lama and the symbolic capital that Tibetans enjoy in Western societies: they are the 'gatekeeper' in the transnational community. An Australian senator, Bob Brown, expressed this recognition of the Global Tibet Movement's debt to Tibetans:

> Your Holiness, everyone from Tibet, you have given so much to the world. It is our job to give back to you, and it is an honour to be part of the quest for freedom for Tibet. May it come rapidly, may it come without conditions, and may we then all be able to breathe the air of freedom with you as you return to your beautiful country. (Department of Information and International Relations and Friedrich-Neumann Stiftung 2001: 4)

De Voe (1983), who examined the relationship between Tibetans and their Western patrons, was perhaps the first to suggest that the *mchod yon* relationship had been integrated into the dynamics of development. At the time of the study she described the patrons as being almost exclusively Christian organizations, which worked with Tibetans and justified their assistance on the basis of Christian charity. Nowadays, in the context of secularization, a quest for new spirituality and the place of Tibetan Buddhism in the New Age, it can be argued that Western patrons assist the Tibetans in a modern form of *mchod yon*, motivated, moreover, by the spiritual values of the Tibetan themselves.

In Chapter 1, we observed the presence of several Christian NGOs supporting the Tibetans during their rehabilitation phase in exile. Thereafter, most of these NGOs departed and new ones arrived during the development phase, especially after the launch by the Tibetans of the International Campaign for Tibet. These new NGOs constitute the core of the Global Tibet Movement, and one can observe that their main motivation for helping the Tibetans goes beyond a Christian impulse to help a population in need.

This new relationship between the Tibetans and their benefactors follows what is nowadays sought after in development, namely, the empowerment and active participation of the helped population. The relationship with Tibetans became a model partnership that increasingly attracted organizations seeking to be part of this success. For these organizations, working for Tibetans means not only being certain to raise funds, thanks to Tibetan popularity in the West, but also being able to work in a well-organized network, with a strong and empowered local partner, the CTA, as well as working with a population that shows gratitude and spiritually gratifies the organization itself, and diminishes the risk of misunderstanding and grievances.

This type of assistance, then, is loaded with spirituality, which is a real bonus in the relationship. These many elements have made the Tibetan refugees a model community for Western developmental agencies, which regularly face virulent critiques because of the frequent failure of their programmes. In that sense, assistance to Tibetans can save the Western model of development by being an example of success. As the 'good students' of development, Tibetans attract assistance in a dynamic where success breeds more success.

The mchod yon *Relationship and the Western Dharma Followers*

As representatives of a new phenomenon of religious conversion, Western Dharma followers already have a spiritual link with Tibet. Since it is linked closely with their beliefs, they have accepted the *mchod yon* relationship readily. The result of their assistance is impressive, as the monasteries have greatly increased their wealth since the early period of exile, thanks in particular to Dharma centres established in the West.

The Tibetan leadership made the same assessment about the wealth of religious institutions and remarked on their lack of contributions; the Dalai Lama asked them to become more involved in the community and to launch social projects as 'Christian institutions do'.[17] If the 'compassion in action' motto is developed by the transnational community, the Christian concept of *caritas* can hardly be observed among Tibetan refugees themselves. Although religious institutions in exile can be very rich materially, few try to address issues of poverty or the needs of the lay population. Indeed, in the many settlements I could visit and study, the only humanitarian initiative linked with a religious institution was created by a Tibetan monk to help low-caste Indians living on the outskirts of lower Dharamsala (the charity is called 'Tong Len', see http://www.tong-len.org/). The project was financed almost entirely by Western donors, and employed Western volunteers.

Some organizations created by Dharma centres or spiritual masters – aptly called 'Dharma brokers' by Ström (2001) – insist on the religious merit the potential donors would earn.

We are humbly requesting your help to rebuild the monastery so that the Dharma can spread in the remote Solu Khumbu region and sentient beings may benefit. *Just as the ocean is made of small drops, your contribution, however small, will be greatly appreciated, and will immensely increase the merit and karma of the donors* ... The [name] Rinpoche and his nuns will pray for donors to be happy in this life and all future lives, and for all their Dharma wishes to be successful. (From a monastery presentation flyer, emphasis added)

Different observers, as well as my own informants, nevertheless noticed that these Dharma followers are not politically or materially engaged in the Tibetan cause beyond involvement in their own religious institutions. According to these observers, Dharma followers lack a sense of awareness of the political problems with which Tibetans are confronted. One working group in the third TSG Conference wrote as an objective: 'getting Dharma centres to become more active in the political arena' (Department of Information and International Relations and Friedrich-Neumann Stiftung 2001: 89). I think this is a subjective vision of Dharma followers because they are in contrast with other militant Westerners. However, talking with many of them, I did not feel that they had less awareness on the Tibetan issue or less concern to do something to help. But it is true that because these Dharma followers already have a religious link with Tibet, some feel no need to be more involved with its cause. Other helpers, however, still seek a religiously centred exchange with Tibetans, who present their assistance in a religious framework. So, in a way, the assistance from lay Westerners to lay Tibetans shares the characteristics of the help provided by religious Westerners to religious Tibetans: characteristics of the *mchod yon* relationship.

Adaptability of the Model

The success of Tibetan refugees in the West raises the question of whether such a model can be replicated. As seen from the previous chapters, the Tibetans in exile managed to develop two agendas which guaranteed them a unique identity made of different elements: strong spirituality, non-violence, environmental awareness, a charismatic leader, and more. This identity was perceived as such by the main donors, thanks to different positive stereotypes in the West, as well as a strong appropriation of these values.

Given these conditions it is difficult to imagine that such a model is replicable: it is unique by its main characteristics which are not all controllable. Indeed, it is difficult to find another population as much respected in the West for its spirituality. With the exception of the Tibetan context, a too-strong degree of spirituality is often perceived as religious extremism (Muslims, for example). Other groups considered in the West as 'exotic', like the Touaregs, do not induce the same empathy as Tibetans. To illustrate this point, it is useful to detail another population close to the Tibetans. The Sherpas, with their Tibetan origins, are such a population, and their relationship with Westerners has been well studied by different authors (Fisher 1990, Adams 1996b, and Ortner 1978, 1989 and 1999). Like the Tibetans, the Sherpas are perceived in the West through various strong stereotypes. Ortner describes, in *High Religion* (1989: 24ff.), the emergence in the Western psyche, from the outset of the twentieth century in Darjeeling, of the Sherpas as astonishing mountaineers. From this image of relentless mountaineers the Sherpas gained a respect from Westerners, who soon attributed to them other qualities like strength, endurance, willingness and more. Fisher writes: 'Westerners have developed a positive image of Sherpas: that of an egalitarian, peaceful, hardy, honest, polite, industrious, hospitable, cheerful, independent, brave, heroic, compassionate people' (1990: 124). In the same way, Adams notes that in the West the word 'Sherpa' became synonymous with strength and reliability, and that companies label their products 'Sherpa' to give the impression of such robustness (1996b: Chapter 1).

In Chapter 3 of *Life and Death on Mount Everest* (1999), Ortner describes exhaustively the evolution of the images of Sherpas, a process that reminds one of the transformations of Western views of Tibetans. Considered at the outset as 'peons, load carriers' and 'support troops', in the 1970s the Sherpas began to be seen as 'something closer to partners, equals, or collaborators' (ibid.: 185) when the mountaineering counterculture stood against the technical and human competition in the mountains. In parallel, as the Sherpas became economically richer with Western support, they gained access to education and improved their self-esteem. From then on, they stopped calling the Westerners 'Sahibs', a term used during colonial times in India (ibid.: 210). Later, they even began employing members of other Himalayan ethnic groups to carry the mountaineers' equipment, keeping leadership roles for themselves. Hence, similarly to the Tibetans, the consideration of Sherpas evolved from a Western sense of superiority[18] to something akin to respect and admiration. Given this fact, the Sherpas were eventually able to negotiate an identity to be shown to the Westerners and maintain the latter's respect.

Fisher notes that the Sherpas do not understand the Western interest in climbing: do they do it for fame or money? The Sherpas did not launch mountain expeditions before the arrival of the first Westerners, and they do not share the Western romantic or male values of climbing that were described by Bishop (see the beginning of this chapter). The Sherpas undertook other activities if they paid more (Fisher 1990: 129). But, knowing that their clients want the Sherpas to be mountaineers, the Sherpas 'wear a mask' and are 'what clients want'; 'successful trekking Sherpas realize that they are, in part, paid professional actors and entrepreneurs' (ibid.: 125). Adams (1996b) also describes this shown identity, and talks of 'virtual Sherpas', thus noting the fact that this identity is a creation, a construction of an ideal 'Sherpahood', disconnected from what the Sherpas were before encountering foreigners. Going further, Fisher remarks that 'Sherpas are so massively reinforced [by the Westerners] at every point for being Sherpas that they have every reason not only to [stay] Sherpa but even to flaunt their Sherpahood' (Fisher 1990: 137). Moreover, '[r]ather than becoming Westernized or nationalized, then, Sherpa culture has been intensified. That is, Sherpas have come to value some of their traditions even more than they did prior to the advent of tourism' (ibid.: 139).[19] Another interesting point about Sherpas is their economic situation, which has improved drastically over time thanks to their attraction of Western support. Ortner (1999) describes how rich they became compared to neighbouring populations. Fisher describes also how modern education became important to the Sherpas through their contact with Westerners: 'The Sherpas realized ... they needed modern schools if they were to have hopes of dealing with the outside world in any but subordinate, submissive way' (Fisher 1990: 76). Finally, Adams remarks that the relationship between the Sherpas and Westerners goes beyond a simple economic link:

> Westerners envision the ability to become like Sherpas by becoming intimately involved with them in a social relationship that they perceive as having special qualities: 'We have brought them a deal of money, but between these people and ourselves a relationship has been clearly established that is something more than a material contract. These men are "engaged" also in the moral sense of the word, and they bring us not only their muscles, but also their willingness, their pleasure and their participation ... for deep within them is a taste and an aptitude for exceptional activities'. (Adams 1996b: 56)

These aptitudes given to the Sherpas, which go beyond their tasks as expedition leaders, help also to explain their success in the West, in a process quite similar to that of Tibetan refugees.

Nevertheless, after having noted the similarities between the relationships of Westerners with Tibetan refugees and Sherpas, it is important to show an intrinsic main difference. This difference is simple, but makes for a profound gap between the two situations. If the Sherpas are admired in the West, it is thanks to their qualities as mountaineers; the Tibetans (not only the refugees) are admired in the West thanks to their religion, as shown throughout this book. Hence, the first relationship – with the Sherpas – is ultimately about qualities that are not traditionally Sherpa (as seen, the Sherpa were not climbers before the arrival of Westerners), while the second is directly linked to the religion of the Tibetans.[20] The relationship between Westerners and Tibetan refugees is indeed constructed around the religion and the norms and values of the Tibetans themselves, all of which serve to consolidate this relationship much more strongly than the relationship between Westerners and Sherpas.

We have seen so far how the Tibetans constructed themselves, through their religion, as universalists, followers of a world religion, which goes far beyond the values projected onto mountains and climbing. As a result, the images and perceptions of Tibetans in the West are much more powerful than those for the Sherpas.

The Tibetan model of relationship teaches us that development never works better than when the exchange is equal and balanced, when each party has something to receive from the other. Since social sciences study the gift, one knows that it is never free and always engages the giver as well as the receiver. The organizations involved in development (especially the NGOs) understood this a long time ago and try to communicate on the counter-gift, such as a good conscience ('give to feel better') or a shock ('give to never see that again'). For the assistance to Tibetans, the reasons to give are various and quite separate from these traditional ways of communicating: the counter-gift is simply assured by the beneficiaries themselves and this is very successful. A businessman would talk of a 'win-win' situation. This equality is fundamental in the new thinking about development, which wants to end the paradigm of power in the development relationship: if the two involved partners nourish each other, the relationship can be ideal. The Tibetan model is a good illustration of this, even if some problems cannot be avoided. This all helps to explain the uniqueness of the Tibetan model as well as the difficulty to replicate it.

Notes

1. Lopez (1998: 169ff.) rightly describes how these fantasies also attract researchers to Tibetan studies.
2. See 'The West in Need' section, Chapter 4.
3. For the Western reception of Buddhism see, among others, Lenoir (1999b), Obadia (1999), Snodgrass (2003) and Kay (2004).
4. See Hervieu-Léger (1993), Delumeau (1993) and Balandier (1985) amongst others.
5. See Bourdieu (1980) and Touraine (1992) for a critique of the subjectivist sociology.
6. For an analysis of development anthropology, see, among others, Long and Long (1992); Gardner and Lewis (1996); Mosse, Farrington and Rew (1998); Crewe and Harrison (1998); Gow (2002); and Edelman and Haugerud (2005).
7. See the excellent article of Leys (2005) on the 'rise and fall of development theory'.
8. An original and leading piece of research that began a lively debate within anthropology.
9. Olivier de Sardan explains that his 'arena' is more descriptive than Bourdieu's *champ* (ibid.: 174).

10. A similar call was made in anthropology: D'Andrade (1995) and Scheper-Hugues (1995) together initiated a debate in *Cultural Anthropology* about the consideration of the moral and the 'primacy of the ethical' in anthropology.

11. Interestingly, as we have seen, Buddhism is regarded in the West as a self-development technique per se.

12. Zetter's subject is the Greek Cypriot refugees on their own island after the Turkish invasion of 1974. These refugees have common characteristics with Tibetans: their home was invaded, they have been economically successful in exile (partly thanks to a generalized assistance), and they want to return to a mythologized home. This brilliant article offers a solid theoretical framework and a new perspective on refugee transition and the 'myth of return home'.

13. The *mchod yon* relationship in exile was studied by authors like DeVoe (1983), Klieger (1978 and 1991), and Lopez (1998).

14. Here Bob does not directly cite support to Tibetans, but he does detail it later in his book.

15. This argument, moreover, has rather eugenic overtones: if the cultures worth saving must have something to 'offer' to the West or their patrons, what happens to those that are not categorized as such?

16. See, among others, McLagan (1996, 1997), Lopez (1998) and Frechette (2002).

17. Personal communication #25 2006.

18. Ortner (1999: 42) remarks that the Westerners at first considered the Sherpas as 'childish'.

19. The same fact of tourism or contact with Westerners fuelling a cultural revival in the Himalaya was also remarked on by Mumford (1989) for Gurung shamanism in rural Nepal.

20. Interestingly, Ortner (1999) shows that the Sherpas are also respected by Westerners because the latter identify the religion of the former with Tibetan Buddhism.

7

Challenges to the Model

The Globalization Phase

The American Lottery

After the demonstrations in Lhasa at the end of the 1980s (see Chapter 1), Tibetan officials like Tenzin Namgyal Tethong, then president of the International Campaign for Tibet (ICT), and American officials like Congressman Barney Frank, had the idea of bringing a number of refugees to the United States (Rinchen Dharlo 1994: 14). The idea was discussed further with the Dalai Lama himself during a visit to Washington in 1989. Precedents for such an exercise existed, such as the Fulbright scholarships, financed partly by the U.S. government, provided to Tibetan refugees working for the Central Tibetan Administration (CTA) from 1987 onwards. Many Americans, Richard Weingarten (the expert who wrote the report leading to the Integrated Development Plans) among them, nevertheless opposed the idea on the grounds that Tibetans would undergo a negative acculturation in the vast American melting pot.

But the Tibetans found more advantages than disadvantages to the repatriation solution. Amongst the advantages were higher living standards in the United States and better education for the children: 'These Tibetans [who would resettle] may be in a position to help their relatives and the community in India' (Rinchen Dharlo 1994: 14). The argument proceeded that these Tibetans would also be able to promote the Tibetan cause in the United States and 'contribute towards saving the cultural and national identity of six million Tibetans inside Tibet and bring [the] long-cherished goal of Tibet's independence closer to realisation' (ibid.: 15). The Dalai Lama and his government then gave their approval, and the 'Tibetan US Resettlement Project' (TUSRP) commenced in Boston. Section 134 of the U.S. Immigration Act 1990, passed on 27 October, granted one thousand visas to 'displaced' Tibetans living in India and Nepal (ibid.). The CTA acted as the counterpart organization of the U.S. State Department. The CTA consequently designated the TUSRP as its representative. In India and Nepal, the process of selection was launched under the supervision of the CTA. Different categories of people were created to avoid multiple applications, and the final allocation of visas was left to chance: a draw was organized.

In April 1992 the first Tibetans arrived in the United States. As early as 1994, Rinchen Dharlo, then representative of the Dalai Lama for America and an organizer of the resettlement, could write that the project was a 'stunning success' and that '[there are] many [Tibetans installed in the United States] who, through hard work, have earned quite a lot of money ... Some enterprising Tibetans have quickly turned to business and some even have managed to open restaurants. Many of the Tibetan immigrants have already bought cars' (Rinchen Dharlo: 17). He also wrote (ibid.: 15) that several thousand Tibetans applied to get one of the American visas – however, different informants have told me that at that time only a few understood the prospects offered by U.S. resettlement. Most of these were officials and educated people who knew the opportunities. As a result, the project became a real 'brain drain', with many skilled and educated Tibetans, especially teachers, leaving their community to settle in the United States.

Now, more than twenty years after this resettlement project, the memories are still vivid among Tibetans, who recall the project as 'the lottery'. With the success of the project, and with unbroken attempts since then by many Tibetans to reach the United States or another Western country by any means, 'the lottery' acquired an almost mystical significance. Those granted an American visa had won a real jackpot.

This lottery began what many Tibetans and experts feared could lead to a mass exodus of the Tibetans in Asia to richer countries. Since the end of the 1990s, something that resembles a second resettlement in Western countries leaves the leaders of the Tibetan community in exile with new challenges, and the prospect of witnessing the disintegration of the community. Decades after the first forced migration of Tibetans, another occurred for economic reasons, pulling some refugees out of their Asian settlements. This period, the 'globalization phase', is still going on today.

New Opportunities in Western Countries

The craze to 'go West' – initiated by the 'lottery' and the ensuing testimonies of a better life in other countries – took, and still takes, different shapes. In the community in Asia, all possible means are used to get a precious visa for a Western country: marriage; 'faking monkhood' (Markey 1999);[1] asking a foreign friend for an invitation letter (required to get a visa); trafficking fake invitation letters or buying real ones (a business sometimes organized by the Tibetan Dharma Centres installed in the West themselves), and other schemes.[2] This ever-increasing trend worries Tibetan officials because it 'spoils' the name of the Tibetans in the world by showing that they are able to lie and deceive,[3] and also because more than 250 people leave their settlements in Asia every year for a Western country, as estimated by the Planning Commission.

The material success of Tibetans installed in Western countries varies from person to person, but most have been able to help their families back in the South Asian settlements to improve their standard of living substantially. It is now common to see large, beautiful houses, of an Indian middle-class standard, in the settlements where a member of the family has left for a Western country.

As in every immigration situation, those who testify to their situation or come home to visit never talk about hardship they encountered or still encounter.[4] They represent their new country as a heaven, and rarely admit that they have low social status or menial jobs. One of my Tibetan friends, installed in London for seven years, is experiencing a hard life in an expensive capital city. His present situation is far from the one he imagined back in India when I met him in 1998. But when he tells me that his life was easier in India and I advise him to go back, he explains to me that he cannot because it would be too shameful to come back unsuccessful. Another friend who has been in Switzerland for four years is able to help his family back in Tibet. But he will never tell them that he is employed as a dishwasher in a restaurant, because this is looked down upon in Tibetan society. As a consequence, the Tibetans in South Asia and also in Tibet hear only success stories, and this further increases their desire to go to the West.

The situation in the settlements since the 1990s has changed drastically. People are less and less interested in farming because relatives in the West send regular remittances, at least as much as what they could earn through their difficult work. Thus big houses are appearing, and people are improving their lot. As one informant told me, people who were riding bicycles began to buy motorbikes, and many now own cars. The same informant told me jokingly how the next step would be an aircraft for each family. The plan of many people is now to educate their children and make them fluent in English, in order for them to settle in a Western country. The same informant told me that the social atmosphere of the settlement has changed consequently; farming used to generate a strong sense of togetherness and common activities, whereas people now are more individualistic and share fewer social activities.

Economic Development

The globalization phase is not only marked by the exodus of Tibetans, but also by the material uplifting of the entire community. As seen during the 'development' phase, international support for Tibetans grew rapidly in the 1990s and the material situation of the community improved considerably: the CTA could provide a real 'welfare state', with free schooling, healthcare, care for the elderly, and more. Nowadays, as one official told me, the CTA has to refuse project proposals by foreign organizations because there are not enough resources to manage these new projects.

The globalization phase is hence characterized by an improvement in the material conditions of the Tibetan refugee community, together with a profound transformation of the community itself. Many young people are leaving to resettle in a Western country or to work in large Indian cities. Ethnically Tibetan populations[5] are attracted by the opportunities offered by the refugees' success and join their schools, monasteries and hospitals. Before the Lhasa uprising of 2008, the annual number of newcomers arriving from Tibet was around two thousand. Since then, China has locked down Tibet and the annual number of escapees is low.

In parallel, the refugees are exhilarated by their own success, and can forget their refugee identity in favour of their temporal situation, which is not an end in itself. As a Tibetan observer writes:

> We pride ourselves on establishing one of the most successful resettlement programmes in modern history, as if the final goal were to live as 'proud refugees'. Our goal is to regain freedom for Tibet. Or have we changed our course? Surely our goal is not to be 'model citizens of the world … *We are so drunk with being the 'best refugees' in the world that we are delirious* … We have become model settlers and resettlers. (Ngawang Dorjee 1992: 11, emphasis added)

The Present Economic Profile of the Refugees

The 2009 survey showed that as many as 14.4 per cent of the workforce in the Tibetan community are involved in the sweater-selling business, which the refugees call 'winter business' (Planning Commission 2010: 56). This activity, consisting of buying wholesale garments in Punjab (mostly in Ludhiana) and selling them throughout India during winter, considerably improved the refugees' economic conditions. Tibetan businessmen send their merchandise by train or truck, after buying in bulk, to the location where they will stay for the winter. Most of them have a stall in a market, sometimes called the 'Tibetan market' thanks to the massive presence of Tibetans, and the luckiest have a shop in a building or a commercial complex.

During the season, one can meet Tibetans in cities or at tourist sites all over India, and these vendors are sometimes far from their settlements. The work is physically demanding, especially for those who have only a stall and have to sleep there to protect the merchandise. Therefore, winter selling is rarely operated by only one person; most of the time entire families work together. As a result, the first demographic survey conducted in 1998 showed that this activity involved as many as 63 per cent of the Tibetan population in India (Office of Planning Commission 2004: 18), a figure that shows the importance of this economic activity and its potential consequences for Tibetan society. The winter business is now the primary source of self-generated income in the Tibetan community in India, even in the agriculture-based settlements (ibid.: 26). As one informant told me, the local Indian populations sometimes envy the economic success of the Tibetans, forgetting that 'the refugees have merited this success, working very hard in Indian cities and markets with the winter business, with wife and sometimes children', to reach their situation. When the Tibetans come back to the settlements after their season, they 'relax', and the local people think that they do not work.

Another important source of revenue for the refugees is the Special Frontier Force (SFF) in the Indian Army. In remote settlements where winter business is not possible, like Tezu, every family has a member in the army. These soldiers often provide the main income for many refugee families. This activity is secret by nature, there are no official figures, and the salaries are not mentioned in either of the two demographic surveys.

A third important source of income for the refugees, increasingly important, is remittances from abroad. This income is often substantial, and the family is able to enjoy a good lifestyle. Finally, Western sponsors help Tibetans directly or through organizations. Most schoolchildren and students have a sponsor, as do most of the destitute and elderly. Many clerics also have foreign sponsors.

The 85,147 Tibetan refugees living in India who were officially surveyed in 1998 (Planning Council 2000: 59; the 2009 census states that 94,203 Tibetans were living in India at this date) had, that same year, an average annual income comparable to the Indian one, regardless of urban or rural zones (Office of Planning Commission 2004: 82). Such a figure, however, tells us nothing about the situation of the Tibetans vis-à-vis their local hosts, given the economic disparities in India. A comparison of the Indian rural zones, where the Tibetan settlements are located, is more appropriate, and tells us that the average Tibetan income is triple that of the Indian in these regions. For each settlement, the Tibetan average annual income is at least double that of their local hosts, and can be up to four times higher – specifically in Shillong (Meghalaya), Shimla, Dalhousie (Himachal Pradesh) and Kalimpong (West Bengal) (ibid.).

Transformations of the Refugee Community

Throughout this book, we have seen different transformations that affected the Tibetan community in exile. Chapters 1 and 7 present the different phases that the refugees went through, and how they are now in a 'globalization phase' where economic development has led to a second migration towards Western countries. Chapter 3 shows how different social values were introduced into the community, as well as how the establishment of a democratic political system and a generalized education system occurred; and Chapter 4 shows how a religious strategy introduced different transformations into the Tibetan religion.

I identified six principal consequences of these social transformations,[6] all interconnected: (1) a decline in fertility; (2) the emptying of the settlements; (3) a new social status based on economic factors; (4) a new face for religion in exile; (5) the limits of democratization; and (6) a new education model.

Decline of Fertility Rate

The most obvious change in Tibetan society in exile has been an extreme decline of the fertility rate:[7] the 1998 survey found that this was only about 1.22 children per woman, among the lowest in the world (Planning Council 2000: 27). The latest survey confirms this trend, showing an even lower fertility rate of 1.18 children per woman (Planning Commission 2010: 30). This discovery shocked the Tibetans because it is a direct threat, originating inside the refugee community, to the survival of that community.

The main reason given for this very low rate is the migration to Western countries – especially the United States – of young people in their fertile years. Other marginal explanations include Tibetan mothers postponing having children; education was only indirectly identified as a reason for low fertility (Planning Commission 2010: 28). In 2004, analysts studied how such a decline could be possible. The methodology adopted by the planning office involved research and surveys in fourteen settlements and scattered communities. Their conclusions are the following:

> Besides well-known socio-cultural uprooting, [the 1998 survey] revealed [an] exceptionally low total fertility rate of 1.22[8] ... This low fertility could be ascribed primarily to late marriage linked to the economic factor of unviable income for raising a family. The same factor seemingly hindered families from having more children, for they could not afford the desired standard for raising, upbringing and providing quality education. *No part of our finding indicates the beginning of any demographic transition where low fertility is a voluntary choice.* (Office of Planning Commission 2004: 13, emphasis added)

In my view, this last sentence was written to reassure the community about itself, but it is not convincing. Although economic reasons are rightly identified as the main cause of fertility decline,[9] a demographic transition is happening right now in Tibetan settlements in India. Moreover, the last demographic survey confirms this transition in the Tibetan community in exile (Planning Commission 2010: 13). This is similar to that which industrialized societies experienced after the Second World War. With the structural change of the economy, from agrarian to industrial, large families were not 'useful' and sustainable any longer, and so decreased in number. From then on, families became aware of the importance of education, which was being made generally available at the same time. Thus, nowadays, low fertility is a choice taken amidst the constraints in societies that experienced this transition. I did not conduct research on fertility among young Tibetan refugees, but I came to realize that they are fully aware of contraception (different ways to control fertility), and that those living as couples are choosing, under economic constraints, to have only one or two children.

It is indeed increasingly rare to see large families among Tibetans born in exile or educated in exile. Such is the case in the large settlements and scattered communities of North and South India where I conducted my fieldwork; the population under fifteen years old is composed largely of young people who escaped from Tibet. Those whom I asked about the decline in fertility gave me the same economic reasons: the 'modern way of life' adopted by refugees implies seeking the best education possible for a better life. Hence, men and women are going for higher studies and postponing marriage; and they want to provide the best education to their own children. Education (21 per cent) is indeed the second most important budget item for a Tibetan refugee household after food (42 per cent); housing accounts for only 6.1 per cent, and clothing 7.6 per cent (Office of Planning Commission 2004: 87). An exception to this trend of declining fertility is Tezu, where the fertility rate remains high because the main activity is still agriculture and the way of life has changed far less than in other Tibetan communities in exile. This fact may well also be true in other settlements in North East India, however these settlements are no more than exceptions to the overall decline in fertility.

The Tibetans, like other refugee communities, are experiencing a decline in fertility. But the main reason for the Tibetan demographic transition is economic, unlike with other refugee groups who have succumbed to factors like social depression and lack of prospects (see Office of the United Nations High Commissioner for Refugees 2000).[10] The consequences of this demographic decline are devastating, as stated in the conclusions of the 2004 survey:

> In conclusion, delay in marriage has made a crucial impact on [the] exile Tibetan population's birth rate. Out migration of the young is [an] additional factor. Both will soon change the demography of Tibetans in exile (in [the]

Indian subcontinent) to that of an aging population. (Office of Planning Commission 2004: 43)

These conclusions, nevertheless, fail to mention what could follow this demographic change: extinction of the refugees and their objectives. They also do not mention the flow of young people escaping from Tibet to receive a better education in exile and who could potentially sustain the birth rate in the future if they can continue to flee Tibet.

Settlements Are Emptying

The Tibetan community now has to cope with a second migration, where people leave the Asian settlements and settle outside the community.[11] The last demographic survey shows that as many as 31 per cent of the total population living in India, Nepal and Bhutan intends to migrate in the future: 6.43 per cent within these three countries (like leaving the settlements to settle in cities) and 24.75 per cent abroad. A finer observation shows that intentions to migrate abroad are higher for the active population: 33 per cent of those aged 20 to 29; 30.5 per cent of those aged 30 to 39; and 23.75 per cent of those aged 40 to 49. The intentions to migrate are higher in the more developed settlements and in those that have contacts with tourism (Planning Commission 2010: 35ff. and 69). This second migration is not motivated by political reasons, which is the case when Tibetans escape from their country, but by economic reasons. One official from the Planning Office told me that the refugees are looking for better opportunities, because they are influenced by 'first, the modernization introduced by the West and its example, and second, by the modernization introduced by the establishment of members from the community in modern Indian cities'. This official was presumably pinning responsibility for the present economic migration on the influences of modernity. Modernity has been introduced by the contact of Tibetan refugees with Western culture through the media, through tourists coming to visit the settlements, and through the Western organizations; but also through refugees who live in modern Indian cities and experience daily a modern way of life that they bring back to the settlements. In India today, around 100 to 150 people leave the settlements each year to resettle on their own, according to the same informants, and around 250 leave for the West.

This trend is increasing and is taken seriously by the Tibetan authorities. The community's leadership is becoming increasingly aware of the danger of such new migration to the West, whereby the Tibetans are scattered and hence have fewer opportunities to sustain their culture. The Dalai Lama, during a visit to Switzerland, told the Tibetans there to try their best to retain their culture and language and to avoid the danger of acculturation.[12]

Moreover, even if the leadership has no real power to keep the refugees in the settlements, it sees hope in the fact that the money sent back to the settlements from abroad reduces the economic dependency on the CTA and hence lightens its burden. Furthermore, a new trend observed by CTA officials is that some Tibetans who successfully settled in the United States or other Western countries have expressed the desire to come back to India or Nepal, and could hence bring back their economic power to the community, which would then depend less on international assistance. For the moment, however, no such return is observable.[13]

Inside the community, the will to settle in a Western country is seen as both dangerous for the survival of the community itself, and as a good opportunity to ameliorate one's life: thus social and individual interests are in conflict. A discourse increasingly heard is the lack of both opportunities and ties in India and Nepal, and that, since the Tibetans are refugees, they would rather be such in a rich country. On another level, Tibetans leaving the settlements are fully aware of being part of a collective plan to safeguard Tibet's culture.

Economic and educational development have contributed to the emptying of the settlements: the young and well educated try to find jobs in cities, jobs that the Tibetan community cannot provide. The CTA employs around three thousand staff, and these are the only high-skilled jobs that the Tibetan community can offer. Educated Tibetans thus have no other choice but to leave the settlement and to look for jobs in the health sector, like nursing, or in information technology (IT) as computer or Business Processing Outsourcing (BPO) technicians (BPO are mainly call centres).

To increase their chance of employment, some young Tibetans take the identity of the Indian so-called 'scheduled tribes' of Tibetan background, like the Monpa from Arunachal Pradesh or the Bhotia living in the Himalayan regions of North India. In doing so, they acquire both Indian citizenship and access to special privileges accorded to scheduled tribes as part of 'affirmative action' – for example, reserved posts in companies, or reserved seats at universities. Taking on Indian identity[14] is not well received in the Tibetan community, according to Tibetans I talked to, and is seen as a direct threat to social cohesion. I would add that if the Tibetans become Indians they will also lose their attractiveness to their Western friends. Nonetheless, more and more young educated refugees are using this subterfuge to ameliorate their lives. In order to settle in Western countries, Tibetan refugees can claim to be monks and gain quite a high status in Western societies, whereas to get a job in India they adopt the identity of scheduled tribes, which have low status in India.

The Tibetan leadership, aware of this outmigration, tries to develop employment inside the settlements to retain its educated young population. Hence, different projects or the creation of BPO or other sources of employment are being developed in various settlements, such as Bylakuppe.[15]

Moreover, 'Tibetan centres' have been opened by the CTA in cities where Tibetans work, like Bangalore and Delhi. There the Tibetans can live together and recreate a Tibetan community away from the settlements, in order to avoid their acculturation into Indian society.

New Status and Continuity of Social Inequalities

The 'U.S. lottery' in 1991 had consequences for the Tibetan community, even inside Tibet, by showing the Tibetans that there were better economic opportunities for them in Western countries. In the refugee community, families with a member settled in the West receive support from abroad and are able to improve their life, sometimes drastically. As a direct consequence, the number of external signs of wealth, like houses, cars and other commodities, is increasing throughout the Tibetan settlements in Asia. This phenomenon further encourages Tibetans to settle in a Western country. The Tibetans inside Tibet are also aware of these opportunities, and many are motivated to escape to India, from where they will be able to organize their resettlement in a richer country. Arrival in Dharamsala is sometimes seen as a stepping stone on the way to the West.

Indeed, the economic changes of the Tibetan community in exile have transformed the traditional hierarchical social system. In exile, social status is no longer based on birth and one's position on the social scale; it is now also based on economic power. I would argue that economic power is nowadays the main social fixer, along with the prestige of leadership (that is, working for the CTA), for two main reasons. First, as refugees, the Tibetans experienced, along with the development of democracy, equality in treatment, which weakened the traditional hierarchical system; and second, the collective objective to develop economically was transferred to the individuals who internalized it. As Schrader (1990: 205) bluntly puts it, '[i]f the slogan formerly was to "love the neighbour for the sake of karma", now the individual "battle for survival and profit" is taking place'.

As a consequence, to become wealthy is seen as a symbol of success, both individually and collectively, and this confers social prestige and respect. However, this is also a factor of disunity in the community, as the distribution of wealth is very uneven. In Bylakuppe, access to economic opportunities is exceedingly unequal amongst the settlers, and one can observe an important gap between, say, camps five and six, with old and poor houses, and camp four, with an Indian middle-class way of life. The inhabitants of camp four profit from the network of the world-known spiritual master Penor Rinpoche, unlike the settlers in camps five and six. In Tezu, by contrast, there are few contacts with foreigners, and the settlement seems to be much more homogenous. Almost every family has a member in the Indian army, and the incomes seem to be quite equal.

The welfare state (described in Chapter 2), financed by Western organizations and the Indian government and organized by the CTA, is distributed evenly among the refugees and tends to increase these inequalities. Hence, rich and poor have access to the same infrastructure for education, health and social payments. Another fact that I observed is that access to Western sponsors is not talked about in the community. People know who has and who does not have a sponsor, but such matters are rarely acknowledged, and the sponsored people keep the information secret. I saw rich Tibetans who had sponsors, in addition to free schooling, for their children.

The Western organizations that sponsor within the Tibetan community rely for the distribution of their assistance on local staff, who assess individuals' needs. These organizations are oblivious to the Tibetan way of sharing resources, which is dependent not only on financial conditions but also on social ones, like personal and hierarchical relations. In such an organization, I could read the application for a school sponsorship of a family I know, very wealthy, living like an Indian middle-class family, in which they described themselves as needy and without means of support. I was surprised and enquired further: the school staff had apparently validated their situation as desperate. Whether the staff was aware of the real situation of the family or not, I do not know,[16] but it is a fact that the organizations I observed take for granted the representations of the refugees as equally poor and in need of support.

Today, as the settlements disintegrate and refugee society becomes increasingly unequal, the community is less united than during the difficult times of the rehabilitation phase, and some of my informants noted that volunteering is quickly declining: fewer and fewer people are giving their time or energy to the community.[17] A rich Tibetan refugee in Nepal is often cited as an example,[18] as he is financing dozens of young schoolchildren, but his example is an exception, and many informants told me that, in general, Tibetans prefer to give their money to religious institutions.

Indeed, one important sign of wealth is to sponsor religious activities, by donating to monasteries, financing festivals, paying for private celebrations, or building large family altars. The religious institutions are thus materially developing at the same time as wealthy Tibetans, and they are also gaining power.

New Face for Religion

In exile, one of the first tasks of the refugees after their rehabilitation was to re-establish the religious institutions. This is nothing new, and Ortner (1989), working on the Sherpas, has described how, historically, economic prosperity in Tibet and the Himalayan region has been translated into the development of religious institutions. For these populations, mundane success depends on the strength of the clergy and the religious institutions. As a direct consequence of this social fact, the religious institutions and the clergy profited from the economic expansion of the Tibetan refugee community. Moreover, thanks to the success of Tibetan Buddhism in the West, these institutions and clergy became increasingly prosperous and powerful in the exiled society.

Several Tibetan monasteries in India and Nepal now have genuine socio-economic power: they control land and own businesses (hotels, guest houses, restaurants), lend money to lay borrowers, influence local communities, and represent for some a gateway to the West.[19] To give back power to monastic and religious institutions, after they had been totally undermined in Tibet itself, is perhaps the most important source of pride for the refugees (Ortner 1989).[20]

Abbots and religious leaders now manage increasing numbers of monasteries and Dharma centres abroad, and raise funds through them. Ström (2001: 70) calls them 'Dharma brokers' because they live between their monasteries in exile and their centres in the West.[21] Going further, Obadia (1999) sees this phenomenon as proselytizing planned by the Tibetan clergy. Moreover, Forbes recounted as early as 1989 that, 'according to one survey, 77 per cent of all Tibetan lamas in exile have travelled to the US or Europe, and 51 per cent have emigrated to the US, Canada, France, Germany, Switzerland, Britain, Australia or New Zealand to resettle in Dharma Centers' (Forbes 1989: 213; she does not reference the survey). These powerful 'Dharma brokers', most of them Rinpoche who are respected as much by Westerners as by Tibetans, are also the indirect cause of tensions between the population and democracy, as seen below.

In 1998, at the time of the first demographic survey, 11,067 Tibetan monks were living in India and Nepal, representing 20 per cent of the 55,159 Tibetan males who were living in these two countries (Planning Council 2000: 71).[22] This is more significant than the 10 to 15 per cent of the Tibetan male population who were monks in pre-1950 Tibet, as estimated by Goldstein (Goldstein and Kapstein 1998; see also Chapter 4). Actually, the monastic population in exile has more than doubled since 1980.

This boom has not been sustained by the population in exile, where the tradition for every family to give one male member to the monastery is declining, but by other populations. Indeed, given their economic success, maybe for the first time in history Tibetans have access, in exile, to other possible outlets (Sen talks of 'capabilities' [Sen 1999]) than monasteries alone for improving their socio-economic conditions. The religious centres today compete in exile with other institutions like schools, and employment opportunities. As a result the refugees who have access to these other possibilities tend to choose them: they do not send their children to the monasteries any more, even in remote Tezu, where other possibilities nonetheless exist.

Most of the refugees who join the monasteries are those with no other choices, or those who come from Tibet where this vocation was difficult or not possible. Hence many newcomers join the Tibetan monasteries and nunneries. Some newcomers join a monastery because they have no other means by which to live, and others because they fled Tibet specifically to join a monastic institution and to live out their vocation in freedom. In Tibet, the monastic institutions are still seen both as the symbol of Tibetan culture and of its oppression, as the clerics are closely monitored by the Chinese authorities, who control the vocations, limit the number of members, and more. To join a monastic institution is therefore seen as a patriotic act (the pro-independence demonstrations in Tibet are led by monks and nuns) and a way to save the culture.[23]

Another category of clerics, which is growing in the religious institutions in exile, are those from the Himalayan regions (but not from Tibet proper). As with the schools, they are attracted by the opportunities offered by the Tibetan institutions, as they do not have the same possibilities in their own societies. They now increasingly join Tibetan monasteries, not only local monasteries of the Tibetan settlements in the Himalayan regions, but also the large monastic universities in South India.[24]

Hence, although the symbolism and importance of these institutions has not faded for the Tibetan refugees, the tradition of each family giving one monk to a monastery has not survived, contrary to what Goldstein predicted in 1975 when he observed the revival of the religious institutions thanks to the economic development of the refugees (Goldstein 1975b: 409). This fact actually contradicts the religious agenda displayed by the Tibetans, who present themselves as continuing legatees of the religious traditions in Tibet.

My observation that the religious strategy was at first directed towards foreign supporters of Tibet, in what I called the spiritualization of received support, was strengthened by my findings in the remotest settlement in India, Tezu (in present-day Arunachal Pradesh), which has practically no contacts with or visits by foreigners. In 1969, two monasteries in Tezu housed thirty-nine monks (Office of His Holiness the Dalai Lama 1969: 46). In 2006 there were ten old monks living in the settlement, apparently the survivors of the original thirty-nine. In thirty years, not one new monk (or nun) had been given by the community. This is remarkable because the way of life in Tezu has not changed drastically since the 1960s, as it has in other settlements (especially Dharamsala). The Tezu community did not lose its faith and there is no apparent process of secularization: the old people meet every night in the prayer hall to pray for the long life of the Dalai Lama, and this meeting is mandatory on Wednesdays. The Dalai Lama has visited the settlement three times, and many of its inhabitants, especially the old, told me they were proud and happy about this. They feel that they live in a place given by their god and leader. Thus, one can notice that even in a traditional and religious Tibetan refugee community, families no longer give children to the monastery. Rather, they prefer to send their sons into the army than to the monastery, and this seems to be an economic choice.

Tezu's only Rinpoche is currently trying to build a new monastery to provide a religious education, on the grounds that the absence of new clerics is being caused by this lack. Different informants told me, however, that this was certainly not the reason, and that if any motivation to give a monastic education to children was present, people could easily send their children to the big institutions in northern India, as they do with school after grade VIII. I would therefore posit that the intention of the Rinpoche to build a large monastery is related to his wish to create a network beyond the settlements of Dharma followers, as he must have in mind the present plan of the state government to open the region to tourism.

Many observers, and even Tibetan leaders, blame modern influences and secularization brought by Westerners for this decline of monastic vocations.[25] In Tezu, however, Western or even Indian influences are clearly not to blame for such a situation: it seems that the exile situation proves that Tibetans sent their children to the monasteries before 1950 *because they had no other alternatives.* Hence, it can be said that the religious agenda is more a discourse deployed strategically by Tibetans towards their Western supporters than a practice observable in exile among the privileged population. Still, Tibetan religious institutions are flourishing, full of monks and nuns, who are refugees in the eyes of most foreign visitors and organizations.

For the Tibetan refugees, to re-create their religious institutions was a way to be linked to their past through the continuation of religious lineages. They were able to avoid a severe disconnection from their past – and the psycho-social trauma that would have followed – by re-creating in exile their religious institutions and following their incarnated rulers.

One could argue that religion saved the refugees through the way it linked them to their past, and that this is why they insist on their culture being religions above all else, and that their religion can save the world (see Chapter 4 and following chapters). The Tibetan religious culture, even when linked to the past, was always able to adapt to new contexts. Hence, under the influence of both the new situation in exile and the community of Western Dharma followers (see Chapter 6), new forms of institutions and rituals developed (Chapter 4 studies these changes). Indeed, the close relationships between Tibetan clerics and Western Dharma followers not only transform the former, but also indirectly affect the *apparatus* and identity of the Tibetan religion.

Money has a special importance in the relationship between Western Dharma followers and their lamas. Yet while this relation is something normal for Tibetans, it can be a source of trouble for Westerners. Moran remarks relevantly that the lamas are 'commodified' by their Western adepts, and enter thus into competition to attract the most foreign followers, who will confer on them prestige, reputation and financial capital (Moran 2004: 84). This special relationship between a Tibetan master and his Western followers, which can reach levels of identification unknown in the Tibetan community,[26] can lead to sectarian splits. A clear example of this is the community of followers of the Shugden deity (see below).

Some religious masters made contacts with Westerners soon after arriving in India. They thus acquired good experience in teaching their tradition to Westerners, and some made the assessment that they should invent new forms of Tibetan Buddhism, more compatible with a Western audience. Such is the case of the Shambala[27] network, which Chögyam Trungpa Rinpoche (1939–1987) established in the 1980s in the United States. Chögyam Trungpa left Tibet in 1959 and moved to England in 1963, where he studied comparative religion and philosophy at the University of Oxford. Trained in the Kagyu and Nyingma traditions, Chögyam Trungpa sought to create a non-sectarian movement, a syncretism of the different Tibetan traditions that could be easily understood by his Western students. In 1969 he disrobed, got married and settled in the United States. After his death, his eldest son, Sakyong Mipham Rinpoche, took over the direction of the Shambala network.

These Dharma centres and networks adapted in new ways, even recognizing Westerners as reincarnations of lamas or *sprul skud* (see Chapter 4). This interesting development of the Tibetan tradition needs further study in order to assess the impact of the recognition of these Western reincarnations on the Tibetan population.[28] The reincarnation of the founder of the Foundation for the Preservation of the Mahayana Tradition (FPMT),[29] Lama Thubten Yeshe (1935–1984), was found, and recognized by the Dalai Lama himself, in a Spanish boy, Osel Hita Torres, known now as Lama Osel and whose parents were Lama Yeshe's devotees (see Mackenzie 1988). Born in 1985, Lama Osel is expected one day to take on responsibilities at the FPMT, together with its co-founder, Lama Zopa. Lama Osel is said to be the first young Tibetan reincarnation born from Western parents, but others have been recognized since 1984.

Similarly, new institutions were created in exile to answer new religious needs of both Tibetans and Westerners. For example, the Central Institute of Higher Tibetan Studies, established in 1967 in Sarnath (Uttar Pradesh), recognized as an Indian university in 1988 and entirely financed by the Indian government, was the first Tibetan lay institution for religious studies, and the first to accept women. Another creation in exile in the 1970s was a new form of religious university: the Institute of Buddhist Dialectics. This institution, based in Dharamsala, is the first-ever Tibetan institution to teach religious higher degrees to Tibetans and foreign lay people and clerics from both genders, in a non-monastic institution. The diplomas conferred are non-sectarian and based on the qualifications of Western universities (bachelor's, master's and doctorates). The institute is successful and has attracted more and more students, foreigners and Tibetans in the last decade.

Finally, I would like to conclude this section by looking at foreigners and the Shugden controversy, described in Chapter 4. Western worshippers of Shugden and their Tibetan masters are based principally in the United Kingdom, and have over time increased their denunciation of what they see as a violation of a human right. These Shugden followers have regrouped in associations and societies like the Shugden Supporters Community (SSC) based in London, the New Kadampa Tradition (NKT) based in Cumbria with branches all over the world, and the recent Western Shugden Society also based in London. Since 1996, these different groups have launched media campaigns to denounce the Dalai Lama and his government as violating their religious freedom. They also demonstrate loudly whenever the Dalai Lama visits the West. Indeed, the Shugden followers argue that they have been expelled from the monasteries in exile, that their statues and shrines have been desecrated, that the CTA is organizing forced signature campaigns denouncing Shugden (the Chinese do the same in Tibet with the Dalai Lama), and that Shugden worshippers are being persecuted, brutalized and forced from their jobs (Western Shugden Society 2008: 10). Their denunciations of the Dalai Lama accuse him of being the instigator of their plight, a 'professional liar', a 'Buddhist dictator' (ibid.: 11), an 'oppressor of religious freedom' (Lopez 1998: 193, quoting an article in the *Guardian*), and so on.

These groups denounce not only religious persecution, but also its political implementation through the CTA. Moreover, recognizing the Dalai Lama as a religious and political leader, the Shugden groups attack him on both fronts. They allege that this Dalai Lama is not the true Dalai Lama and was wrongly chosen over other boys (Lopez 1998: 191), that he came from a Muslim family (Western Shugden Society 2008: 13), that he has a secret organization led by his brother to destroy any opponents, and finally that he truly seeks independence from China, contrary to his public statements (ibid.).[30] By acting in this way, the Shugden groups try strategically to dismiss the Dalai Lama's political and religious legitimacy, using every possible argument against him.

The Western organizations' perception of the Shugden controversy is simpler. In order to avoid being drawn into the religious or political debates, they declare that it is an internal religious matter that does not concern them. Those organizations that I interviewed about this controversy all gave me the same justification, along with the fact that, because they worked with the CTA, they avoided contact with institutions linked to Shugden in order to preserve their relations with the Tibetan administration. In the same way, Mills analyses the answer of the NGO Amnesty International (AI), which has received from Shugden groups complaints of violations of their human rights. AI said that these violations were not within its remit, as they were not 'grave violations of fundamental human rights including torture, the death penalty, extra-judicial executions, arbitrary detention or imprisonment, or unfair trials' (Mills 2003: 56). To close, the organization stated that '[w]hile recognising that spiritual debate can be contentious, Amnesty International cannot become involved in debate on spiritual issues' (ibid.). Through the Shugden controversy we can see how, with the success of Tibetan spirituality, there are cases where the world is 'depossessing' the Tibetans of this spirituality, actually following the Tibetan agenda of a universal religion. This is another challenge the Tibetans have to cope with, given their religious agenda.

Limits of Democratization

Tibetan refugees face a dilemma over democracy. In order to be democratic, they have to elect their head of state, but in doing so must reject their past – where the head of the state is an incarnation – and it is precisely this past that they want to safeguard. Actually, the person who most wants democracy for his people is also its principal brake: the great majority of the Tibetans do not want the slightest diminution in the Dalai Lama's power. The 1991 Charter makes this clear:

> Executive Power – Article 19. The executive power of the Tibetan Administration shall be vested in His Holiness the Dalai Lama, and shall be exercised by Him, either directly or through officers subordinate to Him, in accordance with the provisions of this Charter. In particular, His Holiness the Dalai Lama shall be empowered to execute the following executive powers as the chief executive of the Tibetan people: [here follows a list of the Dalai Lama's various competences, which invest him with supreme power]. (http://tibet.net/about-cta/constitution/)

Nevertheless, the Dalai Lama is slowly preparing the Tibetan population to elect his successor in a democratic process, but these intentions are not really welcomed by the Tibetans. In his statement of 10 March 1992, the Dalai Lama declared that, should he return to Tibet, he would hand over all his responsibilities to the new leadership in Tibet (Dalai Lama 2005: 101). He also declared in 2007[31] that the next Dalai Lama could be elected by a college of high-ranking monks, hence reconciling, in a limited way, Tibetan Buddhism with democracy.[32] Finally, he declared in March 2011 that he would withdraw from his political responsibilities for the sake of democracy, and his decision was indeed executed in the following weeks.

A real democracy would not only lead to a formal end of the supreme power of the Dalai Lama, but also to a more profound break with the past that the refugees are trying to save. Democracy would mean an end to recognition of the ruling religious lineages, and an end also of the *chos srid zung 'brel*. In short, there is an ontological incompatibility between Tibetan culture and democracy. Lobsang Sangay (2006), a lawyer and scholar who worked on these issues (and who was elected prime minister in April 2011), remarks that another limitation of the democratic process is about authority: a Tibetan democratic system should be built by every Tibetan in the world, which is obviously not possible.

Because 'democracy' is a general concept, it can be understood differently in different societies. I recall a political meeting organized jointly by the Tibetan Youth Congress (TYC), a powerful Tibetan organization (self-styled a 'Tibetan NGO'), and the Students for a Free Tibet (SFT)[33] to commemorate the Seventeen-Point Agreement (see Chapter 1). Two speakers were present, one a former minister and the other a member of the Assembly of Tibetan People's Deputies (ATPD), the Parliament-in-exile. The former minister recalled the events that led to the signature of the agreement in Beijing, before raising his voice and passionately shouting his opposition to the Dalai Lama's middle-way policy and the subsequent abandonment of the claim to independence.[34] At this point, the audience, composed of 150–200 Tibetans of different ages, origins and social backgrounds, felt disturbed by such a public display of opposition to their ultimate leader's policy choice. The former minister went on to assert just as strongly that the community was now in a democracy, thanks to the Dalai Lama, and that he had thus the perfect right to oppose his leader's or government's policies. The audience then approved loudly: some shouted '*mang gtso, mang gtso*', and everybody applauded. This situation made clear to me the contradictions that democratization has brought to the Tibetan community: on the one hand, it was still difficult to state one's opposition to the Dalai Lama's position. On the other hand, one could claim this opposition in the name of democracy, which had itself been granted by the Dalai Lama. Similarly, I met a few intellectuals who had in the past publicly voiced their opposition to the middle-way policy. They told me that they were then physically threatened into changing their position; one even received death threats. Some of them had left Dharamsala for these reasons, while others had vacated the public stage in bitterness. They all told me that democracy was still only a veneer in the community, and that it had not been taken to heart by the Tibetans.

I once had a conversation with the abbot of a monastery, who told me of his strong disagreement with the behaviour of other abbots, who were, according to him, 'falling into the trap of materialism'. He then said that such behaviour was not at all 'democratic', and should be changed. The legitimation or rejection of behaviour according to 'democracy' is something I heard often, evidencing both different understandings of democracy (some far from the Western understanding) and the power of the narrative of democracy among Tibetans.

I do not want to analyse further what democracy means for the Tibetan refugee community,[35] but the fact that the first elected prime minister,

Samdhong Rinpoche, was a conservative religious leader is illustrative of their will to compromise between democracy and their traditional mode of governance. Samdhong Rinpoche, who was elected in July 2001 with 82 per cent of the vote, declared in his first speech as prime minister that he wanted to withdraw his name from the candidates' list,[36] but added: 'I also realised that my refusal to participate in the election would deal a blow to the very first democratic exercise of this kind, *which – I feared – would make His Holiness the Dalai Lama unhappy*' (Samdhong Rinpoche 2001: 25, emphasis added). In the same speech the then prime minister declared his strong allegiance to the Dalai Lama: '[I] would like to make a pledge to undertake my administrative responsibilities efficiently so as to cause minimum disturbances and troubles to His Holiness. I trust His Holiness will consider my request with loving-kindness … The new Kashag will hold His Holiness the Dalai Lama's principles of truth, non-violence and genuine democracy as sacrosanct' (ibid.: 26). When a journalist asked the then prime minister if the fact that he was a monk had any influence on his election, he replied: 'From the feedback from people who voted for me I gather they trust me not to disobey His Holiness. *Therefore, they have not chosen me as a great democratic leader but they have chosen me as a faithful follower of His Holiness* (Himal 2002: 28, emphasis added).

In the same way, the political bodies are still organized on the basis of the three regions of Tibet and the five religious schools (four Buddhist and one Bon); there is no system of political parties organized around a majority and an opposition party in the Parliament. These limitations can also be found on the local level, where settlement leaders are still chosen mostly by the CTA, even though, under the 1991 Charter, they should be elected. By 2006, only two of the fifty-four settlements had elected their settlement officer (Thinley 1996: 13). Lugsum Samdup Ling (shortened as Lugsam), a very large settlement close to Bylakuppe[37] (Karnataka, India), houses more than 10 per cent of the Tibetan population in exile.[38] One of the settlement's significant political characteristics is that it has no Local Assembly, the local democratic Parliament defined and guaranteed by the 1991 Charter.[39] This situation is exceptional: only three of the seventy-seven settlements and scattered communities in exile are in the same situation. Yet, given the importance of Lugsam, the exception is significant. The Local Assembly, contrary to the ATPD, is independent of regional origins.[40] If such were the case, there would be problems in settlements where one or more of the regions would not be represented. In Lugsam, however, the majority of the population is from Ü-Tsang, and they did not want to lose their power to a non-provincial-based Local Assembly. Thus some stakeholders supported this view, and blocked the democratic process in the settlement. A political leader who supports this approach told me that, although the settlement has no Local Assembly, it has a cooperative, where all the population are farmers and hence shareholders. He was thus mixing the idea of a farmers' trade union with that of a parliamentary assembly.

In remote Tezu (Arunachal Pradesh, India), the introduction of democracy has been an interesting process. At first, the old people did not understand why the political situation should be changed from that whereby they lived under the leadership of the Dalai Lama. The settlement officer (an official sent by the CTA as manager of the settlement) had to explain pedagogically to the settlers, together with Local Assembly members and different organizations like the Tibetan Youth Congress, the importance and relevance of democracy to their lives. The secretary of the Settlement Office told me that even if some people did not really understand what democracy was, they accepted it as the choice of the Dalai Lama. Moreover, the same person told me how, at first, some people asked him what they would receive in exchange for their vote. They were thinking it would be as in India, where vote-buying is widespread.

Pema Thinley, editor of the *Tibetan Review*, sees the limits of democracy in the Tibetan community as being induced by the top-down process and the lack of education:

> Democracy is, from any point of view, a desirable goal to achieve. But the dangers inherent in a virtually enacted, and, therefore, an unearned democracy, must be realized at once. When people fight for democracy they know what they want. But when it is something which has been dealt out of them, they must be told what it is all about. That is not an easy task, especially when the audience comprises predominantly of illiterate and uneducated masses, ignorant in the ways of democratic systems of governance. The question here is essentially one of educating the public. (Pema Thinley 1990: 11)

The education of the public has been made possible by the creation of a generalized education system. Moreover, the recent penetration of the new technologies into the refugees' community created the possibilities for more exchanges and debate amongst the Tibetans. Indeed, different forums, groups on social networks, and websites discuss of democracy and its principles in the Tibetan community. They have opened new forms of communications where everything can be discussed, certainly more openly and easily than before, such as the policy of the government and the issues around complete independence. Then, the recent election of a scholar and lawyer, Lobsang Sangay, as prime minister also carries the possibilities of democratic transformations, as these were the main studies of Mr Sangay. These are all trends that need to be monitored in the future.

Education

Two major transformations induced by generalized education (see Chapter 3) affect the Tibetan refugee community. The first is the Tibetan ethos: the young, educated generation is developing a new perception of the world that often conflicts with that of their parents. The second is economic: the community is unable to provide employment for youth who have undergone a generalized education.

The Tibetan education system, even if still partly based on traditional – in other words, religious (Nowak 1983) – pedagogical methods, is leading to a reconfiguration of traditional knowledge and beliefs. Nowak showed back in the 1980s that the education system adopted in exile, which incorporates both traditional and modern teachings, has made Tibetan youth aware of different and new 'options'. She describes the Tibetan youth as being in a 'state of limbo ... caught between a country that doesn't exist anymore and a modernity that they are not allowed to embrace' (Nowak 1978a: 252).

This new confrontation in the education system between 'tradition' and 'modernity' is a factor of change among the young educated population. Ström remarks: 'The students are trained according to Western modes of analytical thinking which, although to a certain extent in conformity with the traditional Tibetan monastic debate, has fundamentally different premises and objectives' (Ström 1994: 841). A direct result of such a fact is that the perception of the world of the educated young Tibetans is sometimes incompatible or at odds with that of their parents, and I often heard some beliefs of the latter being dismissed as 'superstition' by the former.

From the 1960s until recently, the Dalai Lama used to declare that the Tibetan education system needed to teach modern subjects:

> [The] educational system [in Tibet, before 1950] completely ignored scientific subjects, concentrating on the study of philosophy, and though such a system might have suited the needs of the people in Tibet as it was then – isolated and unaware of the rest of the world – we feel it needs a thorough overhauling to suit the present situation [in exile]. *We need to modernize our education with the introduction of scientific subjects and the humanities, using contemporary methods of instruction while at the same time preserving the Tibetan language and literature which have contributed so abundantly to our rich culture.* (Redding 1976: 77, emphasis added)

Today, the Tibetan leadership is taking stock of the transformations that education has caused, especially the schizophrenic dichotomy between keeping the culture 'as it was' and giving students the possibility of living in a modern context. Under the guidance of the prime minister, a recent Basic Education Policy (Department of Education 2005) took a conservative turn by promoting Tibetan as a language for education and developing the teaching of Tibetan culture and history in place of other subjects. This new education policy has been born out of the observation that the youth in exile is losing its Tibetan roots, and that modern education has pushed young Tibetans out of the settlements in search of jobs, as expressed by Samdhong Rinpoche, the then prime minister, to Western donors:

> A standard intelligence of a younger generation that we were used to in Tibet is no longer there in exile. If we look back to the last thirty years' graduates, they just belong to mediocre. The community has not succeeded to produce a single genius Tibetan. This makes me worry. Back in Tibet every year hundreds of outstanding genius people did appear without any education facility, but this is not the case here, although school education has become universal, where not a single Tibetan refugee child is left out. (Office of Planning Commission and SARD 2005: 13, grammar respected)[41]

This represents a kind of backlash, whereby the Tibetan leadership implicitly recognizes that it does not want modern education any more, but instead the traditional selective one. A model primary school was thus recently launched, near Dharamsala, where the only language taught is Tibetan, where the programmes in Tibetan culture and history have been reinforced, and where the mandatory uniform is the traditional dress called *chuba*. Under the Basic Education Policy, all schools are intended eventually to follow this model.

Such a turnaround represents fear on the part of the authorities of seeing their youth acculturated in the increasingly modernized world. In doing so, the leadership also placates its Western donors, who are pleased to see such proactive measures to save Tibetan culture. In India I met several Western organizations that were praising what they identified as a 'return to authenticity', while commenting on the charming image of these children in *chuba*. One consequence of this model, however, may be that the Tibetans educated within it will be even less able to find jobs, or be self-reliant.

Tibetan society in exile has only limited job opportunities to offer its educated youth. These young Tibetans have few alternatives after their schooling: if they are not employed by the CTA,[42] they can only work with their parents in activities such as farming, or for petty or 'winter businesses', which are unattractive. The young educated people thus increasingly seek employment outside the settlements. Some join the Indian army (in the SFF), which is relatively well paid, or engage in higher studies so as to be able to have better jobs in Indian cities. Others plan to leave for a Western country to enhance their chances of success.

Another strategy is to take up Indian citizenship in order to get easier access to Indian jobs. By claiming to be natives from 'scheduled tribes' with Tibetan origins, like Bhotia or Monpa, they have access to the Indian 'Compensatory Discrimination' scheme, which facilitates their access to employment. One of my good friends did precisely this. Arriving in exile from Lhasa at the age of eleven, he made outstanding educational progress in exile, quickly becoming one of the best students in his classes. After grade XII, he sat the examinations that would have qualified him for employment by the CTA, and obtained the highest marks. However, due to 'corruption', he failed to get the position, which went to a nephew of a minister. Disgusted and dejected, he decided to pursue his higher studies in an Indian college, where he was also an excellent student (and one of the first Tibetans to graduate). Later on, a bank engaged him, and he is now a successful trader working and living on his own (outside a Tibetan community) in Delhi. Some years ago, in order to get access to the Indian job market, he obtained a birth certificate from Darjeeling, for which he had to bribe an official, and is now an Indian citizen. Stories like his are increasingly frequent, and are seen by the CTA as a danger to the perpetuation of the Tibetan settlements.

As a result of the successful Tibetan education system, financed and praised by Western organizations, there is a real 'brain- and youth-drain' in the Tibetan community. Even more worryingly for the community, the paucity of jobs leaves many young people unoccupied, in disarray, and without life goals: drug addiction is growing steadily amongst the young generation (see Carlson 2003), together with suicide. The leadership is aware that these problems destabilize and alienate the youth, who are less willing to get involved in the community and are more individualistic. The CTA's planning officer expressed the following:

> Unlike other minority communities, an *overwhelming 72 per cent* of the respondents cite the individual-based *values such as economic self-reliance and better life, as the purpose of education.* Only 28 per cent cite community-based values such as serving the community, carrying forward the vision of His Holiness the Dalai Lama, and contributing towards [the] Tibetan freedom struggle. (Office of Planning Commission and SARD 2005: 26, emphasis added)

Moreover, the entire community is becoming aware of the limited opportunities offered by their education system to its children. To avoid these dead ends and to give their children the best chance of success in the Indian context, those refugees who can afford it send them, from the primary level upwards, to Indian private schools. The best schools are only affordable for a fraction of the refugees, but this goal now seems now to be a growing priority. This discourages people from having large families because of the high costs involved for the education. These Tibetans will indeed strive to finance higher studies for their children in Indian colleges. They are aware that their schools no longer correspond to their economic development and their recent entry into a better lifestyle.

Nonetheless, the Tibetan schools, which are free[43] and whose teaching methods and infrastructure enjoy a good reputation, attract many young people from Tibet, who take high risks to receive a Tibetan education.[44] Similarly, they also attract ethnic Tibetan people from the Himalayas who want to benefit from these resources. These ethnic Tibetans are accepted in some schools (especially in Nepal in those schools financed by Western organizations), but sometimes they also claim to be Tibetan refugees, using different means.[45]

Today, a top priority of the CTA is to create jobs inside the community and thereby keep it united and cohesive. Hence the administration has launched different ventures, such as vocational training courses, but these low-skilled jobs are still looked down upon, and thus the majority of takers for these courses are newcomers. The CTA is also planning to develop projects for high-skilled jobs inside the settlements, such as Business Process Outsourcings (BPO, international call centres). Different Western organizations that finance Tibetan schools also support the CTA in its attempts to create work inside the settlements; an example is the Tibet Relief Fund, based in London, which financed the project Youth Opportunity Trust Asia (YOTA). Another result linked to the emigration of the Tibetan refugees to Western countries is that schools in India and Nepal are emptying and some officials think this is worrying for the future of the Tibetans, and so ask the question: 'Who will fight for the cause of Tibet when there are no people?' (http://www.tibetsun. com/interviews/2013/04/06/ctsa-schools-transfer-to-cta-interview-with-doe-secretary).

In conclusion, it can be said that the Tibetan education system is creating a youth that is questioning what is taught to it, in terms of norms, values and worldview. Moreover, this system is also the best vector for the reconstructed Tibetan identity; it is the place where the Tibetan community imagines itself. Through the teaching of a *lingua franca* (the language of Lhasa), and of a common history and culture, a new Tibetan ethos is being built. But the young people are leaving the Tibetan community, to seek a better future. One can, then, see this process as producing a new diaspora, which, for economic reasons, involves the best elements of the society. These young educated Tibetans become, willingly or not, ambassadors for the Tibetan cause, of a new common identity shaped in exile, even as they experience greater strain on their culture and identity outside the community.

Killing by Kindness

The Tibetan refugee community, while entering the globalization phase, has had to face new changes and a redistribution of its social and economic forces. This profound restructuring was caused by the new conditions in exile, but also by the continuous assistance of Western (and non-Western) organizations and individuals.

Today, as Roemer notes, the Tibetan refugees have not managed to create the conditions for the entire community to have a sustainable economic system. They are still dependant on external assistance, and this has even created a '*rentier* mentality' (Roemer 2008: 119) amongst them.

Some observers judge the Western assistance to Tibetans very harshly. Patrick French, co-founder of the oldest British organization helping Tibetan refugees and who assessed his own assistance in his book *Tibet, Tibet* (French 2003), and described to me this Western assistance as 'killing by kindness'. Similarly, Goldstein (1997: 34ff.) talks of the 'bad friend syndrome', referring to Western material assistance to the refugees without any political counterpart.

The Tibetan refugees, and especially their leadership, are aware of their increasing dependency on Western organizations and sponsors, of new trends of resettlement in Western countries, and of 'Westernalization' (a word one official from the CTA used to explain the widespread fascination with the Western 'way of life'). They have also become aware that these trends could endanger their objective of keeping their culture as it was before 1950, or as close to that as possible. One direct result of this awareness is the recent rise in conservative trends observed throughout the community. In particular, a former prime minister, the respected Samdhong Rinpoche, espoused a politics of trying to recreate the society as it was before 1950, a vision obviously at odds with the 'modernization' desired by the Dalai Lama. An example of this occurred when a Tibetan organized, for the first time, a 'Miss Tibet' competition in Dharamsala in 2002. The official reactions vehemently denounced the pageant because the candidates had to be seen in underwear. Samdhong Rinpoche said:

> Tibet is respected because of its spirituality and its cultural traditions in the world. The Tibet cause stands on that basis. *Just imitating the Western culture will never help the Tibetan cause – it will always damage the Tibetan cause.* That is my opinion and I am very transparent and I am very clear about it, and I will never change my mind and my conclusion is based on rationality. (Thubten Samdup 2004: 15, emphasis added)

The West is thus seen through a kind of inverted 'Stockholm syndrome':[46] the community lives thanks to Western assistance, but it does not think it is the panacea, because, according to them, Western culture has become what the Tibetans want to avoid – acculturated and secularized (ibid.).

As seen throughout this book, Western assistance perpetuates and exacerbates the situation of the exiled Tibetan community: on one side, there is a will to preserve the culture as it was before the Chinese invasion, almost to the point of being 'museumized'; and, on the other, a will to 'modernize', and to make the culture even more attractive.

Notes

1. Until recently, monks and nuns were considered by Western embassies as less likely to stay illegally in their countries after the expiry of their visas. These embassies are now aware of the traffic and check the clerics as thoroughly as they do laypeople. In Switzerland and elsewhere, Tibetans who claim to come from Tibet and are seeking refugee status are subjected to a thorough interview

by a fellow Tibetan to check that they are not lying and do not in fact come from outside Tibet, in which case they would not qualify for refugee status.

2. Julia Hess (2003 and 2009) describes extensively the installation of Tibetans in Western countries.

3. See Chapter 6 for the image of Tibetans in the West.

4. Similarly, but in another context, see Hockenos (2003) on refugees from ex-Yugoslavia and the way they deal with exile.

5. Populations living in the Himalayan regions, on the borders of Tibet, who have Tibetan origins but who are Indian or Nepalese citizens.

6. Recent literature on this subject, concerning the transformations of the Tibetan refugee community, is rare when compared to the large corpus of literature on Tibetans in general.

7. Surprisingly, this is not documented in the available literature on Tibetan refugees.

8. The same study conducted in 2004 shows a new fertility rate of 2.04, which is presented as being accurate and a replacement for the 1998 figure (Office of Planning Commission 2004: 36). This assumption is, however, methodologically unacceptable, as the study was based on a sample of only fourteen settlements, chosen as being representative of the entire community in exile, and as such cannot replace the exhaustive survey of 1998. Moreover, the latest survey of 2009 confirms the very low figure.

9. These economic reasons are late marriage for lack of income (the ratio between married and never married women is very important at 1:5 – Office of Planning Commission 2004: 13), and the cost of a child's upbringing, which has increased with the emphasis on education.

10. Moreover, it seems that, as Childs (2006) showed, the Tibetans *inside* Tibet know also that this demographic decline is for these latter reasons: collective depression and lack of future prospects.

11. This trend is not set to end, given that Canada has decided to welcome one thousand Tibetan refugees living in Arunachal Pradesh, India (which includes Tezu settlement). See http://www.projecttibetsociety.ca/

12. Personal communication #4 2006.

13. Personal communication #143 2012.

14. Actually, following an accord between the Dalai Lama and Nehru, the Tibetans cannot gain Indian citizenship. The only way for them to do so is to claim to have been born in India among the Tibetan ethnic populations there.

15. Personal communication #56 2006.

16. I did not ask further, as I did not want to interfere in such a case.

17. Personal communication #40 2006.

18. Personal communication #17 2006.

19. Personal communication #7 2006 and #102 2012.

20. Pride certainly, but I could identify also discomfort or even shame: more and more refugees – lay and religious – no longer support their religious institutions or the new monks' ethos (personal communication #53 2006). The huge monasteries built in the last few years, like the Golden Temple in Bylakuppe, the new Kagyu monastery under construction in the same settlement, said to be fully air-conditioned, and the monastery in Chauntra, which is said to have

cost US$1 million (a fortune in India), are seen by the refugees with mixed feelings of pride and shame. Pride, because the economic booming of the monasteries reflects the entire community's success, as well as the safeguarding of the religion in exile; and shame, because the critics see this same economic boom as corrupting the monks and diverting them from their religious vows of humility. I heard many criticisms directed against the monks for driving huge cars, wearing expensive watches and owning the latest mobile phones (personal communication #17, #27 and #43 2006). Hence, to the many criticisms I heard against Westerners working with Tibetans – they do it only to 'get fame and make a carrier' (personal communication #43 2006, see also #13 and #17) – there come also critiques against Tibetan clerics who establish relationships with foreigners for similar reasons: charisma and money.

An exception to this picture is the nunneries: most of the ones I visited or heard about are poor, surviving only amongst the richer monasteries. The main reason is that they do not enjoy the same capital of charisma and attraction from Western or other foreign societies, who are less keen to finance them. Moreover, few of the male abbots of these nunneries establish Dharma centres in foreign countries or have any other kind of relationship that could provide them with income. Similarly, it is rare to see nuns touring Western countries as the monks do (the ex-political prisoner nuns in Tibet who tour the West to testify about their plight are maybe the rare examples). The economic boom of the Tibetan monastic institutions bypassed the nunneries and the nuns who still live there.

21. In the West, they give religious teachings, manage their centre and/or perform religious forms of arts in order to raise money (as seen in Chapter 4).

22. This compares to only 1,230 Tibetan nuns out of a total of 43,708 Tibetan women (ibid.).

23. Serthar, a monastic community settled in a remote area of Sichuan by Khenpo Jikphun in the 1980s, has enjoyed enormous success. It is said that ten thousand to fifteen thousand monks and nuns live there, and any religious festival attracts tens of thousands of people from all over Tibet (personal communication #69 2007). The abbot also created a publishing house, which has been very successful; Tibetans welcome this literature in a controlled and suffocating environment. Tibetans see Serthar as the 'hope of Tibet for the future': they consider that, thanks to Serthar, their culture is saved and that the 'Tibetan spirit is still alive' (ibid.). Moreover, by its nomadic nature (it is located in a nomad region and the buildings are quickly built), Serthar represents for the Tibetans the freedom and authenticity of their roots. Its success worries the Chinese authorities, who see the institution as a growing power able to contest their position. They have tried to move Serthar, to forbid it, and to destroy it, but it has always been 'brought back to life' (ibid.). The characteristics of this vivid religious institution, built like a nomad camp, and braving all dangers of control and destruction, were always described vibrantly by my informants, as though it were a symbol of their nation.

24. Personal communication #53 2006.

25. See, among others, Rinzin 1997.

26. I observed different groups where individual egos were dissolved in sometimes worrying fashion into that of their lama. The followers were thus literally

hanging on their lama's good will. As far as I know, this profound and important relationship of dependency has not yet been studied. It would be worthwhile to investigate the reasons that push these Westerners into such a relationship when their main criticism of their own religious background is one of power and dependency.

27. 'Shambala' is a hidden kingdom in the Tibetan tradition, which also served for the wording of the 'Shangri-La' monastery by Hilton (1933).

28. Moran (2004: 30) remarked on the question raised by these Western *trulku*: '[We] are told that in essence they are Tibetan lamas within the form of young Americans. That is, they function semiotically as symbol and are therefore not dependent on a relationship of contiguity to the Tibetan homeland or Tibetan substance in order to represent 'Tibet'. Unlike the Panchen and the Karmapa, these young Western tulkus are not physically tied to the national–cultural matrix of Tibet or to the agonizing condition of exile, but rather signify a Tibet that has been reduced to a floating spirituality capable of manifesting outside the narrative of nation'.

29. A network of more than 150 centres in thirty-three countries throughout the world (http://www.fpmt.org/centers/). Its main objective is 'the transmission of the Mahayana Buddhist tradition and values worldwide through teaching, meditation, and community service', which it conducts through its centres and publications.

30. None of these allegations are referenced, and are only written as 'according to some sources' (never named), 'it is said that', and so on.

31. In an interview given to the daily Japanese newspaper *Sankei Shimbun*, 20 November 2007 (Philip 2007).

32. The Dalai Lama is actually now trying harder to propose different ideas, in order to observe the reactions before taking formal decisions. In the same interview, he also said that he could choose his own successor (Philip 2007).

33. Created by a group of students in 1994 in New York, and which now has many chapters throughout the world (see http://www.studentsforafreetibet.org/).

34. In 1995, the Dalai Lama asked the Tibetan population, through a referendum, what sort of political strategy it wanted. The middle-way policy won, but the referendum methods and conclusions were questioned so much by many that it was finally buried (Frechette 2002: 167).

35. I instead refer readers to Frechette (2007), Roemer (2008) Chapters 4 and 5, and Bentz (2010) Chapter 2.

36. There has so far been no campaigning ahead of elections, as the candidates would find it too 'selfish and shameful to present themselves as the best person' (personal communication). Instead, the voters write the name of the person they want on their ballot papers.

37. The settlement is referred to by the Tibetans as 'Bylakuppe settlement'.

38. Lugsam, created in 1961, was the first Tibetan settlement established in India. It houses around 15,000 refugees, according to Lugsam Settlement Office's figures (personal communication #53 2006). This figure is, however, more than double that of the 2009 survey, which recorded 9,229 inhabitants (Planning Commission 2010: 66). This is explained by the fact that, during the survey, many people, such as monks, nuns, school and college students, were not

counted, as they were outside the settlement. Moreover, the population of the monasteries in the settlement varies greatly.

39. 'The Tibetan Local Assembly of Tibetan Settlements – Article 78.
    (1) There shall be a Tibetan Local Assembly in each of the respective Tibetan settlements.
    (2) [...] Each Tibetan Local Assembly shall be comprised of members, regardless of sex or of lay or ordained status, from among the Tibetan residents of their respective settlement, who shall be entitled to stand for nomination and be elected as a member of the Tibetan Local Assembly as prescribed in Articles 11 and 38 of this Charter'. (http://www.tibetjustice. org/materials/tibet/tibet6.7.html)

40. The Tibetan government-in-exile recognizes Tibet as being the three regions (Tib. *chol kha gsum*) of Ü-Tsang (Tib. *dbus gtsang*), Kham (Tib. *khams* or *mdo stod*) and Amdo (Tib. *A mdo* or *mdo smad*). The representation of these three regions is still part of the democracy process in exile.

41. One can notice here another example of self-sufficiency narrative as the prime minister's message to his donors is basically: 'We were doing much better without you'.

42. CTA staff, including school employees, number around 3,000 (Planning Commission 2010: 56), as against 17,824 Tibetan students in 2009 (ibid.: 58).

43. Thanks to the support of India and the sponsorship system backed up by Western organizations.

44. 'To get an education, to see His Holiness and to flee the lack of opportunities at home are the three main reasons cited by the new arrivals for their decision to come to India' (Dhundup Gyalpo 2006: 9). Many of these young people will return to Tibet once their education has finished in exile.

45. Different populations living in Northern India have Tibetan origins, like the Ladakhis and the Bhotias living in the Darjeeling and Sikkim area, and the Monpas living in Arunachal Pradesh (see Gaborieau 1978), and it is sometimes easy for them to claim to the CTA that they are 'newcomers' from Tibet.

46. Personal communication #43 2006.

Conclusion

Summary and Concluding Remarks

The main objective of this book has been to answer the following question: How, after more than fifty years of exile, are the Tibetan refugees still able to attract such substantial assistance from Westerners, unlike other populations of refugees who are largely or totally forgotten?

The answer was organized from the point of view of the Tibetans, as this approach has not yet been fully attempted. As seen in the course of this book, the Tibetan refugees do not really believe that they owe their survival in exile to their foreign benefactors. On the contrary, they consider that they have created their success themselves, thanks to different factors that I have described throughout this work.

My argument has a linear structure, beginning with a description of the refugees' installation in exile, moving on to their creation of a central administration with two agendas (political and religious), then from the constitution of a Western community of 'friends' to the Tibetan success in the West thanks to these deployments by the Tibetans and other favourable conditions. The last chapter focused on the challenges induced by this model.

I began by describing, in Chapter 1, the rehabilitation of the refugees in exile, and the unique conditions that permitted them to go beyond simple rehabilitation and pass through different phases. Thanks to the willingness of the host countries to welcome the refugees, as well as the international assistance that was organized and centralized from the onset of exile, the Tibetan refugees were able to pass through a 'development phase', wherein they could secure their survival in exile and work to attain their two main objectives: regaining their country and safeguarding their culture.

In Chapter 2, I described how the refugees re-established a community in exile and developed an effective government, characterized by a central and legitimate power, and able to organize a true welfare state in exile. I also described the construction of a common identity, and a shared history and imagination based on the traumas of exile. I showed also how this leadership presented itself as the indispensable local partner for those organizations working with Tibetans. This presentation succeeded in the way that these organizations accepted the legitimacy of the Tibetan leadership and worked with it. The next move, given this recognition, was for the Tibetan leadership to become relatively independent in its choices. Thus, two factors that are considered ideal in the theories of development already presented themselves in the Tibetan example: the centralization of assistance, shown in Chapter 1, and the empowerment of the local partner, shown in Chapter 2. From this position of strength, the Tibetan developmental agency managed to redeploy, in exile, a traditional mode of governance, wherein temporal and spiritual powers were interwoven: the *chos srid zung 'brel*, the 'combination of religion and politics'. Using this form of governance, the Tibetan administration launched two agendas, one political and one religious, which were the subjects respectively of the two following chapters.

The political agenda, studied in Chapter 3, described how the refugees managed to present themselves as an ideal society, able to change by adopting new 'modern' concepts in exile while keeping traditional and religious characteristics likely to please the organizations and individuals helping them. These concepts, which profoundly transformed the exile community, are democracy, education and a particular vision of development. The Tibetans managed to frame these concepts into their religion, thus appropriating them in what seems a natural manner. This religious instrumentalization of what is considered as political in the West is one wing of their success in the West.

Chapter 4 examined the religious agenda, which I called the 'religious strategy'. Here again, the Tibetan refugees reinvented, in exile, a new form of their traditional relationship between a religious master and his pupils, called the *mchod yon*. In doing so, the Tibetans, through their leadership's acting like an institutional church, could position themselves as givers of religious and spiritual guidance in their relations with their benefactors, and this empowered them in that exchange. The same chapter also showed the transformations of religion, which were made strategically in order to match the exiles' new context, and the changes also in *mchod yon*, a relationship that has evolved throughout Tibetan history. Thus the actual *mchod yon* that I describe is not quite the same as it was in the earliest times, yet it has certainly retained the same essence. Ortner talks of 'cultural schema' (1989: 60–61) in relation to concepts that are recreated and adapted through time in a culture: the *mchod yon* is certainly a part of this schema in Tibetan culture. I then showed how the Tibetans strengthened their role of religious preceptors towards their Western helpers by undertaking what I called a 'spiritualization' of the received assistance; that is, they relocated this assistance within a religious analysis and discourse, which further reinforced their place in the exchange with their donors.

The two subsequent chapters examined this exchange. Chapter 5 described how a genuine movement was constituted in the West around the Tibetans – a transnational community that I called, following the CTA, the Global Tibet Movement. This movement acts as the spokesperson of the Tibetan issue in the West, thereby giving a serious voice for the refugees' claims, while assuring them of continued material support. The chapter explored the different discourses on Tibet and Tibetans, all tinted with positive stereotypes, adopted by this movement.

Chapter 6 studied why and how Tibetan culture, and especially its religion, has been a long-standing subject of fascination in the West, as well as how the Tibetans arrived in exile at a key moment in Western society. This was the beginning of the 1960s, a decade that saw profound changes in Western culture. These included a pronounced new interest in foreign philosophy, especially Tibetan Buddhism, and a strong will to redefine development and its model. The chapter showed that the refugees, in their relations with Western benefactors, lived up to these different expectations. This is precisely what has been able to guarantee the perpetuation of the relationship over five decades. The relationship between the two communities went far beyond a simple gift given for free (or presented as such); there is a real exchange, following the principles of the *mchod yon* relationship. The Tibetan refugees are not passive recipients of the Western assistance, but, on the contrary, are party to the exchange at the same, or even a higher, level than their donors.

This is where this book, focused on the exchange between Tibetan refugees and Western organizations, throws new light on the reasons for the undisputed success of this exchange. While a general perception holds that the Tibetan refugees had to accommodate the norms and values of their supporters, I demonstrated the reverse position, namely, the accommodation of the aided population by their Western supporters. As shown, this new form of relationship is empowering the Tibetan refugees, who are far from being passive recipients of the given support. In fact, there is an inversion of power (or at least a balance) between them and their supporters, which also contributes to their success and presents a model partnership. Hence, contrary to the conclusions drawn by other literature on the subject, the Tibetans have been instrumental in their own success, by formulating agendas which use metaphors that make sense to their Western supporters, and by respecting a form of exchange already present in their culture.

The Tibetan refugee community has actually developed, like every population, survival strategies (as soft power). But theirs were successful because they had religion as a strong cultural asset, and an idealized vision of it from their helpers. The Tibetans managed, moreover, to present different social, political and environmental expectations to their helpers. This is where the model becomes unique and difficult to adapt, as shown in Chapter 6. Such a model of partnership shows that development is not always a one-way street that flows from the West to the rest, but rather is a complex process where even populations from the periphery can shape global discourse.

Finally, Chapter 7 showed the challenges to this model and how a development relationship, even if potentially 'ideal', brings changes to the beneficiaries that can be counterproductive. These challenges can make one think that it is difficult to escape the post-modern critique of development, which see it as an anti-political machine. This also reminds us that a gift is never free, as anthropology has long shown. These challenges now have to be dealt with by the Tibetan community in exile in order to prepare for the future.

Perspectives for the Future: Is Compassion Enough?

As seen in the book, the Tibetan refugees quickly passed through the rehabilitation phase, one in which many other refugee communities remain stuck. In entering into a globalization phase, they also had to confront new challenges that could threaten their two main objectives: to regain the freedom of their country, and to save their culture.

The challenge for the Tibetans was already postulated by Western friends in 1967, less than ten years after the arrival of the first exiles:

> [T]he problem of the Tibetan refugees calls not only for rehabilitation but also for an extensive programme *to keep alive the living traditions* of the manifold and rich cultural heritage of Tibet. At the same time the refugees *must assimilate* and *absorb* all the best that science, technology and the modern concepts of man and society have to offer, and incorporate them within the framework of the traditional values of the Tibetan people. (The Tibet Society 1967: 38, emphasis added)

As shown in this book, the Tibetan refugee model is a unique material success, as well as a success in terms of image and awareness. The Tibetan plight has not been forgotten on the international stage even after more than fifty years, unlike so many other refugee stories (to cite only one, the Bhutanese refugees in Nepal – the closest refugee community to the Tibetans). Politically, however, the success of the refugees is less obvious, and might even be considered a failure, as the political situation has failed to evolve at all in fifty years. More worrying still, for the future of the community, are the flight and relocation of members in the West, a falling fertility rate, and unemployed youth, plus other challenges. As seen in Chapter 7, in order to save their culture, the Tibetans will have to deal with these challenges as soon as possible. In the meantime, the political situation seems to be more and more desperate for the Tibetans inside their country, as the self-immolations continue to increase.

Today, the incarnation of spiritual and temporal power through the Dalai Lama, the *chos srid zung 'brel*, still stands at the heart of the Tibetan issue.

The two entities fighting around this issue, practically and symbolically, have opposing understandings of the Dalai Lama's power; the Chinese authorities see the Dalai Lama as a political leader, whereas the Western countries acknowledge him as a spiritual leader. Neither side, however, recognizes the *chos srid zung 'brel*, a concept not compatible with their political concepts. This is to the despair of Tibetan intellectuals like Jamyang Norbu (2004), who note that the compassion shown by Western supporters translates itself too often as mere material assistance rather than political help.

The articulation of the Tibetan leader's power is central to the future of Tibetans. The Dalai Lama has already understood this fact, as shown during the events in Tibet in March 2008 and the subsequent Chinese repression, when he announced that he would resign his temporal power, a decision he implemented three years later. Research is needed on this current transition to a new form of power in the community, at a time when challenges to the power of the Dalai Lama can be seen.

One challenge that has arisen from this situation deals with the generation born in exile, who do not follow the Dalai Lama's stated aim of a Tibetan autonomy inside the People's Republic of China. Hence, the Tibetan Youth Congress (TYC) is still fighting for independence. Moreover, a certain attraction to violence can be seen amongst this youth, as expressed by many of my informants, but respect for the Dalai Lama still holds them back. The self-immolations which continue to happen mostly inside Tibet show also that many Tibetans consider the situation as desperate and are ready to give their lives to settle the issue. This tragic wave leaves many people speechless, and even the Dalai Lama has not yet taken a clear position towards these suicides. Time is needed to fully understand what they involve for the Tibetan population, both inside and outside Tibet.

Another risk for the future looms over the period that will follow the death of the Dalai Lama, nearly eighty years old at the time of writing (b. 1935). Even if he chooses to reincarnate, under conditions still to be decided by him, the months or years between his death and the proclamation of a successor will be filled with uncertainty. As seen throughout this book, the Tibetan success owes a great deal to the fourteenth Dalai Lama's personality, legitimacy, charisma and world popularity. The Dalai Lama is not only the strongest link between the refugees and the Tibetans living in Tibet, and a leader recognized as a world spiritual figure, but is also, as many Indian observers have told me, the reason why India is still tolerant towards the Tibetan refugees – and other observers consider he is the reason why China has not crushed the Tibetan freedom movements more harshly. Without the Dalai Lama, these countries could drastically change their dispositions towards the Tibetans. The continued tolerance of India towards the refugees without the Dalai Lama remains a topic of considerable apprehension. Today, the 17th Karmapa, Ogyen Trinley Dorje (b. 1985), who arrived in India from

Tibet in 2000, is thought to many Westerners to be the spiritual heir of the Dalai Lama. These people project many of the qualities they attribute to the Dalai Lama onto the Karmapa, but it is difficult to assess right now if he will be able to fulfil the same role.

Another issue to be faced by the refugees is their relationship with the Tibetans living in Tibet. This is increasingly a matter of bitterness, as I could observe during my fieldwork. With the economic development of the refugees and the consequent transformations in their community, the gap between them and their compatriots is widening. The difference between the refugees installed in exile and the 'newcomers' is also obvious, and easily observable in the settlements. During my field observations in Tibet, I often heard recriminations against the refugees, who were accused of having lost their objectives in the process of their material development, and, worse still, of keeping the Western assistance and awareness for themselves.[1] If the two communities are ever to live together again, they will surely first have to resolve these differences and areas of mutual incomprehension.

Finally, the future development of relations between the Tibetans and their helpers must face the possibility of dissolution of one community into the other (the likely end of such relations); an alternative would be if the Tibetans prove able to secure sufficient freedom within these relations to preserve their identity whilst nonetheless maintaining foreign support. For Amartya Sen, the Bengali economist and winner of the 1998 Nobel Prize in Economics, development is not to be seen in purely economic terms, but rather in terms of individual freedom and capabilities. He writes:

> Seeing development in terms of the substantive freedoms of people has far-reaching implications for our understanding of the process of development and also for the ways and means of promoting it. On the evaluative side, this involves the need to assess the requirements of development in terms of *removing the unfreedoms front which the members of the society may suffer. The process of development, in this view, is not essentially different from the history of overcoming these unfreedoms.* While this history is not by any means unrelated to the process of economic growth and [the] accumulation of physical and human capitals, its reach and coverage go much beyond these variables. (Sen 1999: 33, emphasis added)

Poverty is seen by Sen as something generated not only by low income, but by the deprivation of capabilities and liberties (ibid.: 87).

It seems that, considering the entirety of Tibetan society, the theory developed by Sen is justified: the 'unfreedoms' of Tibetans living inside and outside Tibet mean that, even with the help of foreign friends, their future remains at risk. Indeed, neither community of Tibetans has any political power over its future, and both are thus strongly constrained. This is actually the biggest risk for their future and their two objectives: to keep

Tibetan culture alive and to regain their country. And therefore it seems that compassion alone is not enough.

Notes

1. Frechette has already written on the appropriation of Western assistance to the refugees. This phenomenon is not only fuelled by the refugees, but also by the Global Tibet Movement. A common argument in the West states that 'the Tibetans are suffering; support the refugees'. Frechette describes this fact, analysing Richard Gere's request to the U.S. Senate to finance the refugees after presenting the situation in Tibet: 'Gere's statement here demonstrates a very interesting jump in logic, typical of many "friends of Tibet" organizations. Tibetans in Tibet, the argument follows, are suffering intolerably under Chinese rule; therefore Tibetans in exile should be assisted. Why does [it] not seem incongruous to "friends of Tibet" that the Tibetans suffering in Tibet are not the ones who receive assistance, and that the Tibetans in exile, most of whom, born in exile, have never suffered under Chinese rule are the ones who do' (Frechette 1997: 148).

Bibliography

Adams, V. 1996a. 'Karaoke as Modern Lhasa, Tibet: Western Encounters with Cultural Politics', *Cultural Anthropology* 11(4): 510–46.

———. 1996b. *Tigers of the Snow and other Virtual Sherpas: An Ethnography of Himalayan Encounters.* Princeton, NJ: Princeton University Press.

Al-Rasheed, M. 1994. 'The Myth of Return: Iraqi Arab and Assyrian Refugees in London', *Journal of Refugees Studies* 7(2/3): 199–219.

Anand, D. 2002. 'A Guide to Little Lhasa: The Role of Symbolic Geography of Dharamsala in Constituting Tibetan Diasporic Identity', in P.C. Klieger (ed.), *Tibet, Self, and the Tibetan Diaspora: Proceedings of the Ninth Seminar of the International Association for Tibetan Studies.* Leiden, The Netherlands and Boston, MA: Brill, pp. 11–36.

———. 2003. 'A Contemporary Story of "Diaspora": The Tibetan Version', *Diaspora* 12(2): 211–29.

Anderson, B. 1991. *Imagined Communities: Reflections on the Origin and Spread of Nationalism.* London: Verso.

Appadurai, A. 1990. 'Disjuncture and Difference in the Global Cultural Economy', in M. Featherstone, *Global Culture: Nationalism, Globalization and Modernity. A Theory, Culture and Society Special Issue.* London: Sage, pp. 295–310.

———. 1996. *Modernity at Large: Cultural Dimensions of Globalization.* Minneapolis and London: University of Minnesota Press.

Ardley, J. 2000. 'Violent Compassion: Buddhism and Resistance in Tibet'. Paper for the Political Studies Association-UK 50th Annual Conference, 10–13 April, London.

———. 2003. *The Tibetan Independence Movement: Political, Religious and Gandhian Perspectives.* London: Routledge.

Avedon, J.F. 1994. *In Exile from the Land of Snows: The Dalai Lama and Tibet since the Chinese Conquest.* New York: Harper Perennial.

Baaz, M.E. 2005. *The Paternalism of Partnership: A Postcolonial Reading of Identity in Development Aid.* London: Zed Books.

Balandier, G. 1985. *Le détour: pouvoir et modernité.* Paris: Fayard.

Bangsbo, E. 2004. *Teaching and Learning in Tibet: A Review of Research and Policy Publications.* Nordic Institute of Asian Studies Press.

Barnett, R. 2001. '"Violated Specialness": Western Political Representations of Tibet', in T. Dodin and H. Räther (eds), *Imagining Tibet: Perceptions, Projections, and Fantasies.* Boston: Wisdom Publications, pp. 269–316.

——. 2003. 'A City, its Visitors, and the Odour of Development', in F. Pommaret (ed.), *Lhasa in the Seventeenth Century: The Capital of the Dalai Lamas*. Leiden, The Netherlands and Boston, MA: Brill, pp. 199–226.

——. 2006. *Lhasa: Streets with Memories*. New York: Columbia University Press.

Barnett, R., and S. Akiner. 1994. *Resistance and Reform in Tibet*. London: Hurst.

Battacharya, T. 1981. Tour Report: ORS-38. OXFAM.

Bentz, A.S. 2010. *Les réfugiés tibétains en Inde – Nationalisme et exil*. Paris: PUF.

Bhabha, H.K. 1994. *The Location of Culture*. London: Routledge.

Bhattacharjea, A. 1994. *Tibetans in Exile: The Democratic Vision*. New Delhi: Tibetan Parliamentary and Policy Research Centre.

Bishop, P. 1989. *The Myth of Shangri-La: Tibet, Travel Writing and the Western Creation of Sacred Landscape*. London: Athlone.

——. 2000. 'Caught in the Crossfire: Tibet, Media and Promotional Culture Tibet in the World Media', *Media, Culture & Society* 22(5): 645–64.

Bob, C. 2002. 'Merchants of Morality', *Foreign Policy* (March–April): 36–45.

——. 2005. *The Marketing of Rebellion: Insurgents, Media and International Activism*. Cambridge: Cambridge University Press.

Bourdieu, P. 1979. *La distinction: critique sociale du jugement*. Paris: Editions de Minuit.

——. 1980. *Le sens pratique*. Paris: Editions de Minuit.

Buijs, G.J. 2004. 'Religion and Development', in A.K. Giri, A. van Harskamp and O. Salemink (eds), *The Development of Religion, the Religion of Development*. Delft: Eburon, pp. 101–8.

Burman, B.R. 1979. *Religion and Politics in Tibet*. New Delhi: Vikas.

Calkowski, M. 1997. 'The Tibetan Diaspora and the Politics of Performance', in F. Korom, *Tibetan Culture in the Diaspora, Proceedings of the 7th Seminar of the International Association for Tibetan Studies*. Vienna: Verlag der Österreichischen Akademie der Wissenschaften 4: pp. 51–58.

Cantwell, C. 2001. 'Reflections on Ecological Ethics and the Tibetan Earth Ritual', *Eastern Buddhist* 33(1): 106–27.

Carlson, C. 2003. 'Substance Abuse Among Second-Generation Tibetan Refugees Living in India'. Emory-IBD Tibetan Studies Program, Dharamsala, India.

Cassinelli, C.W., and R.B. Ekvall. 1969. *A Tibetan Principality: The Political System of Sa sKya*. Ithaca, NY: Cornell University Press.

Castles, S., and M.J. Miller. 1998. *The Age of Migration: International Population Movements in the Modern World*. Basingstoke: Palgrave.

Central Relief Committee for Tibetans. 1960. *Tibetan Refugee Relief and Rehabilitation*. New Delhi.

——. 1961. *Story of the Tibetan Refugees*. New Delhi.

Central Tibetan Relief Committee. 2003. *His Holiness the Dalai Lama's Central Tibetan Relief Committee. Building Sustainable Communities in Exile*. Dharamsala.

Childs, G. 2006. 'Tibetan Transitions: Fertility Declines in Historical, Sociocultural, and Political Perspectives'. Paper given at the 10th Conference of the International Association for Tibetan Studies, Bonn, Germany.

Clarke, G.E. 1998. *Development, Society and Environment in Tibet. Papers presented at a Panel of the 7th Seminar of the International Association for Tibetan Studies, Graz 1995*. Vienna: Verlag des Osterreichischen Akademie der Wissenschaften.

Clifford, J. 1983. 'On Ethnographic Authority', *Representations* 1(2): 118–46.

——. 1988. *The Predicament of Culture: Twentieth-Century Ethnography, Literature and Art.* Cambridge, MA and London: Harvard University Press.

——. 1997. *Routes: Travel and Translation in the Late Twentieth Century.* Cambridge, MA and London: Harvard University Press.

Clifford, J., G.E. Marcus et al. 1986. *Writing Culture: The Poetics and Politics of Ethnography.* Berkeley and London: University of California Press.

Congdon, D.J. 2007. '"Tibet Chic": Myth, Marketing, Spirituality and Politics in Musical Representations of Tibet in the United States'. Ph.D. Pittsburgh: University of Pittsburgh.

Conway, J.S. 1975. 'The Tibetan Community in Exile', *Pacific Affairs* 48(1): 74–86.

Crewe, E., and E. Harrison. 1998. *Whose Development? An Ethnography of Aid.* London: Zed Books.

Crush, J.S. 1995. 'Imagining Development', in J.S. Crush, *Power of Development.* London: Routledge, pp. 1–26.

Dalai Lama. (1962) 1997. *My Land and my People: The Original Autobiography of His Holiness the Dalai Lama of Tibet.* New York: Warner Books.

——. 1995. *Speeches, Statements, Articles, Interviews. 1987 to June 1995.* Dharamsala: Department of Information and International Relations, CTA.

——. 2002. *Love, Kindness and Universal Responsibility.* New Delhi: Paljor Publications.

——. 2005. *Tibet and the Tibetan People's Struggle.* Dharamsala: Department of Information and International Relations, CTA.

D'Andrade, R. 1995. 'Moral Models in Anthropology', *Cultural Anthropology* 36(3): 399–408.

David-Néel, A. (1929) 1971. *Magic and Mystery in Tibet.* London: Corgi.

Dawa Norbu. 1987. *Red Star over Tibet.* London: Oriental University Press.

——. 1999. 'Is Tibetan Culture Congruent with Modernity?', *Tibetan Review* 34(2): 8–14.

——. 2001. 'Refugees from Tibet: Structural Causes of Successful Settlements', *Tibet Journal* 26(2): 3–25.

Delumeau, J. 1993. *Le fait religieux.* Paris: Fayard.

Department of Education. 2005. *Basic Education Policy for Tibetans in Exile.* Dharamsala: CTA.

Department of Information and International Relations. 1996. *The Mongols and Tibet: A Historical Assessment of Relations between the Mongol Empire and Tibet.* Dharamsala: CTA.

Department of Information and International Relations and Friedrich-Neumann Stiftung. 1996. *Second International Conference of TSGs – Germany June 1996 – A Report.* New Delhi: Friedrich-Neumann Stiftung.

——. 2001. *Third International Conference of TSGs – Berlin Germany 2000. A Report.* New Delhi: Friedrich-Neumann Stiftung.

Department of Religion and Culture. 1998. *The Worship of Shugden: Documents Related to a Tibetan Controversy.* Dharmasala: Central Tibetan Administration.

De Voe, D.M. 1981. 'Framing Refugees as Clients', *International Migration Review,* XV(1–2): 88–94.

——. 1983. 'Survival of a Refugee Culture: The Long-term Gift Exchange between Tibetan Refugees and Western Donors'. Ph.D. Berkeley: University of California.

_____. 1987. 'Keeping Refugee Status: A Tibetan Perspective', in E. Colson and S.M. Morgan, *People in Upheaval.* Staten Island, NY: Center for Migration Studies, pp. 54–65.

Dhundup Gyalpo. 2006. 'State of Buddhism in Tibet'; *Tibetan Bulletin* (Jan–Feb): 7–10.

Dorjee Thinley. 2005. *Souvenir. His Holiness the 14th Dalai Lama of Tibet.* Dharamsala: The Department of Information and International Relations.

Dreyfus, G. 1998. 'The Shuk-den Affair: History and Nature of a Quarrel', *Journal of the International Association of Buddhist Studies* 21(2): 227–69.

_____. 2002. 'Tibetan Religious Nationalism: Western Fantasy or Empowering Vision?', in P.C. Klieger (ed.), *Tibet, Self, and the Tibetan Diaspora: Proceedings of the Ninth Seminar of the International Association for Tibetan Studies.* Leiden, The Netherlands and Boston, MA: Brill, pp. 37–56.

Dunham, M. 2005. *Buddha's Warriors: The Story of the CIA-backed Tibetan Freedom Fighters, the Chinese Invasion, and the Ultimate Fall of Tibet.* New Delhi: Penguin India.

Durkheim, E. (1912) 1995. *The Elementary Forms of Religious Life.* Trans. K.E. Fields. New York: Free Press.

Edelman, M., and A. Haugerud. 2005. *The Anthropology of Development and Globalization: From Classical Political Economy to Contemporary Neoliberalism.* Malden, MA and Oxford: Blackwell.

Escobar, A. 1995. *Encountering Development: The Making and Unmaking of the Third World.* Princeton, NJ: Princeton University Press.

Evin, F. 2013. 'La méditation modifie certaines zones du cerveau'. *Le Monde,* 12 October.

Featherstone, M. 1990. *Global Culture: Nationalism, Globalization and Modernity, A Theory, Culture and Society Special Issue.* London: Sage.

Federation of Tibetan Co-operative in India Ltd. 2006. 'Acquisition of Two Hotels and the Export Unit of Tibetan Refugees Self-Help Handicraft. A Business Plan'.

Ferguson, J. 1994. *The Anti-Politics Machine: "Development", Depoliticization, and Bureaucratic Power in Lesotho.* Minneapolis and London: University of Minnesota Press.

_____. 2005. 'Anthropology and Its Evil Twin: "Development" in the Constitution of a Discipline', in M. Edelman and A. Haugerud, *The Anthropology of Development and Globalization: From Classical Political Economy to Contemporary Neoliberalism.* Malden, MA and Oxford: Blackwell, pp. 140–54.

Fischer, A.M. 2005. *State Growth and Social Exclusion in Tibet: Challenges of Recent Economic Growth.* Copenhagen: NIAS.

_____. 2013. *The Disempowered Development of Tibet in China: A Study in the Economics of Marginalization.* Lanham, MD: Lexington Books.

Fisher, J.F. 1990. *Sherpas: Reflections on Change in Himalayan Nepal.* Berkeley: University of California Press.

Forbes, A. 1989. *Settlements of Hope: An Account of Tibetan Refugees in Nepal.* Cambridge, MA: Cultural Survival.

Foucault, M., and C. Gordon. 1980. *Power / Knowledge: Selected Interviews and Other Writings, 1972-1977.* New York: Pantheon Books.

Frechette, A. 1997. 'Statelessness and Power: Transformational Entitlements among Tibetan Exiles in Kathmandu, Nepal'. Ph.D. Cambridge, MA: University of Harvard.

———. 2002. *Tibetans in Nepal: The Dynamics of International Assistance among a Community in Exile.* New York and Oxford: Berghahn Books.

———. 2007. 'Democracy and Democratization among Tibetans in Exile', *The Journal of Asian Studies* 66(1): 97–127.

French, P. 2003. *Tibet, Tibet: A Personal History of a Lost Land.* London: HarperCollins.

Fromm, E., and R. Funk. 1995. *The Essential Fromm: Life between Having and Being.* New York: Continuum.

Fürer-Haimendorf, C. v. 1990. *The Renaissance of Tibetan Civilization.* Oracle, AZ: Synergetic Press.

Gaborieau, M. 1978. *Le Népal et ses populations.* Paris: Editions Complexe.

Gardner, K., and D. Lewis. 1996. *Anthropology, Development and the Post-modern Challenge.* London: Pluto.

Gellner, E. 1983. 'Nationalism as a Product of Industrial Society', in M. Guibernau and J. Rex, *The Ethnicity Reader.* Cambridge: Polity Press, pp. 64–79.

Geshe Kelsang Gyatso. 2002. *Universal Compassion: Transforming your Life through Love and Compassion.* Glen Spey, NY: Tharpa Publications.

Giri, A.K. 2005. *Reflections and Mobilizations: Dialogues with Movements and Voluntary Organizations.* New Delhi and London: SAGE.

Giri, A.K., A. van Harskamp and O. Salemink (eds). 2004. *The Development of Religion, the Religion of Development.* Delft: Eburon.

Godelier, M. 1996. *L'énigme du don.* Paris: Fayard.

Goffman, E. 1959. *The Presentation of Self in Everyday Life.* Garden City, NY: Doubleday and Company.

Goldstein, M.C. 1968. 'An Anthropological Study of the Tibetan Political System'. Ph.D. Thesis. Seattle: University of Washington.

———. 1971a. 'The Balance between Centralisation and Decentralisation in the Traditional Tibetan Political System', *Central Asiatic Journal* 15: 170–82.

———. 1971b. 'Stratification, Polyandry and Family Structure in Central Tibet', *Southwestern Journal of Anthropology* 27: 64–74.

———. 1973. 'The Circulation of Estates in Tibet', *Journal of Asian Studies* XXXII(3): 445–55.

———. 1975a. 'Tibetan Refugees in South India: A New Face to the Indo-Tibetan Interface', *Tibet Society Bulletin* 9: 12–29.

———. 1975b. 'Ethno-genesis and Resource Competition among Tibetan Refugees in South India', in L.A. Despres (ed.), *International Congress of Anthropological and Ethnological Sciences (9th, Chicago, 1973). Ethnicity and Resource Competition in Plural Societies.* The Hague: Mouton, pp. 159–86.

———. 1989. *A History of Modern Tibet, 1913–1951: The Demise of the Lamaist State.* Berkeley: University of California Press.

———. 1994. 'Change, Conflict and Continuity among a Community of Nomadic Pastoralists: A Case Study from Western Tibet, 1950–1990', in R. Barnett, *Resistance and Reform in Tibet.* London: Hurst, pp. 76–111.

———. 1997. *The Snow Lion and the Dragon: China, Tibet, and the Dalai Lama.* Berkeley and London: University of California Press.

Goldstein, M.C., and M. Kapstein. 1998. *Buddhism in Contemporary Tibet: Religious Revival and Cultural Identity.* Berkeley and London: University of California Press.

Gow, D. 2002. 'Anthropology and Development: Evil Twin or Moral Narrative?', *Human Organization* 61(4): 299–313.

Grillo, R.D. and R.L. Stirrat. 1997. *Discourses of Development: Anthropological Perspectives.* Oxford: Berg.

Groupe France – Tibet. 2005. Le Tibet en exil: A l'école de la démocratie: Rapport du groupe parlementaire France – Tibet.

Gupta, A., and J. Ferguson. 1992. 'Beyond "Culture": Space, Identity and the Politics of Difference', *Cultural Anthropology* 7(1): 6–23.

____. 1997. *Culture, Power, Place: Explorations in Critical Anthropology.* Durham, NC and London: Duke University Press.

Hall, S. 1990. 'Cultural Identity and Diaspora', in J. Rutherford, *Identity: Community, Culture, Difference.* London: Lawrence, pp. 222–37.

Hanegraaff, W.J. 1996. *New Age Religion and Western Culture: Esotericism in the Mirror of Secular Thought.* Leiden and New York: E.J. Brill.

Harris, C. 2012. *The Museum on the Roof of the World: Art, Politics, and the Representation of Tibet.* Chicago and London: University of Chicago Press.

Hervieu-Léger, D. 1993. *La religion pour mémoire.* Paris: Editions du Cerf.

Hess, J.M. 2003. 'Stateless Citizens: Culture, Nation and Identity in the Expanding Tibetan Diaspora'. Ph.D. thesis. Albuquerque: The University of New Mexico.

____. 2009. *Immigrant Ambassadors: Citizenship and Belonging in the Tibetan Diaspora.* Stanford, CA: Stanford University Press.

Hilton, J. 1933. *Lost Horizon.* London: Macmillan.

Himal. 2002. 'Satyagraha in Exile'. *Himal* (September), Kathmandu.

Hobart, M. 1993. *An Anthropological Critique of Development: The Growth of Ignorance.* London: Routledge.

Hobsbawm, E.J., and T.O. Ranger. 1992. *The Invention of Tradition.* Cambridge: Cambridge University Press.

Hockenos, P. 2003. *Homeland Calling: Exile Patriotism and the Balkan Wars.* Ithaca, NY and London: Cornell University Press.

Holborn, L.W. 1975. *Refugees, a Problem of our Time: The Work of the United Nations High Commissioner for Refugees, 1951–1972.* Metuchen, NJ: Scarecrow Press.

Holtz, T.H. 1998. 'Refugee Trauma versus Torture Trauma: A Retrospective Controlled Cohort Study of Tibetan Refugees', *Journal of Nervous and Mental Disease* 186(1): 24–34.

Huber, T. 1997. 'Green Tibetans: A Brief Social History', in F. Korom, *Tibetan Culture in the Diaspora. Proceedings of the 7th Seminar of the International Association for Tibetan Studies.* Vienna: Verlag der Österreichischen Akademie der Wissenschaften 4: pp. 103–19.

Huber, T., and P. Pedersen. 1997. 'Meteorological Knowledge and Environmental Ideas in Traditional and Modern Societies: The Case of Tibet', *The Journal of the Royal Anthropological Institute* 3(3): 577–97.

Hutt, M. 1996. 'Ethnic Nationalism, Refugees and Bhutan', *Journal of Refugees Studies* 9(4): 397–420.

Inamdar, S. 2005. *Mahatma Gandhi and His Holiness the Dalai Lama on Non-Violence and Compassion*. Dharamsala: Department of Information and International Relations, CTA.

Information Office of His Holiness the Dalai Lama. 1981. *Tibetans In Exile 1959–1980*. Dharamsala: Central Tibetan Secretariat.

Inoguchi, T., and M.Carlson. 2006. *Governance and Democracy in Asia*. Melbourne, Australia: Trans Pacific Press.

Ishihama, Y. 2003. 'On the Dissemination of the Belief in the Dalai Lama as a Manifestation of the Bodhisattva Avalokitesvara', in A. McKay, *History of Tibet*. London: Routledge, pp. 538–53.

Jacobson, E. 2002. 'Panic Attack in a Context of Comorbid Anxiety and Depression in a Tibetan Refugee', *Culture, Medicine and Psychiatry* 26(2): 259–79.

Jameson, F. 1991. *Postmodernism, or, The Cultural Logic of Late Capitalism*. London: Verso.

Jamyang Norbu. 1994. 'The Tibetan Resistance Movement and the Role of the CIA', in R. Barnett, *Resistance and Reform in Tibet*. London: Hurst, pp. 186–96.

———. 1998. 'Dances with Yaks: Tibet in Film, Fiction and Fantasy of the West', *Tibetan Review* 33(1): 18–23.

———. 2004. *Shadow Tibet: Selected Writings, 1989 to 2004*. New Delhi : Bluejay Books.

Karmay, S.G. 1998. *The Arrow and the Spindle: Studies in History, Myths, Rituals and Beliefs in Tibet*. Kathmandu: Mandala Book Point.

Karmay, S.G., and J.Watt. 2007. *Bon, the Magic Word: The Indigenous Religion of Tibet*. New York: Rubin Museum of Art.

Kauffmann, T. 2007. 'Practical Spirituality and Developmental Challenges among Tibetan Communities in India'. Paper given at the Practical Spirituality and Human Development workshop, March 2007. Freiburg: Institute of Sociology, University of Freiburg.

Kay, D.N. 2004. *Tibetan and Zen Buddhism in Britain: Transplantation, Development and Adaptation*. London: RoutledgeCurzon.

Keck, M.E., and K. Sikkink. 1998. *Activists beyond Borders: Advocacy Networks in International Politics*. Ithaca, NY and London: Cornell University Press.

Kharat, R.S. 2001. 'Problem of Bhutanese Refugees: Challenges Ahead', in S.K. Roy (ed.), *Refugees and Human Rights: Social and Political Dynamics of Refugee Problem in Eastern and North-Eastern India*. Jaipur: Rawat Publications, pp. 289–302.

Klieger, P.C. 1978. 'The Nature of the Patron/Priest Relationship in Tibetan Culture', *Tibet Society Bulletin* 12: 1–6.

———. 1991. *Tibetan Nationalism: The Role of Patronage in the Accomplishment of a National Identity*. Meerut, India: Archana Publications.

Knaus, J.K. 1999. *Orphans of the Cold War: America and the Tibetan Struggle for Survival*. New York: Public Affairs.

Kolas, A. 1996. 'Tibetan Nationalism: The Politics of Religion', *Journal of Peace Research* 33(1): 51–66.

Kolas, A., and M.P. Thowsen. 2005. *On the Margins of Tibet: Cultural Survival on the Sino-Tibetan Frontier*. Seattle and London: University of Washington Press.

Korff, R., and H. Schrader. 2004. 'Does the End of Development Revitalise History?', in A.K. Giri, A. v. Harskamp and O. Salemink (eds), *The Development of Religion, the Religion of Development*. Delft: Eburon, pp. 9–18.

Korom, F. 1997a. *Constructing Tibetan Culture: Contemporary Perspectives*. St-Hyacinthe, Quebec: World Heritage Press.

———. 1997b. *Tibetan Culture in the Diaspora: Papers Presented at a Panel of the 7th Seminar of the International Association for Tibetan Studies, Graz 1995*. Vienna: Verlag der Osterreichischen Akademie der Wissenschaften.

———. 2001. 'The Role of Tibet in the New Age Movement', in T. Dodin and H. Räther, *Imagining Tibet: Perceptions, Projections, and Fantasies*. Boston: Wisdom Publications, pp. 167–82.

Korten, D.C. 1990. *Getting to the 21st Century: Voluntary Action and the Global Agenda*. West Hartford, CT: Kumarian Press.

Kumar, B. 1997. 'A Study of Rituals of Tibetan Bonpos at Solan, Himachal Pradesh', *Indian Journal of Buddhist Studies* 9(1–2): 29–37.

Kvaerne, P. 1990. 'The Bön of Tibet: The Historical Enigma of a Monastic Tradition', in C. v. Fürer-Haimendorf, *The Renaissance of Tibetan Civilization*. Oracle, AZ: Synergetic Press.

Kvaerne, P., and R. Thargyal. 1993. *Bon, Buddhism and Democracy: The Building of a Tibetan National*. Copenhagen: Nordic Institute of Asian Studies.

Laeng, D., and P. Broussard. 2001. *La prisonnière de Lhassa: Ngawang Sangdrol, religieuse et résistante*. Paris: Stock.

Lata Manjari Parhi. 1983. Tour Report. ORS 038 Tibetan Resettlement, Chandagiri. Date of Visit 19 April 1983. OXFAM.

Lay Lee, T. 1998. 'Refugees from Bhutan: Nationality, Statelessness and the Right to Return', *International Journal of Refugee Law* 10(1/2): 118–55.

Lenoir, F. 1999a. *Le bouddhisme en France*. Paris: Fayard.

———. 1999b. *La rencontre du bouddhisme et de l'Occident*. Paris: Fayard.

Lévi-Strauss, C. (1949) 1967. *Les structures élémentaires de la parenté*. Paris: Plon.

Leys, C. 2005. 'The Rise and Fall of Development Theory', in M. Edelman and A. Haugerud, *The Anthropology of Development and Globalization: From Classical Political Economy to Contemporary Neoliberalism*. Malden, MA and Oxford: Blackwell, pp. 109–25.

Long, N., and A. Long. 1992. *Battlefields of Knowledge: The Interlocking of Theory and Practice in Social Research and Development*. London: Routledge.

Lopez, D.S. 1998. *Prisoners of Shangri-La: Tibetan Buddhism and the West*. Chicago and London: University of Chicago Press.

Lyotard, J.F. 1979. *La condition postmoderne: rapport sur le savoir*. Paris: Editions de Minuit.

Mackenzie, V. 1988. *Reincarnation: The Boy Lama*. London: Bloomsbury.

Magnusson, J. 2002. 'A Myth of Tibet: Reverse Orientalism and Soft Power', in P.C. Klieger (ed.), *Tibet, Self, and the Tibetan Diaspora: Proceedings of the Ninth Seminar of the International Association for Tibetan Studies*. Leiden, The Netherlands and Boston, MA: Brill, pp. 195–212.

Maillard, D. 2007. *L'humanitaire, tragédie de la démocratie*. Paris: Editions Michalon.

Malkki, L. 1995. 'Refugees and Exile: From "Refugees Studies" to the National Order of Things', *Annual Review of Anthropology* 24: 495–523.

Marcus, G.E. 1995. 'Ethnography in/of the World System: The Emergence of Multi-sited Ethnography', *Annual Review of Anthropology* 24: 95–117.

Markey, M.B. 1999. 'Faking Monkhood for a Visa', *Tibetan Review* 34(1): 26.

Marx, K. 1994. *Philosophie*. Paris: Gallimard.

Masuzawa, T. 1999. 'From Empire to Utopia: The Effacement of Colonial Markings in Lost Horizon', *Positions: East Asia Culture Critiques* 7(2): 541–72.

Mauss, M. (1924) 1950. 'Essai sur le don, forme et raison de l'échange dans les sociétés archaïques', in *Sociologie et Anthropologie*. Paris: PUF, pp. 145–279.

———. 1954. *The Gift: Forms and Functions of Exchange in Archaic Societies*. London: Cohen & West.

McGranahan, C. 2005. 'Truth, Fear, and Lies: Exile Politics and Arrested Histories of the Tibetan Resistance', *Cultural Anthropology* 20(4): 570–600.

McLagan, M. 1996. 'Mobilizing for Tibet: Transnational Politics and Diaspora Culture in the post-Cold War Era'. Ph.D. thesis. New York: New York University.

———. 1997. 'Mystical Visions in Manhattan: Deploying Culture in the Year of Tibet', in F. Korom, *Tibetan Culture in the Diaspora, Proceedings of the 7th Seminar of the International Association for Tibetan Studies*. Vienna: Verlag der Österreichischen Akademie der Wissenschaften 4: pp. 69–90.

Michael, F. 1982. *Rule by Incarnation: Tibetan Buddhism and its Role in Society and State*. Boulder, CO: Westview.

Miller, B.D. 1978. 'Tibetan Culture and Personality: Refugee Responses to a Tibetan Culture-Bound TAT', in J. Fischer, *Himalayan Anthropology*. Paris and The Hague: Mouton Publishers, pp. 365–93.

———. 1988. 'American Popular Perceptions of Tibet from 1858–1938', *Tibet Journal* 13(3): 3–19.

———. 1993. 'Is there Tibetan Culture(s) without Buddhism?', in C. Ramble and M. Brauen (eds), *Proceedings of the International Seminar on the Anthropology of Tibet and the Himalaya: September 21–28 1990 at the Ethnographic Museum of the University of Zürich*. Zurich: Völkerkundemuseum der Universität Zürich, pp. 222–28.

Mills, M. 2003. 'This Turbulent Priest: Contesting Religious Rights and the State in the Tibetan Shugden Controversy', in R. Wilson and J. Mitchell, *Human Rights in Global Perspective: Anthropological Studies of Rights, Claims and Entitlements*. London: Routledge, pp. 54–70.

Moran, P. 2004. *Buddhism Observed: Travelers, Exiles and Tibetan Dharma in Kathmandu*. London: RoutledgeCurzon.

Mosse, D., J. Farrington and A. Rew. 1998. *Development as Process: Concepts and Methods for Working with Complexity*. London: Routledge.

Mumford, S.R. 1989. *Himalayan Dialogue : Tibetan Lamas and Gurung Shamans in Nepal*. Madison: University of Wisconsin Press.

Nebesky-Wojkowitz, R. 1975. *Oracles and Demons of Tibet: The Cult and Iconography of the Tibetan Protective Deities*. Graz, Austria: Akademische Druck- u. Verlagsanstalt.

Nederveen Pieterse, J. 2001. *Development Theory: Deconstructions/Reconstructions*. London: SAGE.

Newland, G. 1992. *The Two Truths in the Madhyamika Philosophy of the Ge-luk-ba Order of Tibetan Buddhism*. Ithaca, NY: Snow Lion Publications.

Ngawang Dorjee. 1992. 'An Assessment of the Exile Situation', *Tibetan Review* 27(2): 11–14.

Norberg-Hodge, H. 2000. *Ancient Futures: Learning from Ladakh.* London: Rider.

Nowak, M. 1978a. 'Liminal 'Self', Ambiguous 'Power': The Genesis of the 'Rangzen' Metaphor among Tibetan Youth in India'. Ph.D. Seattle: University of Washington.

———. 1978b. 'The Education of Young Tibetans in India: Cultural Preservation or Agent for Change?', in M. Brauen and P. Kvaerne, *Tibetan Studies.* Zurich: Völkerkundemuseum der Universität Zürich, pp. 191–98.

———. 1983. *Tibetan Refugees: Youth and the New Generation of Meaning.* New Brunswick, NJ: Rutgers University Press.

Nyima, L. 1978. Application for an OXFAM Grant/Loan: Tibetan Resettlement (Phuntsokling), Chandragiri, Orissa.

———. 1980. Progress Report of an OXFAM Grant/Loan: Multi-purpose Tibetan Co-operative Society Ltd, Chandragiri, Orissa.

———. 1982. Progress Report of Oxfam Grant: Multi-purpose Tibetan Co-operative Society Ltd, Chandragiri, Orissa.

Obadia, L. 1999. *Bouddhisme et Occident: la diffusion du bouddhisme tibétain en France.* Paris: Harmattan.

Office of His Holiness the Dalai Lama. 1969. *Tibetans in Exile, 1959–1969: A Report on Ten Years of Rehabilitation in India.* Dharamsala.

Office of Planning Commission. 2004. *Tibetan Community in Exile: Demographic and Socio-economic Issues 1998–2001.* Dharamsala.

Office of Planning Commission and SARD. 2005. *First Donors Conference 13–15 January 2005.* Dharamsala.

Office of the United Nations High Commissioner for Refugees. 2000. *The State of the World's Refugees, 2000: Fifty Years of Humanitarian Action.* Oxford: Oxford University Press.

Olivier de Sardan, J.-P. 1995. *Anthropologie et développement: essai en socio-anthropologie du changement social.* Marseille: APAD.

Ortner, S.B. 1978. *Sherpas through their Rituals.* Cambridge: Cambridge University Press.

———. 1989. *High Religion: A Cultural and Political History of Sherpa Buddhism.* Princeton, NJ: Princeton University Press.

———. 1999. *Life and Death on Mt Everest.* Princeton, NJ: Princeton University Press.

———. 1996. 'Democracy is an Integral Part of the Tibetan Freedom Struggle', *Tibetan Bulletin* (May–June): 11–13.

Petech, L. 2003. 'The establishment of the yüan-sa-skya partnership', in A. McKay, *History of Tibet.* London: Routledge, pp. 338–61.

Philip, B. 2007. 'Le dalaï-lama songe à assurer sa succession, de son vivant', *Le Monde*, 23 November.

Pike, R.A.D. 2001. 'Campaigning for a Free Tibet: Transnational Activism and the "Universal Rights Strategy"'. Cambridge, MA: Harvard College.

Planning Commission. 2004. *Tibetan Community in Exile. Integrated Development Plan III. Investment and Implementation Guidelines for 2004–2007.* Dharamsala: Central Tibetan Administration.

____. 2009. *Tibetan Community in Exile. Integrated Development Plan IV. 2009-2013.* Dharamsala: Central Tibetan Administration.

____. 2010. *Demographic Survey of Tibetans in Exile - 2009.* Dharamsala: Central Tibetan Administration.

Planning Council. 1990. *CTA Project Needs Support Directory.* Dharamsala: Central Tibetan Administration.

____. 1992. *Tibetan Refugee Community. Integrated Development Plan, 1992-1997.* Dharamsala: Central Tibetan Administration.

____. 1994. *Tibetan Refugee Community Integrated Development Plan II, 1995-2000.* Dharamsala: Central Tibetan Administration.

____. 2000. *Tibetan Demographic Survey 1998.* Dharamsala: Central Tibetan Administration.

Powers, J. 2004. *History as Propaganda: Tibetan Exiles versus the People's Republic of China.* New York and Oxford: Oxford University Press.

Pratt, M.L. 1992. *Imperial Eyes: Travel Writing and Transculturation.* London: Routledge.

Prost, A. 2006. 'The Problem with "Rich Refugees": Sponsorship, Capital, and the Informal Economy of Tibetan Refugees', *Modern Asian Studies* 40(1): 233–53.

Quarles van Ufford, P., and A.K. Giri. 2003. *A Moral Critique of Development: In Search of Global Responsibilities.* London: Routledge.

Quarles van Ufford, P., and J.M. Schoffeleers (eds). 1988. *Religion and Development: Towards an Integrated Approach.* Amsterdam: Free University Press.

Redding, E.Z. 1976. 'The Effects of Modern Education and Western Environment on Tibetan Religious Beliefs and Attitudes'. Ph.D. thesis. Claremont, CA: Claremont Graduate University.

Reynolds, A. 2003. 'Support for Tibet Worldwide', in D. Bernstorff and H. v. Welck, *Exile as a Challenge: The Tibetan Diaspora.* Hyderabad, India: Orient Longman, pp. 447–53.

Richardson, H. (1962) 1984. *Tibet and its History.* Boulder, CO: Shambhala.

Rinchen Dharlo. 1994. 'A Brief History of Tibetans in North America', *Tibetan Review* 29(10): 12–17.

Ringu Tulku. 1997. 'The Rime Movement of Jamgon Kongtrul the Great', in E. Steinkellener, *Proceedings of the 7th Seminar of the International Association for Tibetan Studies, Graz 1995.* Vienna: Verlag der Österreichischen Akademie des Wissenschaften.

Rinzin, T. 1997. 'Is there a Process of Secularization among the Tibetans in Exile?', in F. Korom, *Tibetan Culture in the Diaspora, Proceedings of the 7th Seminar of the International Association for Tibetan Studies.* Vienna: Verlag der Österreichischen Akademie der Wissenschaften 4: pp. 25–32.

Roemer, S. 2008. *The Tibetan Government-in-Exile: Politics at Large.* London and New York: Routledge.

Ruegg, D.S. 1995. *Ordre spirituel et ordre temporel dans la pensée bouddhique de l'Inde et du Tibet.* Paris: Collège de France.

Safran, W. 1991. 'Diasporas in Modern Societies: Myths of Homeland and Return', *Diaspora* 1(1): 83–99.

Said, E.W. 1979. *Orientalism.* New York: Vintage Books.

Salemink, O. 2008. 'Saint Bob and the celebration of Millennial Development Goals: The sacralization of a neoliberal utopia', Paper given at the EIDOS Conference "The Ends of Development: Market, morality, religion, political theology?" Amsterdam, The Netherlands.

Samdhong Rinpoche. 2001. 'New Kalon Tripa Samdhong Rinpoche Speaks', *Tibetan Bulletin* (Sept–Oct): 25–28.

———. 2005. 'Our Sole Objective is to Retain Identity of Tibetan People as Non-Violent Society', *Tibetan Bulletin* (Nov–Dec): 10–12.

Samuel, G. 1993. *Civilized Shamans*. Washington, DC and London: Smithsonian Institution Press.

Sangay, L. 2006. 'Is the Dalai Lama a Democrat? A Paradox between Buddhism and Democracy or a Constitutional Analysis of the Securalisation of the Tibetan Diaspora: The Role of the Dalai Lama'. Paper given at the 11th Seminar of the International Association for Tibetan Studies, Bonn, Germany.

Scheper-Hugues, N. 1995. 'The Primacy of the Ethical: Propositions for a Militant Anthropology', *Current Anthropology* 36(3): 409–40.

Schrader, H. 1990. 'Linked with the World Market: The case of Tibetan Refugees' Community in Nepal', *Kailash* 16(3–4): 187–209.

Schrempf, M. 1997. 'From "Devil Dance" to "World Healing": Some Representations, Perspectives and Innovations of Contemporary Tibetan Ritual Dances', in F. Korom, *Tibetan Culture in the Diaspora. Proceedings of the 7th Seminar of the International Association for Tibetan Studies*. Vienna: Verlag der Österreichischen Akademie der Wissenschaften 4: pp. 91–102.

Schwartz, R.D. 1994. 'The Anti-Splittist Campaign', in R. Barnett and S. Akiner, *Resistance and Reform in Tibet*. London: Hurst, pp. 207–37.

Sen, A.K. 1999. *Development as Freedom*. Oxford: Oxford University Press.

Shakabpa, W.D. 1967. *Tibet: A Political History*. New Haven, CT: Yale University Press.

Shan, Z. 2001. *A History of Development of Tibet*. Beijing: Foreign Language Press.

Skorupski, T. 1981. 'Tibetan g-Yung-Drung Bon Monastery at Dolanji', *Kailash* 8(1–2): 25–43.

Smith, M. 2004. 'Contradiction and Change? NGOs, Schools and the Public Faces of Development', *Journal of International Development* 16: 741–49.

Snellgrove, D.L., and H. Richardson. (1968) 2003. *A Cultural History of Tibet*. Bangkok: Orchid Press.

Snodgrass, J. 2003. *Presenting Japanese Buddhism to the West: Orientalism, Occidentalism, and the Columbian Exposition*. Chapel Hill and London: University of North Carolina Press.

Stein, R.A. (1962) 1972. *Tibetan Civilization*. Stanford, CA: Stanford University Press.

Stepputat, F. 1994. 'Repatriation and the Politics of Space: The Case of the Mayan Diaspora and Return Movement', *Journal of Refugees Studies* 7(2/3): 175–85.

Ström, A.K. 1994. 'Tibetan Refugees in India: Socio-cultural Change', in P. Kvaerne, *Tibetan Studies: Proceedings of the 6th Seminar of the International Association for Tibetan Studies, Fagernes, 1992*. Oslo: Institute for Comparative Research in Human Culture, pp. 837–47.

——. 1995. *The Quest for Grace: Identification and Cultural Continuity among Tibetan Refugees in India.* Oslo: University of Oslo.

——. 2001. 'Continuity, Adaptation and Innovation: Tibetan Monastic Colleges in India'. Doctor rerum politicarum. Oslo: University of Oslo.

Subba, T.B. 1990. *Flight and Adaptation: Tibetan Refugees in the Darjeeling-Sikkim Himalaya.* Dharamsala: Library of Tibetan Works and Archives.

Subedi, B.P. 2001. 'The Problem of Bhutanese Refugees and Comparison with Tibetan Refugees in Nepal', *Contributions to Nepalese Studies* 28(1): 73–90.

TCV (Tibetan Children's Village). 1980. *Tibetan Children's Village Dharamsala. Information Brochure 20 Years.* Dharamsala.

——. 2000. *Tibetans in Exile. TCV History Book for 8th Class.* Dharamsala.

——. 2006. *Metok. Winter 2006. A Newsletter from the Tibetan Children's Village.* Dharamsala.

——. 2009. *Metok. Summer 2009. A Newsletter from the Tibetan Children's Village.* Dharamsala.

Thinley, P. 1990. 'A Judicial Dimension to Tibetan Democracy', *Tibetan Review* 25(11): 9–11.

Thub bstan chos kyi grags pa and H.I. Köppl. 2004. *Uniting wisdom and compassion: illuminating the thirty-seven practices of a Bodhisattva.* Boston: Wisdom Publications.

Thubten Samdup. 2004. 'I appreciate those who find fault with my administration, says Samdhong Rinpoche', *Tibetan Bulletin* (Mar–Apr): 13–15.

Thubten Zopa and N. Ribush. 1998. *Virtue and Reality: Method and Wisdom in the Practice of Dharma.* Boston: Lama Yeshe Wisdom Archive.

Tibet Society, The. 1967. *The Tibet Society Newsletter.* Bloomington, IN.

Tincq, H. 2008. 'Le dalaï-lama à Nantes: "La violence est démodée!"' *Le Monde*, 16 August.

Tölölyan, K. 1996. 'Rethinking Diaspora(s): Stateless Power in the Transnational Movement', *Diaspora* 5(1): 3–36.

Touraine, A. 1992. *Critique de la modernité.* Paris: Fayard.

Tucci, G. 1969. *The Theory and Practice of the Mandala: With Special Reference to the Modern Psychology of the Subconscious.* London: Rider.

UN General Assembly. 1964. Account of the Mission of the Director of Operations to India and Nepal (Submitted by the High Commissioner). Report A/AC.96/INF.31, 23 October.

United Nations High Commissioner for Refugees. 2008. *The 1951 Refugee Convention. Questions and Answers.* Geneva.

U.S. Committee for Refugees and Immigrants. 2008. *World Refugee Survey 2008.* Washington DC.

Vernette, J. 1992. *Le New Age.* Paris: Presses Universitaires de France.

Vertovec, S. 1997. 'Three Meanings of "Diaspora", Exemplified among South Asian Religions', *Diaspora* 6(3): 277–99.

Weber, M. (1905) 1964. *Éthique protestante et esprit du capitalisme.* Paris: Plon.

Weber, M., et al. 1989. *Max Weber's "Science as a Vocation".* London and Boston: Unwin Hyman.

Weingarten, R. 1987. 'Tibetan Economic Development Project Report' (unpublished).

Western Shugden Society. 2008. 'The Western Shugden Society'. Unpublished flyer.

Wolch, J. 1989. 'The Shadow State: Transformations in the Voluntary Sector', in J. Wolch and M.J. Dear, *The Power of Geography: How Territory Shapes Social Life*. Boston: Unwin Hyman, pp. 197–221.

Wood, A.T. 2004. *Asian Democracy in World History*. New York: Routledge.

Woodcock, G. 1970. 'Tibetan Refugees in a Decade of Exile', *Pacific Affairs (Vancouver, B.C.)* 43(3): 410–20.

Yeh, E. 2003. Taming the Tibetan Landscape: Chinese Development and the Transformation of Agriculture. Ph.D. dissertation. Berkeley: University of California.

____. 2013. *Taming Tibet: Landscape Transformation and the Gift of Chinese Development*. Ithaca, NY: Cornell University Press.

Zetter, R. 1999. 'Reconceptualizing the Myth of Return: Continuity and Transition amongst the Greek-Cypriot Refugees of 1974', *Journal of Refugees Studies* 12(1): 1–22.

Index

10 March – Uprising Day, 16, 49, 155, 168, 185

Amdo, 3, 180
Arunachal Pradesh, 3, 7, 8, 21, 33, 52, 160, 164, 171, 177, 180
Assam, 17, 47
authenticity, 92, 117, 124, 126, 130n21, 133, 173, 178n23. *See also* orientalism

Bangalore, 161
Bangladesh, 20
Barnett, Robbie, 30, 33, 57, 71, 72, 129, 130
Beijing, 14, 15, 16, 169
Bengal, 15, 17, 21, 65, 156
Bhutan, 3, 16, 17, 27, 32, 39, 67, 82, 83, 159
Bon, 6, 11, 73, 88, 89, 91, 170
Bourdieu, Pierre, 127, 150

Calcutta, 14, 15
Canada, 33, 35, 36, 163, 177
Central Relief Committee for Tibetans (CRCT), 17, 18, 19, 22, 23, 32, 39
Central Tibetan Administration (CTA). *See* Chapter 2
    Bod gzhung (the Tibetan government), 46, 47, 51
    Corpus Fund, 37, 38, 39, 78
    creation of a community, 48–51
    creation in exile, 21–22, 46–48
    Department of Education, 53, 109

Department of Finance, 7, 38
Department of Home, 52, 53
Department of Information and International Relations (DIIR), 50, 70, 101, 105, 129
Department of Religion and Culture, 53, 92
    as a developmental agency, 7, 9, 19, 27, 28, 39, 182
    jurisdiction, 27
    Kashag (*bka' shag*, the Tibetan Cabinet), 13, 46, 47, 48, 62, 170
    as a local partner, 36–46
    parliament, Assembly of Tibetan People's Deputies (ATPD), 31, 61, 90, 118, 122, 169, 170
    Planning Commission, 7, 38, 45, 68, 154
    Tibetan government-in-exile (TGIE), 1, 2, 44, 47, 48, 55, 63, 66, 88, 90, 120, 180
    welfare officer, 27, 52
    welfare state, 5, 28, 39, 45, 46, 48, 51–53, 120, 155, 162, 181
    See also chos srid zung 'brel; political agenda; political agenda: democracy; religious agenda; development relationship
Central Tibetan Relief Committee (CTRC), 19, 39
Central Tibetan Schools (CTS), 66
China, People's Republic of China (PRC), 8, 13, 14, 15, 16, 17, 18, 20, 30, 43, 51, 55, 61, 63, 72, 75,

79, 85, 87, 90, 95, 96, 99, 109,
118, 120, 121, 125, 126, 130, 140,
155, 167, 169, 185
chos srid zung 'brel ('religion and politics
combined'), 2, 10, 28, 49, 54–57,
59, 60, 61, 86, 91, 141, 142, 168,
182, 184, 185
Christianity, Christian, 18, 19, 27, 40,
94, 107, 131, 135, 140, 141, 145,
146
colonialism, 94, 136
neocolonialism, 138
compassion, 92–99, 104, 106, 107, 108,
110, 123, 124, 125, 130, 135, 142,
146, 148, 184, 185, 187

Dalai Lama, His Holiness the
Fourteenth
and democracy, 60–63. *See also*
political agenda: democracy
escape to exile, 13–16, 18
Five-Point Peace Plan, 30
as a gatekeeper, 119, 120, 145
history of his power, 46–48
installation in exile, 21–22, 55
leadership, 25, 28
middle-way policy, 68, 72, 80, 169
Nobel Peace Prize, 31, 100, 127
temporal and religious leader, 55–
57, 168, 184–185
See also political agenda; religious
agenda; Tibetan Buddhism
Delhi, 16, 18, 27, 91, 161, 174
development
critique of development in terms of
power, 137–139
critique of development in terms of
values, 139–141
development agencies, 9, 19, 39,
139, 146, 182
development anthropology, 137,
150n6
development projects, 27, 35, 39, 42,
43, 53, 69, 101, 111, 115, 116, 121,
138, 142
non-governmental organization
(NGO), 9, 29, 36, 38, 40, 42, 44,

45, 74, 104, 114, 115, 116, 124,
167, 169
See also development relationship;
Tibetan development; utopia
development relationship
donation, 38, 39, 41, 66, 67, 78, 103
donor agency, 22, 38
embodiment, 54, 56, 109, 118, 119,
126, 127, 129, 133, 143, 144
ideal 'Tibetanness', 65, 127, 144
mchod gnas, 54, 86
mchod yon relationship, 11, 54, 84,
85, 86, 87, 88, 94, 97, 104, 107,
108, 144, 145, 146, 147, 151, 182,
183
model of partnership, 10, 146, 150,
183. *See* Chapter 6
partner, 10, 35, 36, 38, 39, 41, 42,
46, 107, 112, 114, 139, 140, 146,
148, 150, 182
partnership, 100, 121, 131, 133, 135,
137, 139, 141, 143, 144, 145, 146,
147, 149, 151
portrait of donors, 116–117
in the religious agenda, 102–107,
127–128
sbyin bdag (sponsor in Tibetan), 84,
86, 88, 102, 103, 104, 105, 109
sponsor, 43, 53, 76, 84, 88, 102, 103,
104, 105, 112, 113, 116, 127, 156,
162, 176
volunteer, volunteering, 44, 73, 111,
116, 123, 125, 127, 128, 146, 162
voluntourism, 128
Western donors and supporters, 29,
62, 63, 66, 76, 82, 87, 109, 146,
172–173
See also Global Tibet Movement;
orientalism; TSG
Dharamsala (MacLeod Ganj), 1, 7, 17,
21, 23, 28, 33, 43, 44, 47, 52, 58,
63, 65, 66, 73, 82, 91, 100, 103,
104, 113, 117, 118, 123, 124, 125,
127, 129, 130, 146, 161, 164, 166,
169, 173, 176
diaspora, 7, 9, 23, 25, 26, 33, 49, 101,
175

Dorje Shugden, 89, 90, 91, 108, 166, 167, 168
Durkheim, Emile, 97, 98

Escobar, Arturo, 137, 138, 139, 140

Ferguson, James, 11, 137, 138, 139
Foucault, Michel, 24, 50, 137
France, 1, 55, 63, 100, 111, 163
Frechette, Ann, 44, 58, 63, 81, 144, 151, 179, 187
Fürer-haimendorf, Christoph Von, 26, 33

Gaborieau, Marc, 180
Gandhi, 82, 100, 109
Gere, Richard, 29, 122, 187
Germany, 68, 82, 163
Giri, Ananta Kumar, 139, 140
Global Tibet Movement, 10, 30, 70, 71, 99, 101, 105, 106, 111, 115, 116, 117, 118, 119, 120, 121, 122, 123, 124, 127, 128, 129, 136, 141, 142, 144, 145, 183, 187
Goldstein, Melvin, 11, 14, 26, 29, 31, 46, 109, 163, 164, 176
Great Britain, 19, 163, 167

Hervieu-Léger, Danièle, 134, 143, 150
Himachal Pradesh, 1, 6, 21, 23, 24, 27, 52, 65, 105, 156
Himalaya, Himalayan regions
  culture, 82n24, 148, 160, 162, 164, 174
  geography, 1, 17, 18, 20, 24, 107
Hobsbawm, Eric, 48–49, 139

immigrants, immigration, 11, 152–154
India, 1, 3, 4, 5, 6, 7, 9, 11, 13, 14, 15, 16, 17, 18, 20, 21, 22, 23, 24, 25, 27, 32, 33, 34, 38, 39, 40, 41, 42, 43, 45, 47, 50, 51, 53, 55, 58, 60, 61, 64, 65, 66, 67, 92, 95, 109, 111, 118, 119, 123, 129, 134, 148, 152, 153, 154, 155, 156, 158, 159, 160, 161, 163, 164, 165, 166, 170, 171, 173, 175, 177, 178, 179, 180, 185

informant, 2, 8, 9, 23, 24, 32, 50, 69, 77, 79, 82, 87, 91, 92, 93, 102, 116, 125, 126, 129, 130, 147, 153, 159, 162, 165, 178, 185
International Campaign for Tibet (ICT), 28, 29, 30, 31, 43, 45, 56, 63, 72, 74, 97, 101, 122, 123, 145, 152

Jammu-and-Kashmir, 20
Jamyang Norbu, 31, 50, 136, 185

Karmapa, 16, 89, 179, 185, 186
Kathmandu, 39, 42, 113
Kham, 3, 4, 5, 11, 30, 31, 61, 180
Kublai Kahn, 85, 86, 87

Ladakh, 3, 27, 77, 180
Lenoir, Frédéric, 102, 135, 136, 150
Lhasa, 3, 8, 13, 15, 16, 28, 30, 46, 47, 49, 50, 52, 125, 126, 130, 133, 152, 155, 173, 175
Lopez, Donald, 93, 94, 102, 128, 131, 150, 151, 167

Mao Tse Tung, 13, 15, 16, 109
Mclagan, Meg, 29, 87, 88, 101, 118, 136, 151
Mongolia, 33, 34, 47

Nehru, Jawaharlal, 16–18, 20, 47, 55, 177
Nepal, 1, 3, 4, 5, 6, 11, 16, 21, 22, 23, 32, 39, 41, 42, 43, 50, 51, 53, 67, 111, 114, 118, 119, 134, 151, 153, 159, 160, 162, 163, 174, 175, 177, 184
Nowak, Margaret, 33, 50, 59, 67, 172
nunneries, 164, 178

Obadia, Lionel, 96, 102, 132, 134, 135, 150, 163
orientalism, 49, 131, 133, 136, 137
  archetypes, 25, 124, 135
  authentic Tibet, 26, 117, 119, 121, 122, 124, 125, 128, 135, 142

myth(s) of Tibet: Shangri-La, 59,
102, 127, 128, 132, 133, 179;
Shambala, 102; Deshangrilised,
50
stereotypes, 10, 121, 122, 124, 125,
126, 133, 147, 148, 183
See also utopia

Pakistan, 20
Panchen Lama, 14, 89, 130, 179
Phagpa, 85, 86, 87, 88, 108
political agenda, 10, 57, 60, 61, 63, 65,
67, 69, 71, 73, 75, 77, 79, 80, 81,
83, 94, 100, 113, 182. *See* Chapter
3
Basic Education Policy, 53, 172–173
democracy, 25, 33, 42, 48, 53, 60,
61, 62, 63, 64, 67, 68, 80, 81, 125,
161, 163, 168, 169, 170, 171, 180,
182
democratization, 57, 61, 62, 63, 64,
157, 168, 169
ecology, 72–75, 82, 136, 142
education, 44, 47, 48, 50, 51, 53, 60,
64–68, 104, 114, 148, 149, 152,
157–160, 162, 165, 171–175, 182
greening, 73, 74, 82
self-sufficiency narrative, 25, 78–79,
82, 97, 180
victim narrative, 75–79
See also chos srid zung 'brel;
development; development
relationship
Punjab, 155

Qinghai, 3, 121
Quarles van Ufford, Philip, 139, 140

Ranger, Terence, 48–49, 139
religious agenda, 2, 10, 28, 57, 79, 80,
84, 85, 87, 89, 91, 93, 95, 97, 99,
101, 103, 105, 107, 109, 121, 164,
165, 168, 182. *See* Chapter 4
essentialization, 92–94
sacralization, 97–98
spiritualization, 10, 97, 98, 104, 105,
106, 107, 129, 145, 164, 182

universalization, 94, 95, 98
See also chos srid zung 'brel;
compassion; development
relationship: in the religious
agenda
Rumtek, 17

Samdhong Rinpoche, 47, 58, 88, 96,
99, 100, 106, 108, 170, 172, 176
Sangay, Lobsang, 48, 62, 169, 171
secularization, 97, 134, 143, 145, 164,
165
Sen, Amartya, 186
Seventeen-point agreement, 14, 169
Sherpa, 119, 148–151, 162
Sichuan, 3, 178
Sikkim, 3, 14, 16, 17, 27, 180
Ström, Axel, 58, 93, 146, 163, 172

Taiwan, 43, 58, 109
Thailand, 5, 33
Tiananmen, 30
Tibet Autonomous Region (TAR), 3, 4,
15, 16, 66
Tibet Support Group (TSG), 42, 43, 44,
45, 95, 119, 125, 128, 129
TSG conference, 74, 99, 105, 106, 118,
120, 122, 147
TSG desk, 122, 129n13
Tibetan Buddhism, 34, 43, 49, 55, 84,
87, 88, 91, 92, 93, 94, 95, 96, 101,
108n11, 128, 132, 134, 135, 136,
143, 145, 163, 166, 168, 183
Avalokiteshvara, 33n17, 54
Bodhisattva, 54, 100, 104, 109n21
Buddha, 5, 61, 62, 81, 84, 86, 106,
109
Dharma, 4, 5, 6, 43, 44, 45, 54, 59,
70, 84, 92, 93, 99, 102, 104, 106,
108, 109, 117, 119, 128, 134, 146,
147, 154, 163, 165, 166, 178
Dharma follower, 43, 44, 45, 92, 117,
119, 128, 146, 147, 165
Gelug, 5, 6, 47, 61, 88, 89, 90
Hinayana, 135
Kadampa, 167
Kagyu, 5, 61, 166, 177

Kalachakra, 29, 34, 102, 106, 109, 110

karma, 98, 107, 145, 147, 161

Mahayana, 85, 109, 135, 166, 179

mandala, 88, 101

Nyingma, 5, 61, 89, 90, 166

Om mani padme hum, 93

rime movement, 91

Sakya, 5, 61, 85, 86, 88, 108

tantrism, tantra, 5, 90, 109

Vajrayana, 5, 106

See also compassion; religious agenda

Tibetan Children's Village (TCV), 24, 65, 66, 67, 73, 81, 82, 104, 105, 114

Tibetan Demographic Survey (TDS), 4, 5, 7, 14, 32, 67, 155, 156, 157, 158, 159, 163

Tibetan development
challenges, *see* Chapter 7
development phase of the Tibetan refugees, 27, 35, 39, 145, 181
Integrated Development Plan (IDP), 28, 38, 52, 58, 68, 69, 72, 75, 77, 78, 79, 82, 152
rehabilitation phase, 17, 23, 27, 35, 39, 42, 76, 145, 162, 184
See also development relationship; political agenda; religious agenda

Tibetan Institute for Performing Arts (TIPA), 45, 118

Tibetan settlement, 2, 7, 8, 16, 22, 25, 37, 42, 43, 44, 52, 53, 65, 73, 74, 91, 95, 102, 104, 105, 111, 112, 113, 114, 117, 121, 156, 158, 161, 164, 174, 179, 180

Buxa Duar, 17, 19

Bylakuppe (Lugsam Samdup Ling), 7, 21, 25, 26, 74, 103, 160, 161, 170, 177, 179

Chandragiri, 21, 40

Chauntra, 65, 105, 177

cooperative, 40, 41, 53, 114, 136, 170

Dalhousie, 21, 65, 156

Darjeeling, 8, 15, 18, 21, 65, 67, 103, 174, 180

Dharamsala (MacLeod Ganj), *See* Dharamsala (MacLeod Ganj)

Dolanji, 6

handicraft, 21, 37, 40, 52, 58

Kalimpong, 15, 18, 65, 156

Kollegal, 74

Majnu-ka-tilla, 91

Miao, 33

Missamari, 17, 19, 32

Mundgod, 21

Shillong, 156

Shimla, 8, 24, 65, 156

Tezu, 1, 7, 21, 52, 53, 65, 74, 76, 156, 158, 161, 163, 164, 165, 171, 174, 177

Uighur, 3

UNHCR, 19, 21, 23, 32, 35, 39, 41, 42

United States, 14, 15, 19, 20, 22, 28, 29, 30, 36, 44, 61, 80, 94, 152, 153, 157, 160, 166

utopia, utopianism, 133, 140–141, 144

Ü-tsang, 3, 4, 5, 61, 170, 180

Weingarten, Richard, 27, 36, 27, 38, 39, 44, 45, 52, 58, 152